Metaphor and Meaning

SUNY series in Chinese Philosophy and Culture
───────────
Roger T. Ames, editor

Metaphor and Meaning

Thinking Through Early China with Sarah Allan

Edited by
CONSTANCE A. COOK,
CHRISTOPHER J. FOSTER,
and SUSAN BLADER

Associate Editor
WILLIAM NELSON FRENCH

Assistant Editor
GAIL PATTEN

Cover Credit: From *Old Pines* 歲寒圖 (2023). Six images from a folding album. Ink on rice paper. © Wang Mansheng 2023.

Published by State University of New York Press, Albany

© 2024 State University of New York

All rights reserved

Printed in the United States of America

No part of this book may be used or reproduced in any manner whatsoever without written permission. No part of this book may be stored in a retrieval system or transmitted in any form or by any means including electronic, electrostatic, magnetic tape, mechanical, photocopying, recording, or otherwise without the prior permission in writing of the publisher.

For information, contact State University of New York Press, Albany, NY
www.sunypress.edu

Links to third-party websites are provided as a convenience and for informational purposes only. They do not constitute an endorsement or an approval of any of the products, services, or opinions of the organization, companies, or individuals. SUNY Press bears no responsibility for the accuracy, legality, or content of a URL, the external website, or for that of subsequent websites.

Library of Congress Cataloging-in-Publication Data

Names: Cook, Constance A., editor, author. | Foster, Christopher J., editor. | Blader, Susan, 1943– editor. | Allan, Sarah, honouree.
Title: Metaphor and meaning : thinking through early China with Sarah Allan / edited by Constance A. Cook, Christopher J. Foster, and Susan Blader.
Description: Albany : State University of New York Press, [2024] | Series: SUNY series in Chinese philosophy and culture | Metaphor and Meaning is part of a three-book series, with Myth and the Making of History and Bone, Bronze, and Bamboo, that celebrates Allan and the integral role she has played in the immense growth and development of early China as a field.—Galley | Includes bibliographical references and index.
Identifiers: LCCN 2023050399 | ISBN 9781438498300 (hardcover : alk. paper) | ISBN 9781438498324 (ebook) | ISBN 9781438498317 (pbk. : alk. paper)
Subjects: LCSH: Chinese language—To 600. | Philosophy, Chinese—To 221 B.C.—Sources. | Philosophy, Chinese—221 B.C.–960 A.D.—Sources. | China—Civilization—221 B.C.–960 A.D.—Sources. | China—Civilization—To 221 B.C.—Sources. | China—Antiquities.
Classification: LCC DS741.65 .M48 2024 | DDC 951/.01—dc23/eng/20240320
LC record available at https://lccn.loc.gov/2023050399

To Sarah Allan

Photo of Sarah Allan by C. A. Cook, Yantai, China, 2014.

Contents

Foreword: Appreciation of Professor Sarah Allan's
Scholarly Contributions   ix

Preface   xi

Acknowledgments   xvii

1. A Fluid Cosmos: Cosmologies of Creative Flow in Early China   1
   Erica Brindley

2. Water as Homology in the Construction of Classical Chinese Medicine   19
   Vivienne Lo and Gu Man

3. Destruction of Temples and Arresting Spirits: Metaphors of War, Illness, and Health in Daoist Conversion Narratives   51
   Gil Raz

4. Patterns in Stone: The Third Metaphor of Chinese Philosophy   75
   Edmund Ryden

5. Humans Can Broaden the Way, Sages Can Continue and Carry Out the Workings of *Tian*: 人能弘道, 聖人能繼天立極   93
   Roger T. Ames

6. Exorcism and the Spirit Turtle   117
   Constance A. Cook

7. Transcription Notes on the "Mind as Ruler" Section in the Tsinghua Bamboo Manuscript *The Heart Is Called the Center* (*Xin shi wei zhong* 心是謂中) 147
   Chen Wei

8. Texts, Historicity, and Metaphors in Early China: Reading *Tang Resides Near the Mound of Tang* (*Tang chuyu Tangqiu* 湯處於湯丘) in the Tsinghua Collection of Warring States Bamboo Manuscripts 163
   Shirley Chan

9. Some Remarks on the Value and Inner Meaning of the Way of Archery 189
   Cheung Kwong-yue

10. The Meaning of the Graph and Word *ge* 革 in the Huayuanzhuang East Oracle Bone Corpus and Related Questions 201
    Han Yujiao

11. Notes on a Cornerstone of Early Chinese Argumentative Rhetoric: The Function Word *gù* 故 211
    Rudolf G. Wagner

List of Contributors 241

Index 243

Foreword

In Appreciation of
Professor Sarah Allan's Scholarly Contributions

Editors' Note: The following remarks by Li Xueqin 李學勤 were written just before the International Conference on Human Nature, Morality, and Fate in the Tsinghua University Bamboo Manuscripts: *Tang chuyu Tangqiu* 湯處於湯丘, *Tang zai Chimen* 湯在啻門, and Yin *Gaozong wen yu Sanshou* 殷高宗問于三壽 held at the Friedrich-Alexander University, Erlangen–Nuremberg, Germany, May 10–12, 2016, and read there by a colleague because he was unable to attend for health reasons. Professor Li passed away on February 24, 2019.

Ladies and Gentlemen:

Some time ago, in Beijing, I heard that a grand celebration of Professor Sarah Allan's scholarly achievements would be held during this academic forum. I was extremely delighted about this.

I have had the good fortune to know and work with Professor Allan for many years, already more than thirty. I remember, in 1986, Professor Allan and I traveled together all over Germany to examine the Chinese artifacts collected in each place. We traveled from Sweden to what was at that time East Berlin and then to West Berlin. I will never forget that day, because it was precisely on that day that the nuclear accident occurred in Ukraine at Chernobyl, now already thirty years ago.

As a very old friend of Professor Allan, I would like to say a few personal words here, based on my superficial understanding and experience, about her extensive and extraordinary scholarly achievements.

First, what I wish to talk about is this: the breadth of erudition in Professor Allan's scholarship. Professor Allan has, for decades, concentrated her research on early Chinese culture, paying particular attention to the history of early Chinese thought. She has continued the Western sinological tradition and has meticulously studied the Classics; moreover, she has been able to gain mastery of new archaeological finds and excavated documents. The range of her research is extremely broad; but the issues she has addressed are complex and subtle. From oracle bone inscriptions and bronzes up to Warring States, Qin, and Han manuscripts on bamboo, wood, and silk, in all of these fields, there are problems that she has paid attention to and contributions that she has made—this is extremely difficult and very valuable.

Second, I wish to say that, in her research, Professor Allan has keen insight and is able to grasp issues opportunely; moreover, she has stamina and perseverance, and wholeheartedly delves into her research. Over these several decades, she has completed an enormous number of undertakings, some of which were pure contributions. For example, people do not necessarily know how arduously she worked on arranging and publishing in China all the [non-Buddhist] Dunhuang materials in British collections, even though Dunhuang research is not within the main sphere of her concerns. It is precisely because of Professor Allan's broad erudition, keen insight, and steadfast spirit that she has achieved such extraordinary scholarly results, which are generally respected throughout the scholarly world.

Her past works have already been translated into Chinese in four volumes as *The Collected Works of Sarah Allan* and published in Beijing. Now, I suggest that everyone heartily congratulate her on the publication of her new book, *Buried Ideas*. The Chinese version of this important book, which specifically focuses on newly discovered bamboo-slip manuscripts will very soon be published as the fifth volume of her *Collected Works*. Professor Allan's scholarly achievements are ever innovative, as she is continuously forging new paths. I know that we are all looking forward to even more research from Professor Allan in the future.

Respectfully wishing Professor Allan good health, success, and happiness.

—Li Xueqin

Preface

The advent of scientific archaeology and the discovery of oracle bones more than one hundred years ago opened up the field of early China studies in dramatic ways. The constant unveiling of new archaeological discoveries, including inscriptions and manuscripts, has forced scholars of early China to broaden the scope of their research beyond the traditional sources of our received corpus. At the same time, novel theoretical approaches and methodologies have been brought to bear alongside this wave of new data. The field has been bursting with innovation and recalibration ever since.

There has been no scholar more attuned to these developments than Sarah Allan. Over the past fifty years, she has published pathbreaking scholarship on early China. Utilizing both received texts and archaeological discoveries as her sources, she has helped mold early Chinese studies with pioneering research on a remarkable range of topics and time periods—from the Neolithic up through the Han—in disciplines as varied as paleography and conceptual metaphor theory.

Metaphor and Meaning is part of a three-book series, with *Myth and the Making of History* and *Bone, Bronze, and Bamboo*, that celebrates Allan and the integral role she has played in the immense growth and development of early China as a field. Scholars throughout the world, who have collaborated with her as mentors, colleagues, and students, were invited to contribute essays in her honor, which we have compiled into these three books. While the range of specialist essays presented here testifies to the expanding boundaries of the study of early China, we believe that, as with Allan's scholarship from the very beginning, there is a compelling and overlapping concern: to understand early China on its own terms. Whether through uncovering the root metaphors of the culture, articulating the interplay between myth and history, or examining newly discovered artifacts, Allan has sought to detach from our modern vantage, to enter into the minds of the ancient peoples of China, understand how they thought, and discern how they communicated those ideas.

∽

Metaphor and Meaning explores early Chinese philosophy, religion, and the language through which they were communicated—both metaphoric and linguistic. While picking up on numerous topics that Allan has discussed over the years in her collected works, the present volume pays special homage to her methodological interest in the application of conceptual metaphor theory to the study of early China. Conceptual metaphor theory, as first advanced by George Lakoff and Mark Johnson in *Metaphors We Live By*, treats metaphors not just as linguistic expressions but as fundamentally structuring thought processes that define one's conceptual system and perception of reality.[1] To understand a worldview adopted by members of another culture, then, hinges upon identifying the right metaphors, through which it becomes possible to navigate between shared and unshared experiences.[2]

It is this mission on which Allan embarks in her *The Way of Water and Sprouts of Virtue*.[3] Allan argues that "early Chinese thinkers, whatever their philosophical school, assumed that common principles informed the natural and human worlds."[4] She places this observation in contrast to Western philosophical traditions, which embedded root metaphors from Indo-European religious mythologies that assumed transcendence. For the holistic worldview of early Chinese thinkers, however, the "natural world was the source of the root metaphors used in the formulation of abstract concepts and its imagery is embedded in the language and structure of Chinese philosophy."[5] This insight allows Allan to explicate many of the most central—and yet also perplexing, from our now-distant purview—philosophical terms employed in early Chinese philosophy (e.g., *dao* 道, *wuwei* 無為, *xin* 心, *qi* 氣, *wanwu* 萬物, *de* 德, *xing* 性, *cai* 材, *duan* 端, *ren* 仁, *ziran* 自然, and *wei* 偽), through metaphors based on attributes of water and the plant life nourished by water.

When compiling *Metaphor and Meaning*, we selected essays from the invited contributors that pursued lines of argument that complement, enhance, or challenge Allan's prior investigations into these root metaphors of early Chinese philosophy, whether by explicitly engaging with conceptual metaphor theory or, more indirectly, addressing meaning construction in a broader sense. The crucial role played by attributes of water in early Chinese thinking serves as a point of departure for several chapters. Erica Brindley looks at "watery actions and modes of being," particularly acts of creativity or even cosmic creation, within the philosophical narratives of the "Natural Way" (Dao) from the Warring States through Han, distinguishing between cosmologies of creative flow (her reoriented "Daoism") and cosmologies of resonance (often referred to as "Five Phase" theory). Vivienne Lo and Gu Man analyze newly discovered medical manuscripts and artifacts to show how the Han imperial conception of the human body as a hydrological landscape derives from a water homology indebted to Warring States natural philosophy—and perhaps even the geographical texturing that springs from life along the Yangzi itself. Medical healing thus came to involve knowledge of the liquid flow of *qi* 氣 through bodily channels and manipulating the riverine named system of acupuncture points that regulated it. As Gil Raz shows, basic metaphors about the flow and management of *qi* as water likewise informed Celestial Master religious healing. The deviance of backward flowing or stagnant *qi* was mapped over onto demonic illness and the rectification of *qi*'s proper stream required a new type of demonic management, which demanded demons' arrest or violent removal through spirit warfare. Yet, as Edmund Ryden contends, the dynamism of flowing water and growing plants presented a conceptual obstacle for describing unity. Ryden argues how in the Song dynasty, metaphors based on *li* 理, or the patterning of veins in jadeite stone, navigated this dilemma and successfully combined unity with multiplicity.

Fundamental to Allan's application of conceptual metaphor theory to early Chinese thinking is an assumed holistic worldview that joins humanity to the larger cosmos. Although nature may have dictated the root metaphors Allan identifies, Roger T. Ames warns that we cannot cast the dyadic yet constitutive relationship between humanity and *tian* 天 (the cosmic) as one in which the former is unilaterally shaped by the latter. Rather, the mutuality of *tian* and humanity, expressed by the saying *tianren heyi* 天人合一, in fact, permits human sagacity an affect upon the natural order in turn. By again addressing the relationship between "the one and the many," Ames calls for us to treat Chinese philosophy in a whole new light. In the chapter by Constance A. Cook, the relationship between humanity and the cosmos finds religious expression with Shang oracle bones. Cook notes how it is through the microcosm of the human body, reflected in the bone media, that the macrocosm of the greater cosmos is experienced most intimately. Focusing on the language for healing recorded on turtle plastrons, she contextualizes words that suggest ancient iatromantic binding techniques meant to contain "toxin" (*du* 毒). Cook connects the cosmic layers of the turtle plastron with the royal "body"—itself conceptually expandable from the physical into the four directions of the political and supernatural realm. Treating the king's body also cured the world, while burning the turtle plastron healed the king's body in turn.

Other chapters delve into the intimate connection between the body and state in early China as well, expanding upon the political dimensions to metaphors of and for bodily experience, specifically in manuscripts from the Tsinghua University collection. In an analysis of the *Xin shi wei zhong* 心是謂中 (The Heart Is Called the Center) manuscript, Chen Wei conducts a close reading of the first section of the *Xin shi wei zhong*, which he titles "Xin jun" 心君 or "Mind as Ruler." Chen's copious textual annotations, providing justification for word choices and interpretations, are a model of modern Chinese paleographical approaches to deciphering unearthed manuscripts, especially those without parallels in our received corpus. Treating another manuscript from the Tsinghua collection, *Tang chuyu Tangqiu* 湯處於湯丘 (Tang Resides Near the Mound of Tang), Shirley Chan explores how natural metaphors drawing from bodily experiences—such as eating and illness—were linked to historical allegory as a way of guiding the body politic. In this manuscript, the legend of Yi Yin's culinary skill, with his proper blending of ingredients into nourishing food, provides a lesson in statecraft, where harmonization allowed for the health of the state, as it does for the human body.

The conceptual systems and worldviews adopted by a given community find tangible expression in their lived political and religious practices. The chapters by Gu and Lo, Raz, and Cook, already briefly introduced, draw direct connections between, on the one hand, metaphoric thinking based on the attributes of water and a presumed holism to the human-cosmos relationship, to, on the other hand, specific healing practices conducted in early and medieval China. With Cheung Kwong-yue's survey of descriptions for ritualized archery competitions, drawing from Shang to Han period sources, we are again invited to reflect upon how specific practices developed out of larger cultural orientations and ways of thinking. This is true as well for the chapter by Han Yujiao, who explicates 革 (skin, leather) and related terms found on the Huayuanzhuang East oracle-bone inscriptions (Huayuanzhuang dongdi jiagu 花園莊東地甲骨), arguing that these name a sacrifice requiring animals to be skinned with their hides presented.[6] Another curious observation raised by Han, however, is that the Huang 黃 diviner group produced bones with omen cracks uniquely directed away from the central axis of a given plastron or carapace. This differs from the majority of omen cracks found on other Shang oracle bones, complicating assumptions of any overarching Shang royal style (or indeed, divination technique). Han calls for a more refined view of Shang practices, reminding us of the often subtle diversity exhibited internally within the communities we study.

The last chapter of *Metaphor and Meaning* deserves special recognition, as the final scholarly contribution by Rudolph G. Wagner before his passing.[7] Language mediates meaning construction, with linguistic analysis a necessary preliminary for any scholar who works on ancient texts and the ideas they express. To this end, Wagner's chapter turns to the function word *gu* 故 (that is why), as the cornerstone of early Chinese argumentative rhetoric. He traces the historical development of *gu* and challenges common misconceptions about its definition (e.g., as establishing a cause-effect relationship, "therefore"). He shows how *gu* links an *explicandum* and an *explicans* in an implied dialogic situation, with variations to the argumentative logic behind this linkage that may map over onto generic boundaries (e.g., histories versus Masters literature).

With *Metaphor and Meaning*, we celebrate Allan's dedication to understanding early China on its own terms and, specifically, her interest in conceptual metaphor theory. The chapters in this volume do so by asking a wide array of questions, at various registers of analysis and using a broad range of methodologies. When and how do particular metaphors emerge, and with what other conceptual systems did they compete? How did this relate to humanity's perceived relationship to nature and a larger cosmos? What role did political institutions play in formulating a language for understanding bodily experience, and vice versa? How did certain worldviews manifest themselves as tangible political and religious practices? How were they expressed through linguistic articulation? It is through Allan's work that we have been invited to explore these questions and more.

—Constance A. Cook, Christopher J. Foster, and Susan Blader

Notes

1. George Lakoff and Mark Johnson, *Metaphors We Live By* (Chicago: University of Chicago Press, 1980). Lakoff and Johnson have continued to develop the field, for instance by examining the role of embodied experience in structuring cognition; see their *Philosophy in the Flesh* (New York: Basic Books, 1999).

2. Lakoff and Johnson, *Metaphors We Live By*, 232–33.
3. Sarah Allan, *The Way of Water and Sprouts of Virtue* (Albany: State University of New York Press, 1997).
4. Allan, *Way of Water*, 4.
5. Allan, *Way of Water*, 4.
6. Portions of chapter 10 have been previously published as Han Yujiao 韓宇嬌, "Huadong buci 'ge' zi shiyi ni Huang lei bujia zhao zhixiang wenti chuyi" 花東卜辭'革'字釋義及黃類卜甲兆指向問題芻議, *Jiaguwen Yin Shang shi* 甲骨文殷商史 10 (2020): 238–42.
7. For a tribute to Wagner and his career, see Barbara Mittler, "Rudolf G. Wagner—A Man of Many Dreams," *T'oung Pao* 106 (2020): 1–7, as well as her more extensive piece, with Monica Juneja, "The Joys of Transculturality—or Research and Teaching between China and the World: A Tribute to Rudolf G. Wagner," in *China and the World—the World and China: Essays in Honor of Rudolf G. Wagner*, ed. Joachim Gentz et al. (Gossenberg: Ostasien Verlag, 2019), vol. 1, ix–xiv.

Acknowledgments

We would like to express our most heartfelt appreciation to our colleagues for their enthusiastic engagement with this project, their insightful scholarly outputs, and their extraordinary patience. We are certain that, as a result of their care and attention, the essays in the three books—*Myth and the Making of History: Narrating Early China with Sarah Allan*; *Bone, Bronze, and Bamboo: Unearthing Early China with Sarah Allan*; and *Metaphor and Meaning: Thinking Through Early China with Sarah Allan*—will be welcomed by scholars and students in the China field, as well as by individuals interested or involved in the study of any ancient civilization.

These three books could never have been brought to completion without the editing expertise of four colleagues. Gail Patten[1] did the first complete editing and compilation of the pieces. The editorial and computer expertise of Ehud Z. Benor[2] was indispensable in creating the template required by SUNY Press to unify the formatting of each chapter. William N. French III,[3] at an exceptionally busy and stressful time, took on the huge task of finalizing *Metaphor and Meaning*, for which we are immensely grateful. Amy Matthewson[4] beautifully finalized both *Myth and the Making of History* and *Bone, Bronze, and Bamboo*. We also wish to express our gratitude to James Peltz[5] for his support of this massive project, and to the anonymous reviewers of *Metaphor and Meaning*, who offered much helpful advice.

Our thanks go to Lehigh University for providing Constance A. Cook[6] with research funding as part of her position as an NEH Distinguished Professor. The project began when Cook was an active member of the Institute for Advanced Study in Princeton, New Jersey, whose support is much appreciated. Christopher J. Foster[7] is grateful for the support he received from Pembroke College, University of Oxford, when Stanley Ho

Junior Research Fellow; and from the British Academy and SOAS University of London, during his British Academy Postdoctoral Fellowship.

Finally, Connie and Chris both wish to acknowledge the profound contribution of Susan Blader,[8] who conceived of the project as a felicitous tribute to Sarah, nurtured it constantly, and ensured—through all manner of trials and tribulations—that it grew to adulthood.

Notes

1. Administrator, Department of History, Dartmouth College, Retired.
2. Emeritus, Department of Religion, Dartmouth College.
3. PhD ABD, Chinese History, East Asian Languages and Civilizations, Harvard University; Dartmouth College '08.
4. PhD, History, SOAS University of London.
5. Associate Director and Editor in Chief at SUNY Press.
6. Professor and Chair, Modern Languages and Literatures, Lehigh University.
7. PhD Chinese History, East Asian Languages and Civilizations, Harvard University; Dartmouth College '06.
8. Associate Professor Emerita, Asian and Middle Eastern Languages and Literatures, Dartmouth College.

1

A Fluid Cosmos

Cosmologies of Creative Flow in Early China

Erica Brindley

Flow: Watery Actions and Modes of Being

By the fourth century BCE, some groups of early Chinese thinkers propounded an expansive cosmological vision that differed significantly from visions passed down from the early Zhou period. Instead of a world in which the dominant deities were animated spirits (whether gods such as Shangdi 上帝 or the spirits of human ancestors, animals, or other creatures), this cosmology presented a more unified, monistic image of a divine cosmos—rooted ultimately in Heaven (Tian 天) and the Way (Dao 道) of Heaven—from which humans derive and of which they are a part. Humans and all creatures, according to this religious view, are but creative manifestations of the intrinsic force and power latent in the heavenly cosmos.

In this chapter, I will build on Sarah Allan's in-depth work on the role of water in early Chinese mythology and thought. Allan's work examines the many rich representations and meanings of water, which was linked in some traditions to the early cosmos.[1] Rather than analyze the concrete image of water itself as a metaphor, I discuss watery actions and modes of being—movements and activities associated with the Dao of the cosmos, such as creativity, spontaneity, and flow. In the end, my analysis aligns with

Allan's goal of showing how the natural and human orders were supposed to merge in a single continuum.

When Allan links water to associated root metaphors in early Chinese philosophy, she considers the views they stem from to be starkly secular, separate from any religious, spiritual order. She states that the early Chinese found root metaphors "in the natural world rather than religious mythology."[2] The conceptual split between nature and religion, however, is very much a Euro-American conceit, grounded in the ways in which these traditions define religion and pit it against the workings of the natural world. At the same time that I agree with Allan that the study of ancient China compels us to step outside of our conceptual world, I also think we need to do so by stepping away from Euro-American tendencies to strip "nature" of any religious heritage or meaning. We might begin by pointing out what some of our thinkers seem to take as self-evident: that nature and the natural order are fundamentally spiritual and nonsecular, and that the divine inheres in the natural.[3] Indeed, it is precisely by analyzing root metaphors in Chinese philosophy that we begin to consider different ways of ordering and arranging the world around us, helping us redefine what we mean by "religion" and "nature" as well.

In early China, some cultures were grounded in a belief that the natural cosmos was tantamount to the Way of the cosmos, an idealized or utopic vision of "the Natural." Ultimate good could be acquired, it was thought, via a reconciliation of the human world with this natural Way. A central question in this type of belief system, then, was how humans were supposed to reconcile themselves with the Way. Intriguingly, the answer to this question among a variety of thinkers who idealized the Natural Way (hereafter "Dao") was very similar: it was a matter of returning to, recovering, or embracing the constant agency of the Dao in one's life and person. In other words, one must essentially embody and become a true and unique manifestation of the Dao in this world.

In analyzing a few early Chinese creation stories and cosmologies, I will underscore the largely convergent ways in which thinkers who ascribed to this type of "Dao-embodiment" approach tried to characterize the natural simplicity and efficiency of the Dao itself, showing how their characterizations were intended to be guidelines for human behavior. The fact that so many different authors ascribed to this view of the cosmic-human relationship suggests a shared spiritual or religious outlook that stressed the unmediated spiritual embodiment of the Divine rather than obedience to Heaven's divine preferences or desires, and laws—all of which are mediated through society in some fashion.

Warring States texts reveal a plethora of religious views concerning Heaven (Tian) and its interactions with humans and creatures on Earth (Di 地). The textual tradition is so diverse that it is often difficult to ascertain whether there were dominant ways of conceiving of the cosmos, and if so, what those dominant ways were. And, of course, we must always ask, "Dominant for whom, during what period, and for how long?" While I think it fair to say that there was a dominant religion of the elites rooted in the power of Heaven and Shangdi during the early Zhou period, authors during the later Zhou presented very different interpretations concerning how Heaven acted in the world and how humans were supposed to interact with Heaven and the spiritual world. Many scholars studying the fifth century BCE and later have fallen back on the ancient Chinese categorization of texts and thinkers into "schools of thought," such as Confucian, Daoist, Mohist, Sophistic, Agriculturalist, among others. This approach has been thoroughly problematized in recent years, especially with the introduction of newly excavated manuscripts that do not fit neatly into such categories and suggest a much more complicated picture. Nonetheless, as I will argue here, there are merits to some basic distinctions among these alleged groups, as long as we understand them to be our own hermeneutical categories and do not take them as necessarily emic groupings or institutional affiliations that corresponded to shared sociopolitical realities at the time.

The bulk of my analysis is organized around the concept of creativity, a category under which I group many linked actions or activities, including spontaneity, self-generation or self-arising, and flow (English terms that can be used to translate concepts like *wuwei* 無爲, *ziran* 自然, *zizuo* 自作, *shun/tong* 順/通).[4] This set of English terms helps translate ancient Chinese descriptions of idealized human actions or interactions with things in the world. Taken together, they serve as an interpretive cluster characteristic of a religious orientation that began to enter into Chinese mainstream philosophy around the fourth century BCE, becoming quite visible with the onset of more systematic cosmological thinking at the time. Since our early authors never just restricted themselves to one term or way of describing idealized action in accordance with the Dao, it is advisable that we examine as many related ideas as possible. Intriguingly, the way water moves and interacts with objects is a superior metaphor that links these actions together and may be the best way to describe what is salient and important about the ideal of Dao-embodiment.

Scholarship abounds on how some early authors, such as those of the *Zhuangzi* 莊子, *Laozi* 老子, *Huainanzi* 淮南子, and so forth, argue for an idealized congruence between human and cosmos, or the idealized natural world around us.⁵ One thing that is readily apparent in many Dao-embodiment accounts, however, is not that idealized modes of action in the human realm are linked to the Dao of the spiritual cosmos but that the primary agency of the individual is identical to the functionality of the Dao. I therefore begin with a basic provocation that refines the notion of human-cosmic congruence, arguing instead for identification. In other words, humans must not be congruent with the cosmos; they must tap into it and its very functionality. Since the idealized cosmic Dao functions according to a certain mode, humans should also function according to that very same mode. Indeed, the more appropriate way to conceptualize this approach is not that we mimic cosmic behavior and act similarly to it, but that our behavior is cosmic behavior.

Michael Puett has written extensively on the early Chinese notion of a human becoming a god or divinity. He discusses such a notion primarily in terms of discrete ideologies of what he dubs "self-divinization," which began in the fourth century BCE but flourished especially during the imperial period. Explaining the growth of such ideologies as intentional, oppositional claims made to redirect power away from major courts and their practices of sacrifice and divination, Puett positions self-divinization movements as alternative, theoretical stances advocated by a few intellectuals, as opposed to large-scale religious practices stemming from alternative religious cultures such as "shamanism."⁶ While I agree with Puett that one should not draw a genetic link between so-called "correlative cosmology" and "shamanism," I picture a rather different image of the intellectual and religious movements of the period. Mine is not one in which a few elite men are engaged in self-conscious debate with each other to found new movements at court, but one in which the viewpoints presented in these texts, which we can presume elite men wrote and presented to some extent in various early Chinese courts, were not the sole possession of these men and their fellow intellectuals. Rather, many of these elites were representing and drawing upon larger and rather extensive religious and cultural practices, either imported or more local to a particular region. And such practices implicated people from all walks of life, not just the educated or literate elite. So, whereas Puett speaks of a few main actors who created agendas, rebelling against contemporary norms and innovating at the top of society, I would like to propose that these few main actors were acting within a larger sphere of embedded religious practices and a more general religious orientation. My conclusions in this chapter—concerning the continuities and similarities among Dao-embodiment outlooks and ways of expressing idealized human action—support this view.

My discussion of concepts such as creativity, spontaneity, and flow thus reveals a diverse yet largely convergent way that many authors characterized the natural simplicity and efficiency of the idealized cosmos. I show how this convergent approach, which I argue corresponds approximately to typical uses of the category "Daoist," differs from others in the Central States sphere in its view of the human potential to embody the divine cosmos. And to make sure that this approach to Dao-embodiment is not confused and conflated with another type of cosmology that was gaining traction around the same time in early China—Five Phases correlative cosmology—I further outline fundamental differences between the two. I thereby draw a distinction between Dao-embodiment "cosmologies of flow" and Five Phases "cosmologies of resonance." By identifying the category of "Daoist" as a noteworthy spiritual orientation on embodied (cosmic) creativity in society, I also show how the concept of "Daoism" might be fruitfully used to underscore cosmologies of flow in ancient China.

Creativity as the Functionality of the Cosmos

In the middle part of the twentieth century, Joseph Needham spoke of the Chinese predilection for self-generated creation rather than creator gods and myths.[7] In subsequent decades, Western scholars such as Frederick Mote, Derk Bodde, and Chang Kwang-chih, for example, picked up on Needham's insight to discuss the so-called lack of a "creation myth" in early Chinese culture, basing their claims on arguments about the "inner necessity" or "spontaneously self-generating" nature of the cosmos. These claims by twentieth-century scholars have since been convincingly refuted by Paul Goldin in his article "The Myth That China Has No Creation Myth."[8] Most contemporary China scholars would have a hard time not agreeing with Goldin's arguments. There are creator gods—and many of them—in early Chinese traditions. We see this in the pantheon of gods associated with the ancient state of Chu, as well as in the *Taiyi sheng shui* 太一生水 (Taiyi Gives Birth to Water) excavated manuscript, among other sources.[9]

Nonetheless, there is indeed a way in which Mote, Bodde, and others were right: certain cosmological outlooks in early China do not describe creation in terms of anthropomorphic acts of will, intent, and active fashioning.[10] Rather, creation is sometimes described in terms of organic, biological metaphors of self-generation, coupling, and spontaneous emergence or arising. Bodde describes this process in the following terms: "[The Chinese] cosmic pattern is self-contained and self-operating. It unfolds itself because of its own inner necessity and not because it is ordained by any external volitional power. Not surprisingly, therefore, Chinese thinkers who have expressed themselves on the subject are unanimous in rejecting the possibility that the universe may have originated through any single act of conscious creation."[11] In trying to encapsulate a singularly "Chinese" approach to creation, Derk Bodde most certainly oversimplified the matter. But his description of the cosmic pattern as something that unfolds is very helpful in underscoring what is important about a particular, more naturalistic or organic vision of cosmic creation.

A new bamboo-slip text called *Hengxian* 恆先 (hereafter: *The Primordial State of Constancy*) provides us with a rare opportunity to familiarize ourselves more precisely with one version of cosmic creativity and flow in the world. It is helpful to start our analysis with this text because it depicts the spiritual cosmos quite clearly as something fundamentally creative. Moreover, the natural creativity of the cosmos expresses itself in a liquid manner: every creation, indeed every living being, both comes into being and functions according to a localized, unique version of spontaneous generation. This is best described as a process of cosmic flow or unfolding.[12]

In *The Primordial State of Constancy*, we find one of the most complete accounts of cosmic creation in early Chinese texts. The text begins:

> In the primordial state of Constancy, there is no material existence. There is simplicity, stillness, and emptiness. Simplicity is Great Simplicity; stillness is Great Stillness; emptiness is Great Emptiness.[13] It fulfills itself without repressing itself. [Bounded] space arises.[14] Once there is [bounded] space, there is *qi*; once there is *qi*, there is material existence; once there is material existence, there is a beginning; once there is a beginning, there is the passage of time.

> 恒先無有，樸，靜，虛。樸，大樸；靜，大靜；虛，大虛。自厭，不自忍。域作。有域，焉有氣；有氣，焉有有；有有，焉有始；有始，焉有往者。[15]

In this passage we see how, out of nowhere, the primordial state of Constancy—defined as Great Simplicity, Great Stillness, and Great Emptiness—encounters or experiences change. This occurs through the arising of (bounded) space (*yuzuo* 域作).[16]

The text goes on to show that the process of change and creation intrinsic to the cosmos is a process of the spontaneous arising (*zizuo* 自

作) or spontaneous generation/birthing (*zisheng* 自生) of *qi* 氣 and other ingredients such as space-time. Most intriguingly, the author makes sure to emphasize that such arising and generation occurs of its own accord and is not reliant on some external creator or force: "*Qi* is self-generating; Constancy categorically does not engender *qi*. *Qi* is self-generating and self-arising" (氣是自生, 恆莫生氣, 氣是自生自作).[17] From this passage, we can deduce that cosmic creation involves transformation of *qi*, and that this process is always ongoing, so that every entity or thing that takes shape is always changing in relationship to others at a specific place and time. This process of change within space-time is the creative fulfillment of things. Situations and objects change by arising "of themselves," and not because they are fueled by an "inner necessity" (to use Bodde's terms) or an internal motivator or creator; indeed, there is no absolute "internal" in a ceaselessly changing "self" or "thing." Instead, the motivator that causes change is the intrinsic motor of the cosmos.

The paramount question that this description of the cosmos evokes, then, begins not with "what" but with "how." The author seems interested not in answering the question "What (entity) causes things to be created and transformed?" but, rather "How are things created and transformed?" The answer, as we have seen, lies in the notion that creation is a spontaneous process of boundary-making in which all *qi* is generative and everything has the potential to change according to its proper, cosmic place in space and time. Rather than erroneously attribute the cause of such creativity to either an external creator or internal power (i.e., a power intrinsic to a thing), let us simply call it "cosmic flow."

The second half of the text breaks from a discussion of the idealized creativity of the pre-cosmos and early cosmos to talk about the actions and thoughts of human beings. Blaming humans for the current disorder in the world, the author implies that humans should clean up the mess: "Primordially, there is good, order, and no disorder. Once there are humans, there is not-good. Disorder emerges from human beings" (先者有善, 有治無亂; 有人焉有不善, 亂出於人).[18] Since humans are the cause of all "not-good" (*bushan* 不善) in the world, we should clearly be the ones to fix it, but how? Thankfully, the second part of the text provides suggestions. Humans can reset their primordial relationship with the cosmos by entering into the cosmic flow. To be sure, humans must leave behind their imagined notions of permanent, fixed boundaries that define entities and things and focus instead on a more fluid understanding of creative change and nonstop boundary-making/unmaking.

But how to reengage ourselves in this Constancy? The author states: "Regarding the actions of the world: by neither avoiding nor partaking in them, they can happen of themselves" (舉天下之為也，無舍也，無與也，而能自為也).[19] If one takes this statement at face value, its meaning remains opaque, and it is difficult to guess at what the author means when saying "by neither avoiding nor partaking in [something]" (無舍也，無與也). Yet if one uses the metaphor of water, especially its image of flow and the dissolution of discrete boundaries, the text's message comes into focus. Indeed, the cosmic flow will take its course if we but stop actively meddling around, avoiding things, or inserting ourselves consciously into affairs—if we stop trying to control or dam up the water. Instead, by acting like water, we allow *wei* activity (*wei* 為) to "occur of its own" (*ziwei* 自為). So, while activity of some sort does take place, it is not activity intended by us in any way. This is what spontaneity means in the context of *The Primordial State of Constancy*: it is tapping into the creative flow of the cosmos and thereby reestablishing our connection to the fundamentally creative processes of the cosmos.

Water is famous for taking the shape of whatever container or landscape it finds itself in. The following excerpt reveals the importance of context—of time and space—in shaping who we are at any particular moment and how we proceed in this process of unending change: "[As for] the arisings of the world: if they do not go against Constancy, there will be nothing that opposes its place" (天下之作也，無迕恆，無非其所).[20] Here, arisings that are coordinated with Constancy, presumably those that are right and do not cause disorder by breaking with the cosmic fabric, possess a proper place (*qi suo* 其所). I read "place" here in a metaphysical way, implying one's role or position not merely in the social realm but in a hierarchy of humans, animals, and things in relationship to each other. In the context of the larger cosmogonic argument of the text, I think it appropriate to interpret "place" as the specific site in which Constancy functions, one that is connected to all other sites.

The author exhorts people to find their proper place by allowing the creative processes of the cosmos to work through them to establish proper relationships among things. This does not mean mimicking the Heavenly cosmos but embodying it as we proceed through every moment in space. With respect to water, it means leaving behind any attempt to control or direct it but, rather, to become like water instead. An arising, in any living being, is unique and uniquely connected to other arisings around it; it does not follow along just any generalized path of Constancy, as though proceeding along the same, broad road as everything else. Rather, each arising must obtain and fulfill its particular Constancy (*qi heng* 其恆) at specific locations and moments of time (*qi suo*). Creativity and spontaneity in this context are the cosmic forces that allow each of us to bubble forth from our cosmic, divine source and stream along the grooves and landscapes in which we live.

The Cosmos and Flow

Another recently unearthed manuscript, the *Taiyi sheng shui* (Taiyi Gives Birth to Water, hereafter *Taiyi*), provides a cosmogonic genesis account that directly involves water and its flow.[21] The text, like *The Primordial State of Constancy*, also enjoins followers to embrace and reconnect themselves to creative, organic processes of nature, although *Taiyi* is more obvious in articulating the cyclical aspects of these processes. The details of *Taiyi*'s cosmogony are utterly different from *The Primordial State of Constancy*, insofar as it traces everything back to a creator god, Taiyi. But the main emphasis on a natural process of creative change, along with its exhortation that humans embody such change, is similar. We might therefore include it in our group of texts that support what I have called a "Dao-embodiment" approach.

In the text, water, created initially by a creator god(dess), Taiyi, joins together with first-created cosmic entities such as Heaven and Earth to initiate the natural forces and cycles of the cosmos. Flow in this context is flow that completes a cycle and reverts back to the beginning to start again. It is a divine process initiated by Taiyi and carried out according to a cosmological logic of cyclical progression and completion. The first paragraph of the text describes this well:

> Taiyi gives birth to water, which returns to assist it. In this manner it completes Heaven. Heaven returns and assists Taiyi and thereby completes Earth. Heaven and Earth then mutually assist each other, and in this manner they thereby complete the numinous and bright. The numinous and bright then mutually assist each other, and in this manner they thereby complete Yin and Yang. Yin and Yang then mutually assist each other, and in this manner they thereby complete the Four Seasons. The Four Seasons then mutually assist each other, and in this manner they

thereby complete coldness and hotness. Coldness and hotness then mutually assist each other, and in this manner they thereby complete moisture and dryness. Moisture and dryness then mutually assist each other, and in this manner they thereby complete the year, after which [this process] comes to a halt.

大 (太) 一生水, 水反鋿 (輔) 大 (太) 一, 是以成天. 天反鋿 (輔) 大 (太) 一, 是以成埅 (地). 天埅 (地)【復相輔】也, 是以成神明. 神明復相 鋿 (輔) 也, 是以成盨 (陰) 睸 (陽). 盨 (陰) 睸 (陽) 復相鋿 (輔) 也, 是以成四時. 復【相】鋿 (輔) 也, 是以成倉 (滄) 然 (熱). 倉 (滄) 然 (熱) 復相鋿 (輔) 也, 是以成溼澡 (燥). 溼澡 (燥) 復相鋿 (輔) 也, 成凾 (歲) 而繢 (止).[22]

It is worth noting here that the creation of the "myriad things"—humans, animals, and even *qi*-material force—is, surprisingly, missing.[23] The point of the passage is to depict cosmic acts of creation and self-fulfilling natural cycles—or cycles that automatically propel the world and its creatures forward along an appropriate path. The emphasis, as was the case in *The Primordial State of Constancy*, is not on the manifold things of the world but on the constant movement and inevitability of creative cycles in the cosmos.

In *Taiyi*, in particular, creative flow consists in actions such as proceeding (*xing* 行), cycling back (*zhou* 周), reverting back (*fan* 反), mutually assisting (*fu* 輔), and completing (*cheng* 成). These are all highly interactive and dynamic processes based on cycles of life and seasonal change. Take, for example, the following passage:

> For this reason Taiyi hides in water, proceeds with the seasons, cycles back around and starts again . . . [it takes itself as] the mother of the myriad things.
>
> 是古 (故) 大 (太) 一襐 (藏) 於水, 行於時, 猵 (周) 而或【始, 以己為】冨 (萬) 勿 (物) 母.[24]

Implicated in this never-ending process of cyclical change is an interactive type of creativity in which leading actors mutually participate in a cosmic dance of sorts, helping each other bring natural cycles to fruition. The authors are intriguingly not concerned so much with the single-handed creation of an almighty God, although they concede that an almighty Taiyi started it all in the beginning by creating water. Instead, they seem focused on creativity as a process of mutual aid and assistance, one of completing, reverting back, and beginning again rather than actively fashioning and destroying. Destruction, in fact, is not really part of the vocabulary of these cosmic processes. As parts of cycles that continue over and over again, things are not actively destroyed; they wither and die and new things are born as a natural outcome of the process.

At this point, we might ask how humans are supposed to act in relationship to these divine cycles and forces, and how water might fit back into the story. While the author of *Taiyi* mostly speaks of cosmic cycles, certain passages in the text support the notion that such an interest feeds directly into a primary concern for the health and well-being of society and its individuals. The text states:

> Below, there is earth, and [this region] is called Earth. Above, there is *qi*, and [this region] is called Heaven. The Dao is also its familiar appellation. I beg to ask for its name. When carrying out affairs by way of the Dao, one must rely on its name. Thus, affairs of the world are completed and one's body develops.
>
> 下, 土也, 而胃 (謂) 之趡 (地). 上, 閔 (氣) 也, 而胃 (謂) 之天. 道亦其瞤 (字) 也. 青 (請) 昏 (問) 其名. 道從事者必瘅 (託) 其名, 古 (故) 事成而身長.²⁵

Here, the ideal agency of an individual who must carry out worldly affairs lies not in the "Dao" as a simple label or bounded appellation (*zi* 字) but, rather, in "its name (*ming* 名)."²⁶ The "name" of the Dao presumably refers to some sort of all-encompassing or infinite truth that cannot be put into language. From the context, it appears as though it refers to an ongoing process that helps bring everything in the human and natural worlds to completion, much like the creative, cosmic flow described in *The Primordial State of Constancy*. One might thus compare it to the "Constant Name" of the Dao, referred to in the *Daode jing* 道德經 (i.e., the *Laozi*).²⁷ In both the *Daode jing* and *Taiyi*, the "[Constant] Name" is the motor of the world and a font of inexhaustible creative powers that are referred to as "Constancy" (*heng* 恆) in *The Primordial State of Constancy*. And, in *Taiyi*, the very first and most basic expression of this creative power consists in the creation of water that permeates the universe and helps direct all natural cycles.

Many thinkers who ascribed to a type of Dao-embodiment approach of cosmic flow make use of similar verbs and varied metaphors for describing the spontaneous movement that constitutes both the movement of the cosmos and idealized human behavior. In the texts examined so far, we have encountered early cosmic activities such as spontaneous arising and generation, cycling or reverting back, completing, and mutually assisting. For humans, we find discussion of "relying on its name," "neither participating in nor avoiding," "letting things arise of themselves," and so on, which show that human actions need to be motivated by the same forces that motivate the cosmos. But nothing says "cosmic flow" more clearly than the language of Zhuangzi's concept of *you* 遊, the verb he invokes to describe an aspirant's ultimate freedom in the cosmic Dao (*xiaoyao you* 逍遙遊). Translated by Burton Watson as "free and easy wandering" and by A. C. Graham as "going rambling without a destination," wandering or rambling (*you* 遊), in these contexts, is about floating around, as though on water. In fact, the word meaning "to swim" (*you* 游) is often used interchangeably with "to ramble" in texts like the *Zhuangzi* and *Huainanzi*. This can be seen in the cosmological chapters of the *Huainanzi*, as well as in hundreds of other examples, where authors refer to the ideal person as one who is "roaming in the land of the Inexhaustible" (*you yu wuqiong zhi di* 游於無窮之地).[28] Even the more mundane meaning of *you* 遊—as "to travel," instead of "to ramble/wander"—imparts the dynamic change involved in this mode of acting in the world.

The usages of the two types of *you* 遊/游 in cosmic flow texts frequently follow a formula. Either they describe one's traveling in or around a specific worldly destination, like a state or other locale, or they describe where one rambles psychologically in life, in terms of a spiritual state of mind. When rambling in the latter manner, one goes about one's everyday business but in a cosmic dimension of space-time, with the cosmos as one's motivation for action. The formula appears frequently: one goes "rambling in X" (遊於 X), where X stands for some kind of vast, cosmic space such as the infinite, the murky (*mingming* 冥冥),[29] a "no-man's-land wilderness" (*wuren zhi ye* 無人之野), "with the Dao rambling in the state of Large Nothingness" (*yu dao you yu damo zhi guo* 與道遊於大莫之國),[30] "on the banks of the Murky River" (*xuanshui zhi shang* 玄水之上),[31] "outside the Six Convergences" (*liuhe zhiwai* 六合之外), or the likes.[32]

So far, I have outlined the links that authors in a few early texts made between early cosmic processes of creation and idealized human action. In each of these texts, the solution for avoiding human-made chaos and ensuring cosmic harmony is ultimately a psychophysiological one based on the proper embodiment of the Dao. While the metaphors may change, the type of activity and its source in the Dao remains the same, and it always involves change that creates a new, localized configuration in space and time. Moreover, such an activity does not involve pursuing the desires of oneself or one's close associates; following or changing laws; setting up and abiding in a particular social, political, or ritual order; or divining and sacrificing to spirits outside the self. It involves, quite simply and, in contrast to many other types of approaches in early China, individuals altering their states of mind so that they engage the cosmic flow of the immanent Dao. From the perspective of political philosophy, this type of solution to social order is fundamentally decentralized and based in individual behaviors, not institutional structures or policies. It also presupposes a fundamentally religious belief that the cosmic flow, when properly invoked, will help bring order and other good things to the world.

Correlative Cosmology versus Cosmologies of Flow

How do cosmologies of flow (or Dao-embodiment approaches) differ from other cosmologies that might be labeled "naturalistic" in orientation? By this, I refer to cosmological articulations that became popular in late Warring States China that depicted a cosmos that functioned according to causes that we might deem to be at once "natural," "spiritual," and "physical," rather than due to the intention or will of deities, supernatural beings, or living or deceased beings and ancestors. So-called "correlative cosmologies" (or Five Phases cosmologies) are one such type of cosmology that gained renown around the same time as cosmologies of flow.[33] Although most scholars hold Five Phases cosmology (I will refer to them as "cosmologies of resonance" from now on) to be intrinsically linked to any early naturalistic ways of describing the cosmos, I will argue a slightly different point here. The fact that many authors in early China became interested in articulating naturalistic, largely non-animistic cosmologies during the period cannot be denied.[34] It is also true that such cosmologies were articulated precisely in order to explain how humans should act and interact in the world. But this does not mean that all naturalistic cosmologies are necessarily similar in kind.

It is important to distinguish cosmologies of flow from cosmologies of resonance, as they are based on a divergent way of presenting the idealized cosmic-human connection. Whereas cosmologies of flow ask that humans invoke, engage, and activate cosmic flow through their bodies and minds, cosmologies of resonance demand that humans study all the diverse objects and creatures in the world so as to reveal intrinsic resonances among categories of objects. Humans must then behave so that the natural resonances among objects can be revealed and "sounded" in the world. In other words, a resonance worldview requires that humans concertedly and consciously recreate situations and environments such that the underlying harmonies of the cosmos can be felt and appreciated by all.

In cosmologies of resonance, the goal is to figure out which objects have an automatic, reflexive, or resonant connection with each other. This active search for correlations, along with attempts to arrange and articulate them clearly to rulers and the public, is inimical to the embodied worldview presented by thinkers who promote cosmic flow. As pointed out earlier, the chief trait of this cosmology is creative, cosmic change. In cosmologies of flow, while an individual's embodiment of cosmic flow might actually result in a certain resonance or harmony with surrounding objects and creatures, the act of matching oneself up properly with these objects and creatures should never be taken as the primary goal. Moreover, the underlying resonances cannot be predicted beforehand, as with resonance cosmologies, since the Dao of the cosmos works creatively and spontaneously—that is, according to a process of self-generation that cannot be predicted or prescribed beforehand.

Conclusion

In this chapter I have highlighted what we might productively categorize as a shared approach or religious worldview that emerged sometime during Warring States China. Characterized by both a belief in a cosmology grounded in a naturalistic Dao and the imperative for humans to embody the cosmic flow of the Dao in their everyday lives, this orientation can be found in texts like the *Laozi*, *Zhuangzi*, *Taiyi sheng shui*, *The Primordial State of Constancy*, the *Huainanzi*, parts of *Master Lü's Spring and Autumn Annals* 呂氏春秋, and more. While Sima Qian's 司馬遷 father, Sima Tan 司馬談, is famous for having coined the label "Daoist School" to refer to a particular lineage and way of thought, scholars have recently questioned the legitimacy of thinking of Daoism as a school in early, preimperial times. I wish to present the claim: "Yes. There is something that we might fruitfully refer to as a 'Daoist' spiritual orientation in early China. Although it may not have been a self-conscious school of thought or organized itself in the same ways we currently may wish to organize our source materials, this spiritual orientation seems to have had an extensive reach in the intellectual world of Warring States China."

Building on Sarah Allan's work on water as well as Michael Puett's analyses of self-divinization movements, I argue that there was an overarching spiritual outlook—the Dao-embodiment approach—that viewed idealized human action in terms of cosmic flow and localized, creative, self-generating powers. Such a view might not differ that much from some formulations of "creativity" in the Western world. Cecilia A. Conrad, a spokesperson from the MacArthur Foundation, recently commented on two associated concepts that are popular in American notions of human excellence: genius and creativity. She said, "Genius is a state, but creativity is an activity: It's stuff you're doing."[35] Although there was no concept of genius in early Daoism, there was the notion that anyone who could engage the Dao in his or her life could become a spiritual person. Hence, the Daoist sage in early Daoism is comparable to what we might call a genius. And as for creativity as an activity rather than a state of being, the author(s) of *The Primordial State of Constancy* would mostly agree, although they would probably not care to differentiate between the two. Creativity (*zizuo, zisheng, ziwei/wuwei, ziran*) is an activity as well as a state of being—one that is latent and waiting to be uncovered in every second that passes and every space that exists.

It is important to note, again, that cosmologies of creative flow are different from cosmologies of resonance that became quite popular during the Han period. In cosmologies of resonance, there is an intrinsic connection postulated between two disparate objects merely because of their purported cosmological affinity with each other. Cosmologies of flow associate affinities based not on resonance but on intrinsic cosmological connection. They are based in an early Chinese form of spontaneity or creativity that is powered by the cosmos itself.[36] Affinities among objects and creatures of the world do frequently occur, but they do so because creatures in the world are fulfilling their natural, creative potentials and operating according to fundamental cosmic harmony, not because of a predefined, cosmic correlation.

Notes

1. Sarah Allan, *The Way of Water and Sprouts of Virtue* (Albany: State University of New York Press, 1997).

2. Allan, *Way of Water*, 4.

3. See Ames's essay in this volume for a discussion of the religiosity of early beliefs. I also discuss these issues in more detail in my books *Individualism in Early China: Human Agency and the Self in Thought and Politics* (Honolulu: University of Hawai'i Press, 2010) and *Music, Cosmology, and the Politics of Harmony in Early China* (Albany: State University of New York Press, 2012), and I provide background to the question of religion and nature on pages 1–5 of the latter book.

4. I use the English terms "creativity" and "creative," which also happen to describe the type of "creation" that occurs in creation myths associated with these types of activities. I try to limit my use of the terms to the ways that they are defined in the early Chinese texts, although it is important to recognize that many modern connotations of creativity may not be relevant to the context at hand.

5. In previous work, I have also discussed the human-cosmos relationship in terms of an isomorphism or parallelism.

6. Michael J. Puett, *To Become a God: Cosmology, Sacrifice, and Self-Divinization in Early China* (Cambridge, MA: Harvard University Asia Center, 2002), see esp. chap. 2, 80–121.

7. Joseph Needham, *Science and Civilisation in China*, vol. 2, *History of Scientific Thought* (Cambridge: Cambridge University Press, 1956).

8. Paul R. Goldin, "The Myth That China Has No Creation Myth," *Monumenta Serica* 56 (2008): 1–22.

9. We will discuss the *Taiyi* text later. See also Constance A. Cook and John. S. Major, eds., *Defining Chu: Image and Reality in Ancient China* (Honolulu: University of Hawai'i Press, 1999), esp. 121–65. As John Major states, "Modern scholars, relying on late Warring States and Han texts, have reached a consensus that Chinese cosmogony is unique in having an inception rather than a creation. . . . But the widely held image of the Chinese universe as 'uncreated' is in need of revision; the gods in the Chu Silk Manuscript are depicted unambiguously as cosmic creator-ancestors." *Defining Chu*, 129.

10. Mote claims that the "self-generating" cosmos—one with no god or creator external to itself—is distinctly "Chinese" or "northern Chinese." See Frederick W. Mote, "The Cosmological Gulf between China and the West," in *Transition and Permanence: Chinese History and Culture; A Festschrift in Honor of Dr. Hsiao Kung-ch'üan*, ed. David C. Buxbaum and Frederick W. Mote (Hong Kong: Cathay Press, 1972), 7–9.

11. Derk Bodde, *Essays on Chinese Civilization*, ed. Dorothy Borei and Charles Le Blanc (Princeton, NJ: Princeton University Press, 1981), 81. See also Derk Bodde, "Myths of Ancient China," in *Mythologies of the Ancient World*, ed. Samuel Noah Kramer (Garden City, NY: Anchor, 1961), 367–408; K. C. Chang, "Chinese Creation Myths: A Study in Method," *Bulletin of the Institute of Ethnology* 8 (1959): 47–79.

12. This is an unprovenanced text that was purchased on the illicit antiquities market and published in the many-volume series by the Shanghai Museum. Scholars

agree that it is authentic, written in the Chu script, and likely dates to around the same time as the manuscripts unearthed at Guodian (ca. 300 BCE). All translations of this text are taken from our translation in Erica F. Brindley, Paul R. Goldin, and Esther S. Klein, "A Philosophical Translation of the *Heng Xian*," *Dao* 12 (2013): 2: 145–51. For an analysis of this text in terms of boundary-making, change, and creativity, see Erica Brindley, "Spontaneous Arising and Creative Change in the Hengxian," *Journal of Daoist Religions* 9 (2016): 1–17.

13. See the Mawangdui *Daoyuan* 道原 text, in which both the terms *jing* 靜 and *daxu* 大虛 help describe the beginnings of the cosmos; Guojia wenwuju guwenxian yanjiushi 國家文物局古文獻研究室, *Mawangdui Han mu boshu* 馬王堆漢墓帛書, vol. 1 (Beijing: Wenwu, 1980), 145–46.

14. The manuscript uses *huo* 或, which is generally taken as *yu* 域 in both the received and paleographic literature.

15. Text and translation after Brindley et al., "A Philosophical Translation," 146–47.

16. I have written about the significance of the term *yu* in Brindley, "Spontaneous Arising." I show how the emergence of space and time in the text is linked to boundary-making, which is tantamount to the creative change of the cosmos, or "nature."

17. Brindley et al., "A Philosophical Translation," 146.

18. Brindley et al., "A Philosophical Translation," 148.

19. Brindley et al., "A Philosophical Translation," 150 (end of slip 11).

20. Brindley et al., "A Philosophical Translation," 150 (slip 12).

21. In contrast to *The Primordial State of Constancy*, *Taiyi* was excavated properly and not acquired on the illicit antiquities market. The translation I use is my own. I have consulted Scott Cook's published translation and included a few of his terms or phrases. See Scott Cook, *The Bamboo Texts of Guodian: A Study and Complete Translation*, 2 vols. (Ithaca, NY: East Asia Program, Cornell University, 2012).

22. Jingmen shi bowuguan 荊門市博物館, *Guodian Chu mu zhujian* 郭店楚墓竹簡 (Beijing: Wenwu, 1998), 125.

23. I have written more at length about this text in Brindley, "The *Taiyi shengshui* 太一生水 Cosmogony and Its Role in Early Chinese Thought," in *Dao Companion to the Excavated Guodian Manuscripts*, ed. Shirley Chan (Cham, Switzerland: Springer, 2019), 153–62.

24. Jingmen shi bowuguan, *Guodian Chu mu zhujian*, 125.

25. Jingmen shi bowuguan, *Guodian Chu mu zhujian*, 126.

26. It is worth noting that the true name of the Dao mentioned here is likely equivalent to Taiyi, since the author links creative, cosmic change (of any sort) to both the Dao and "Taiyi hidden in water." See Brindley, "*Taiyi shengshui*."

27. The *Laozi* famously states: 道可道非常道。名可名非常名 (The Dao that can be spoken is not the Constant Dao. The name that can be named is not the Constant Name).

28. *Huainan honglie jijie* 淮南鴻烈集解, comp. Liu Wendian 劉文典, punct. Feng Yi 馮逸 and Qiao Hua 喬華 (Beijing: Zhonghua, 1989), 10.

29. *Wenzi shuyi* 文子疏義, ed. Wang Liqi 王利器 (Beijing: Zhonghua, 2000), 327 ("Weiming" 微明).

30. *Zhuangzi zhuzi suoyin* 莊子逐字索引, ed. D. C. Lau et al. (Hong Kong: Shangwu yinshuguan, 2000), 20/53/25 and 20/54/3–4 ("Shanmu" 山木).

31. *Zhuangzi zhuzi suoyin*, 22/60/3 ("Zhibeiyou" 知北遊).

32. *Zhuangzi zhuzi suoyin*, 66/69/1 ("Xuwugui" 徐無鬼).

33. These developed in the fourth through third centuries BCE and took off in early imperial intellectual circles from the second century BCE through the end of the Han. See the contributions in "Reconsidering the Correlative Cosmology of Early China," ed. Magnus Fiskejö, special issue, *Bulletin of the Museum of Far Eastern Antiquities* 72 (2000): 1–196.

34. It is best not to make a stark distinction between "naturalistic" and "animistic" cosmologies during the period, however, because it is likely that largely naturalistic cosmologies also retained belief in animistic deities who fit and were integrated into the natural picture in some way.

35. Jennifer Schuessler, "MacArthur Foundation Announces 2016 'Genius' Grant Winners," *New York Times*, September 22, 2016.

36. By this I refer to A. C. Graham's note of caution that one need not think of such spontaneity in terms of the Western dichotomy of rational choice versus whimsical, emotional impulse: "The Taoist is somewhere where this dichotomy does not apply. He wants to remain inside nature, to behave as spontaneously as an animal . . . on the other hand, he has a contempt for emotion and subjectivity, a respect for things as they objectively are, as cool and lucid as a scientist's." See Angus C. Graham, "Taoist Spontaneity and the Dichotomy of 'Is' and 'Ought,'" in *Experimental Essays on Chuang-Tzu*, ed. Victor H. Mair (Honolulu: University of Hawai'i Press, 1983), 10–11.

2

Water as Homology in the Construction of Classical Chinese Medicine

VIVIENNE LO AND GU MAN

> Water is the blood and *qi* of the earth; it resembles what courses through the veins and arteries. So it is said that water is the potential for everything.
>
> 水者, 地之血氣, 如筋脈之通流者也. 故曰水具材也.
>
> —*Guanzi jiaozhu* 管子校注

From Philosophy and Religion to a *Techne* of Water

In *The Way of Water*, Sarah Allan describes two fundamental "root metaphors" in Chinese philosophy—water and plants.[1] Images of water, she argues, pervade the discourses of the Warring States philosophers and are variously cast as an allegory for human morality. They illustrate the power and significance of fluidity against the more well-known and rigid aspects of Confucian social hierarchies and rituals. They naturalize spontaneity in the personal and political philosophy of *wuwei* 無為, "non-[purposive] action,"

The epigraph for this chapter is from the "Shuidi" 水地 (Water and Earth) chapter of the *Guanzi* 管子, a text compiled from the fourth to second centuries BCE; *Guanzi jiaozhu* 管子校注, comp. Li Xiangfeng 黎翔鳳 (Beijing: Zhonghua, 2004), 813.

a program for nonaggressive and fluent being-in-the-world that seeks to align behavior with natural-cosmological, rather than human, principles.[2]

Common properties that extend the hermeneutics of water in early China are that water flows downward; it is formless, forever transforming and taking the shape of whatever contains it. Nevertheless, it endures; with no ultimate source or ultimate destination, it is inexhaustible, always replenishing itself; and since it wears away stone it is more powerful than hard and impermeable things. The *Daodejing* 道德經 makes the properties of water very clear:

> In the world nothing is softer or weaker than water; yet there is also nothing that can outdo its ability to attack the hard or the firm; for there is nothing that can substitute for it; water overcomes rock; soft overcomes firm.
>
> 天下莫柔弱於水, 而攻堅強者莫之能先也, 以其無以易之也. 水之勝剛也, 弱之勝強也.[3]

Water has the physical power to overcome other elements, but it also has the power of creation. The ceaseless movement and flow of water inform interpretations of the passage and even the very beginnings of time, at least in the context of the *Daodejing*. Water features in descriptions of cosmogenesis and the creation of the world, and in the same vein refers to the generative power of women.

In a moral universe, these properties of water conflated easily with the description of the sagacity of the true gentleman: his humility, his spurning of the pursuit of high places and good reputation or material gain, his timelessness. In gender analyses, water links to the yielding and the female with positively construed qualities of flexibility and modesty. Ultimately, water was associated with the rise of Yin 陰, in a polar, yet constantly interactive, relationship with Yang 陽.

This chapter draws on artifacts and texts written on bamboo slips and silk scrolls discovered in Western Han (206 BCE–25 CE) tomb excavations in the last four decades and compares them with classical Chinese medical texts that were compiled in later Han and printed one thousand years later.[4] It will argue that over the course of the Han empire evidence from these sources helps us to mark a moment and place in the process between the late Zhou philosophical discourses that Allan described so well and the construction of a new, imperial, hydrological body. In this world, the properties of water accrete to a newly conceived physiology and medical expertise where the body could be brought under control through manipulating the physiology of inner *qi* 氣.

Medical writers in China, throughout the millennia, have assumed that the properties of water were fundamental to imagining the regularities of physiology and associated therapies. The language and principles of water are, therefore, easily accepted and taught by contemporary practitioners who are immersed in the technical legacy. Yet it is difficult to find any academic analysis of the historical process through which the philosophy that Allan presented so well segued into practice.

The emergence of new manuscript sources excavated from late Warring States and Han tombs, in this case at Mawangdui 馬王堆 (Changsha), Zhangjiashan 張家山 (Jiangling), Guodian 郭店 (Jingmen), and the more recently discovered tomb at Laoguanshan 老官山 (Chengdu) help us to understand this process. They provide context-rich political, social, and geographic locations along the course and hinterland of the Yangzi River that permit a new focus on applied knowledge. Through them we can trace how the aesthetics of philosophical theory manifest in technical performance, in this case in the arts of medicine. Where ancient Greeks are thought to have distinguished between a negatively construed "arts" with no utility and a craft with everyday utility (skills of the lower classes), the early Chinese technical manuscripts were written for, and possibly by, a social elite. They were copied and collected by those living in and moving along the course and hinterland of the Yangzi valley, in the territories of the old kingdoms of Chu 楚 and Shu 蜀, who could afford magnificent burials and who believed that ostentatious displays of the ownership of knowledge, both philosophical and technical, would aid them—and those who worked for them—in the afterworld.

Water Is the Most Powerful Agent, the Origin of the Myriad Things

The *Laozi* 老子 (ascribed to a shadowy Master Lao, imagined as a contemporary of Confucius) is the locus classicus for the conflation of the Way (Dao 道) with water. The qualities of water—humility, femaleness, malleability, and strength—are shared in its verses. The writings in this text and others retrospectively elevated by Daoist organizations take a less moral position than those attributed to Confucian traditions. At least the texts do not profess a humanistic style of philosophy and rather reject the significance of moral values that draw on discourses of human nature and experience, or human reason. Water, for example, is not contentious; in flowing downward, it derives power from counterintuitively seeking the lower position:

> The highest good is like water; water benefits the myriad living things; it does not contend and dwells in places everyone detests; it comes close to the Way (the Dao).
>
> 上善若水, 水善利萬物而不爭. 處眾人之所惡, 故幾於道.[5]

The path of the sage in *Laozi* is not guided by collective human values but mimics the principles of water; the Way, water (and eventually *qi*) began to share semantic fields. During the Warring States, concepts of the Way embraced the many paths that philosophers and government advisors promoted for individual and state action. Or in the case of the *Laozi*, the aforementioned philosophy of non-(purposeful) action (*wuwei*) was key, since the Way served as a valley to water, effortlessly leading and guiding action:[6]

> The Way is empty, yet in using it, there is something that needs to fill it. A deep spring, it seems like the ancestor of the myriad living things.
>
> 道沖而用之, 有弗盈也, 淵呵, 始萬物之宗.[7]

As the "ancestor of the myriad living things" the Dao of the *Laozi* drew easily on observable qualities of water, including here the apparent ability of a "deep spring" to self-generate. A tomb text known as *Taiyi sheng shui* 太一生水 (Taiyi Creates Water), connected with *Laozi* material excavated from Guodian tomb no. 1 (Jingmen 荊門, Hubei 湖北, burial dated ca. 300 BCE) although not extant in the received text of the *Daodejing*, bears testimony to the role of a deity and divine-spirit-creator Taiyi 太一 (Grand Unity) in cosmogony, with water designated as the second stage of creation.[8]

This is Donald Harper's translation of the opening passage:

> Grand One generates water. Water rejoins Grand One, thereby perfecting heaven. Heaven rejoins Grand One, thereby perfecting earth. Heaven and earth, in repeat, conjoin, thereby perfecting

spirit illumination. Spirit illumination, in repeat, conjoins, thereby perfecting *yin* and *yang*. *Yin* and *yang*, in repeat, conjoin, thereby perfecting four seasons.

太一生水，水反輔太一，是以成天．天反輔太一，是以成地．天地【復相輔】也，是以成神明；神明復相輔也，是以成陰陽；陰陽復相輔也，是以成四時．[9]

This passage is closely related to the classical account of cosmogony in the *Laozi*, but the identification of Taiyi (Grand One or Grand Unity) as the originator makes for a fundamental difference, and, if we agree with Harper's interpretation, we have to imagine him or it—a divine creator and a conscious being—somehow storing itself and immanent in water.

Therefore, Grand One stores itself in water and moves through seasons. Completing a cycle and beginning again, it takes itself to be the mother of the myriad things. Now deplete, now replete, it takes itself to be the mainstay of the myriad things. This is what heaven cannot kill, what earth cannot bury, and what *yin* and *yang* cannot perfect. The gentleman who knows this is called . . .

是故太一藏於水，行於時，周而又【始，以己爲】萬物母；一缺一盈，以己爲萬物經．此天之所不能殺，地之所不能埋，陰陽之所不能成．君子知此之謂 . . .[10]

The passage describes a process that is not so much an impersonal process of natural cosmogenesis, as the received text is commonly interpreted, but more cosmogenesis by virtue of the creativity of a godlike being. This is a process that can be known by the enlightened gentleman; where spirits, and particularly Grand Unity, animate the world around us so that Yin-Yang divisions of the body, astronomy, astrology, and the planetary gods and spirits exist on a continuum. All are ultimately embraced within one and the same order. Thus, at the fourth stage of a nine-stage cosmogenesis—(1) water 水, (2) heaven 天, (3) earth 地, (4) spirit illumination (*shenming* 神明), (5) Yin and Yang, (6) four seasons (*sishi* 四時), (7) cold and hot (*hanre* 寒熱), (8) wet and dry (*shizao* 濕燥), (9) year 歲—"'spirit illumination' expresses the limitless responsiveness of a numinousness that is everywhere in the cosmos—including particularized spirits—and in the human microcosm, where it constitutes the spiritual and intellectual core of a human being."[11]

As "the spiritual and intellectual core of a human being," spirit illumination represents an expression of consciousness that is something, the text goes on to say in its last sentence, "a gentleman should know." Exactly how or what he should know is lost in the missing text. In the following two centuries, however, the notion of the brilliance of the spirits entailed in the accomplishment of spirit illumination became more and more a part of the expression of human experience and of the techniques of self-cultivation articulated for the literate.

In the manuscripts excavated from Mawangdui tomb no. 3 (located in the old kingdom of Chu, a region with early associations with the cult of Taiyi), we have clear evidence of how a gentleman might know how to nourish spirit illumination.[12] Introducing a text on cultivating spirit illumination through the sexual arts, we find a lyrical passage that associates spirit illumination most closely with the power of water:

> [May it be] like water springing forth, like the [balanced] *qi* of spring and autumn. What is past, I can no longer see, nor can I gain [from it] merit. What is to come, I cannot spy out, yet I may enjoy its benefits [if I am careful]. Oh! be careful! The matter of *shenming* (spirit illumination) depends on that which closes. Vigilantly control the jade closure, and spirit illumination will come. In all cases of mastering the self, the hard work lies in accumulating *jing*.[13]
>
> 如水沫淫, 如春秋氣, 往者弗見, 不得其功; 來者弗覩, 吾饗其賞. 嗚呼慎哉, 神明之事, 在於所閉. 審操玉閉, 神明將至. 凡彼治身, 務在積精.

In other words, the past is gone, we are in the moment, and my practice aimed at spirit illumination follows the spontaneous generation of water and the order of seasonal *qi*. Thereafter, a technical treatise on how to achieve spirit illumination provides sexual partners with a guide to embodying Yin and Yang cosmogenesis, bringing together heaven and earth. The following two excerpts from another Mawangdui tomb text on sexual practice (168 BCE) links moving *qi* and spirit illumination. We lose the explicit presence of water, except that it remains ever-present in the qualities attributed to moving *qi*. The first passage is a record of the technical aim of sexual cultivation, what we believe to be the earliest extant description of female orgasm; the cultivation culminates in the birth of spirit illumination. *Qi* radiates around the body:

> At this point the *qi* extends from the middle extremity and the quintessential spirit enters the internal organs and spirit illumination is born.

> 當此之時，中極氣張，精神入藏，乃生神明。[14]

A second passage codifies the final objectives of successful semen retention in ten stages, with free-flowing water at the sixth. This is a technique for the male partner, exemplified here in the sought-after outcome of spirit illumination.

> If there is no orgasm in the first movement, the ears and eyes will become keen and bright; with the second, the voice becomes clear; with the third, the skin gleams; with the fourth, the back and flanks are strengthened; with the fifth, the buttocks and thighs become sturdy; with the sixth, the waterways flow freely; with the seventh, one becomes sturdy with strength; with the eighth, the patterns of the skin shine; with the ninth, one gets through to an illumination of the spirit; with the tenth, the body endures—these are called the ten movements.

> 出入而毋決。一動毋決，耳目聰明，再而音聲彰，三而皮革光，四而脊脅強，五而尻髀方，六而水道行，七而至堅以強，八而腠理光，九而通神明，十而爲身常，此謂十動。[15]

In these body-based practices for the civilized gentleman, we see spirit illumination described as a sharpness and acuity of the senses combined with clarity, strength, and sturdiness. Cultivating these qualities depends on the free flow of water in the body.

By the second century BCE, spirit illumination could refer to this radiant way of being-in-the-world, expressed and perceived as a combination of physical strength and inner clarity—qualities found in various degrees as the effect of Han exercise routines for the elite, breath and sexual cultivation, as well as the result of religious practice. Water has infused into the language with which records of these practices are expressed, whether explicitly or not; perhaps with an inherited memory of the spirit Taiyi immanent in water, creating Yin, Yang, and spirit illumination.

Successful Water Projects Marked Effective Emperors: A Transition from *Qi* as External Influence to Internal Constituent—Political Physiology

QI AND WATER

The control of water was core to the imagination and evolution of Chinese politics and the conduct of empire, as enshrined in the legend of Yu the Great. Yu was the last of the Three Emperors (Yao 堯, Shun 舜, and Yu 禹), the culture bringers who, according to Chinese histories, brought civilization to the world. Flood was a major natural catastrophe, second only to drought in China. Yu's dedication to protecting the people from the river floods is represented in a story, recorded in many sources, about how he worked tirelessly, excavating dikes and drainage canals, not entering his home for years, and even ignoring the cries of his baby when passing by his house.[16]

The annexing of the southwest territories by the King of Qin 秦, who was to unify the empire for the first time in 221 BCE, was accompanied by innovative irrigation projects that divided the flow of the Min River 岷江 and routed the water into a series of irrigation canals that still function today, notably at Dujiangyan 都江堰 in modern Sichuan. A twenty-mile canal built in 246 BCE drew water from the Wei River 渭河 to irrigate the alkaline lands of central Shaanxi 陝西, making fertile key areas of political control: "Thereupon the land within the passes became a fertile plain, and there were no more bad years. Qin thus became rich and powerful and ended by conquering the feudal lords."[17] Together with the building of walls to the north and the imperial tombs, these monumental state projects involved many hundreds of thousands of men in corvee, convict, and slave labor. So, whether or not Sima Qian 司馬遷 (ca. 145–86 BCE), the Grand Historian of Han, was correct about the real importance of the irrigation projects to the rise of the kingdom of Qin, water control was certainly part of the imaginary of good government.

In the centuries before King Zheng of Qin 秦王政 first unified the Warring States, in large part by drawing on the agrarian resources of the upper Yangzi valley, there had been an important transition. Where *qi* had primarily referred to those external environmental, spiritual, and demonic qualities that could affect the body, it began to feature internally as a part of the body's physiology, first with the breath and then as a body constituent over which anyone could exercise control. Its weaknesses and strengths could be known and trained through micromanaging the sensations of the inner body with ever more sophisticated techniques—first one's own body with proper nourishment, breath control, meditation, therapeutic exercises, and sexual cultivation, and then other peoples' bodies in the practice of medicine.

It was only with the dawn of empire and the extension of bureaucratic power and imperial sway to Tianxia 天下 (All Under Heaven) that we begin to see a literature that standardized *qi* as flowing through the whole body in organized channels. This happened in concert with the imperial standardization of many other aspects of state administration: coinage, script, and road track sizes to grease the wheels of trade and the military. There began the body mapping that we know today in acupuncture charts—imperial control could suddenly chart its way into the very depths of every imperial subject, ordering every aspect of their being.

With the political importance of water control imagined to be at the heart of the imperial process, it is not surprising that we find that images of water pervade early writings that relate to the conception and development of these body maps. The water homology is clearly demonstrated in medically related manuscripts and artifacts that are later adapted into the acupuncture traditions. In them, we will see a transition from drawing on imagery of natural watercourses, seas, lakes, and rivers in the philosophical literature of the Warring States, to a discourse that linguistically elides these waterscapes with the process of controlling and manipulating both the flow of water and physiological *qi*.

A clear demonstration of an early stage of this transition can be seen in the third-century BCE *Lüshi chunqiu* 呂氏春秋 (Master Lü's Spring and Autumn Annals, an encyclopedia of ritual and statecraft, written in the state of Qin by Lü Buwei 呂不韋, ca. 239 BCE). Lü Buwei was regent to King Zheng of Qin, who was to ascend to an imperial throne seventeen years after the completion of the book. Lü was therefore at the epicenter of administrative power.

WATER MOVES AND CLEARS STAGNATION

In the following quotation from a treatise on the cultivation of sagacity from the almanacs of *Lüshi chunqiu*, the analogy between water and *qi* is made explicit. We learn that a door hinge must be kept in constant use to function well, and that flowing water does not stagnate: exercising will keep *qi* flowing in the body and this is consistent with the healthy body and its physiology.

> Flowing water and the pivot of the door do not rot because of their constant movement. The relationship between bodily form and *qi* is the same. If the bodily form does not move, the quintessence does not flow; if the quintessence does not flow, the *qi* will stagnate.
>
> 流水不腐, 戶樞不蝼, 動也. 形氣亦然. 形不動則精不流, 精不流則氣鬱.[18]

Fifty years later, we find most of the same passage excerpted in a manuscript, which was recently excavated from Zhangjiashan tomb 247, in Jiangling, modern Hubei Province (tomb closed ca. 186 BCE). Here we have an extended physiological definition, since the movement described emptied the five viscera and filled the limbs; it also cleared the *mai* 脈, which were the channels and vessels of the body.

> Now the reason that flowing water does not stagnate and a door that pivots does not get woodworm is because of movement. When there is movement, then it fills the four limbs and empties the five viscera; when the five viscera are empty, then the jade body will benefit. Now, one who rides in a carriage and eats meat must (fast and purify themselves?) in spring and autumn. If they do not (fast and purify themselves?) then the *mai* (vessels/channels) will rot and cause the death of the flesh.
>
> 夫留 (流) 水不腐, 戶貊 (樞) 不橐 (蠹), 以其勭 (動). 勭 (動) 者實四支 (肢) 而虛五臧 (臟), 五臧 (臟) 虛則玉體利矣. 夫乘車食肉者, 春秋必浩, 不浩則脈闌 (爛) 而肉死.[19]

The reference to a jade body in the preceding passage is precisely to the new physiological body, which was made up of *qi* and could be supported by body cultivation techniques such as properly conducted sexual relations and forms of therapeutic exercise. What follows this passage is a description of how someone else, presumably a doctor, could normalize the downward directional flow of *qi* in a patient's body by piercing it with a stone needle.

As we will see, the Zhangjiashan text is therefore the earliest extant treatise on acupuncture and marks the moment when the jade body became a medical phenomenon, rather than one of ritual or self-cultivation.[20]

Water Flows Down and Follows Water Courses

We find the properties of water and the essential goodness of human nature brought together as one in writings attributed to the fourth-century BCE philosopher Mengzi 孟子 (Mencius). For Mencius, training *qi* was a moral self-education. Getting up in the morning to breathe the fine morning *qi* would cultivate the sprouts of goodness that were innate in the body as spontaneously as water had a propensity to flow downward and along channels in the earth.

> Gaozi said: "Nature is like a bubbling spring. If you make a channel for it to the east, then it will flow eastward. If you make a channel for it to the west, then it will flow westward. Human nature is not biased toward good or bad; it is like water that is not biased toward east or west."
>
> Mencius said: "Water certainly is not partial to east or west, but is it not partial to above or below? Human nature being good is like water going downward. Among people, there are none who have [as their nature] not being good; of water, there is none that does not descend. Now, supposing water is splashed and made to jump up, it can be made to go higher than the forehead. Or, it can be made to stay on a mountain if it is banked up and caused to circulate. How could this be the nature of water: it is like that because it is induced. Men can be made to do what is not good: but their nature is still the same."

> 告子曰: "性, 猶湍水也, 決諸東方則東流, 決諸西方則西流. 人性之無分於善不善也, 猶水之無分於東西也."
>
> 孟子曰: "信無分於東西, 無分於上下乎? 人性之善也, 猶水之就下也. 人無有不善, 水無有不下. 今夫水搏而躍之, 可使過顙, 激而行之, 可使在山, 是豈水之性哉? 其勢則然也. 人之可使為不善, 其性亦猶是也."[21]

In *The Way of Water*, Sarah Allan states that "it is this tendency of water to move downward that makes it possible to channel water and it is the reason that it will flow along a preestablished course or riverbed."²² By implication human intervention can also channel *qi*. We have no reliable description of a formal physiological movement of *qi* within the body for the period that the *Mencius* was being compiled. *Qi* was breath—ingested into the body, it permeated the body as *haoran zhi qi* 浩然之氣 (floodlike *qi*). But within two centuries the tomb manuscripts demonstrate that once inside the body the "natural" course was to flow downward through the channels of the body, and that this could be assisted by breathing meditations and by doctors. When those channels became blocked, creating weaknesses and obstructions, sickness and death would ensue.

In the same Zhangjiashan tomb no. 247, mentioned just now for its medicalized versions of texts in the *Lüshi chunqiu*, and in other tombs nearby in modern Hunan Province, we find the properties of water shaping treatises about both therapeutic movement and acupuncture. The following exercise seems to treat numbness and discomfort in the head after excessive alcohol consumption by reestablishing the downward movement of *qi* through a form of stepping exercise:

> The prescription for ailing from *liao* [too much liquor]: Grasp a staff in the right hand, face a wall, and do not breathe; with the left foot tread on the wall, resting when tired. Then do likewise with the left hand and the right foot, again resting when tired. When the *qi* of the head flows downward the foot will no longer be immobile and numb, the head will not swell, and the nose will not be stuffed up. Whenever there is free time, practice this often.

> 病瘳 ▲ (疒 + 豊?), • 引之之方, 右手把丈 (杖), 鄉 (嚮) 壁, 毋息, 左足躆 (蹠) 壁, 卷 (倦) 而休; 亦左手把丈 (杖), 右足躆 (蹠) 壁, 亦卷 (倦) 而休. 頭氣下流, 足不痿【痹】, 首不蹱 (腫) 鼽, 毋事恆服之.²³

In the same set of manuscripts, we find that reestablishing the natural propensity for *qi* to flow downward with cautery and piercing with stone was integral to practical, and innovative, medical techniques to resolve rising heat:

> The channels are valued by the sages. As for *qi*, it benefits the lower and harms the upper; follows heat and distances coolness.

So, the sages cool the head and warm the feet. Those who treat illness take the surplus and supplement the insufficiency. So if *qi* goes up, not down, then when you see the channel that is in excess, apply one cauterization where it meets the articulation. When the illness is intense then apply another cauterization at a place two *cun* above the articulation. When the *qi* rises at one moment and falls in the next pierce it with a stone lancet at the back of the knee and the elbow.

夫脈者, 聖人之所貴殹. 氣者, 利下而害上, 從燸而去清, 故聖人寒頭而燸足. 治病者取有徐 (餘) 而益不足, 故氣上而不下, 則視有過之脈, 當環而久 (灸) 之. 病甚而上於環二寸益為一久 (灸). 氣壹上壹下, 當胎 (郄) 與胕 (跗) 之脈而砣 (砭) 之.²⁴

Conditions of deficient or excess *qi* created discomfort and numbness. In other medical and healing texts they described an intensification of sensation, one of heat, pain, digestion, emotion, pleasure, and passion—articulating a uniquely Chinese language for the most intimate experiences of life. These treatises on *daoyin* 導引 and acupuncture respectively do not mention water explicitly, but an acceptance of the downward flow of *qi* has already been established and is a premise of growing medical theory.

We can see this more technical imaginary of water most clearly entering the medical body on the captions marked on a black lacquered figurine excavated in 2012 from a Western Han dynasty tomb (ca. 188–141 BCE) at the Laoguanshan 老官山 site in Tianhui 天回 Township, modern Chengdu. This is the second archaeological discovery of a human figurine covered in black lacquer with red lines, the first and larger figure having been excavated among the burial goods of a military man at the Shuangbaoshan 雙包山 tomb (tomb closed late Western Han) at Mianyang 綿陽, to the northwest of Chengdu. I (Lo) have written extensively on the relationship between the earlier figurine and the therapeutic exercise regimen recorded in the Zhangjiashan manuscripts.²⁵ But there are important differences between the two figurines. Those differences significant to this discussion are (1) the numerous points marked on the Tianhui model's surface, some with captions; and (2) the captions listing the internal organs on the back correlate them to a sequence of wood, earth, water, fire, metal. This was consistent with the *ke* 剋 or conquering cycle. The *ke* cycle listed the inner organs according to their affinities with the Five Agents (*wuxing* 五行) and the control relationship between them: wood conquers earth, earth conquers water, water conquers fire, fire conquers metal. This predated the *sheng* 生 cycle of generation—wood, fire, earth, metal, water, which became more central to structuring classical medical practice.[26]

The points are the earliest extant testimony to acupuncture points. Before the discovery at Laoguanshan the earliest extant evidence had been in the Eastern Han Wuwei 武威 manuscripts, excavated in modern Gansu Province and dated to the first century CE.[27] The points described in the Wuwei manuscripts are all *shu* 輸 (transporting points) that run parallel to the spine on the back of the body.[28]

There are many more points engraved on the body of the Laoguanshan lacquered figurine (figs. 2.1a–c). Among them are two sets of inscriptions that relate to water: the bilateral inscriptions on the axilla, which read *yeyuan* 夾淵 (腋淵, armpit abyss), and the bilateral inscriptions in the gap behind the hip joint, which read *gu* 谷 (valley). On the popliteal fossa there is also the inscription *xi* 奚 (豀、溪, ravines). To understand the exact meaning of these terms we will have to take an extended trip around the waterways of Han-dynasty China.

The textual annotations on the figurines are not simply a process of body inscription, as if the body were a passive repository of knowledge. They are a part of an emerging technoculture of the body specific to the mid-Western Han dynasty. We can triangulate its evidence with manuscript evidence from the tomb as well as contemporary tombs from downriver (Mawangdui and Zhangjiashan as cited earlier) and the later Yellow Emperor's corpus, the locus classicus for classical Chinese medicine that was compiled in the following centuries but not printed in its current form until the Song (960–1279).

There are elements of the medical texts and the figurine that testify to a growing empire-wide medical culture with regional variations, particularly in centers such as Qi and Shu. The evidence of the excavated manuscripts is that references to water and watercourses belonged to textual production on the river networks that stretched along the Yangzi from Changsha to Jiangling to Chengdu. In an archaeological field that is subject both to preservation bias and to exciting new finds practically every year, it would be audacious to make strong assertions. Nevertheless, the existing evidence does show these interesting tendencies that require sustained research and verification. Looking forward, the figurine's captions are one of the earliest indications of a culture of body point naming that explicitly landscapes the human body in terms of body terrains and waterscapes. While the tomb manuscripts give us a concrete place and time where this culture

Figure 2.1a. 夾淵 (腋淵, armpit abyss).

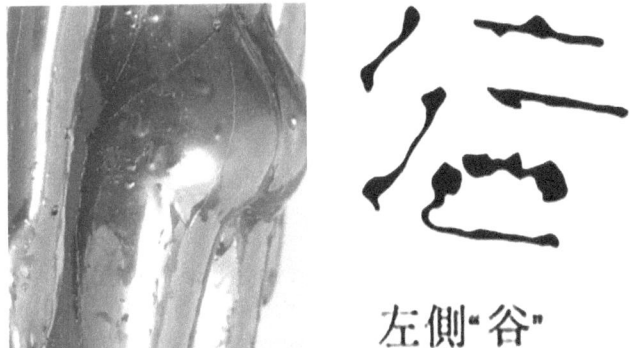

Figure 2.1b. 谷 (valley).

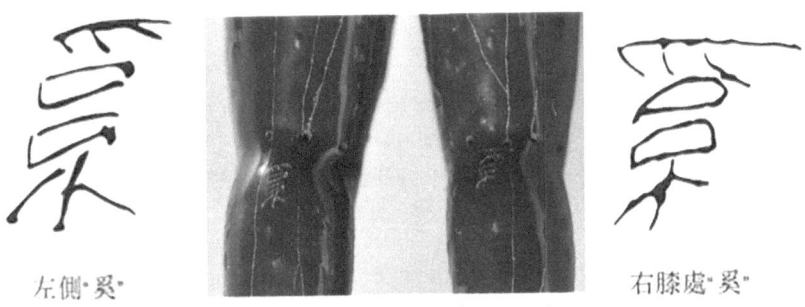

Figure 2.1c. 奚 (谿、溪, ravines).

Figures 2.1a–c. Human Figurine Covered in Black Lacquer with Red Lines. *Source:* Photographs provided courtesy of Dr. Zhou Qi.

flourished, it was soon to become an assumption of the classical medical literature that where

> the earth has high mountains, humans have shoulders and knees; the earth has deep valleys, humans have armpits and the hollows of the knees; the earth has twelve stream waters (rivers), humans have twelve standard channels; the earth has spring channels, man has protective *qi*.
>
> 地有高山, 人有肩膝; 地有深谷, 人有腋膕; 地有十二經水, 人有十二經脈; 地有泉脈, 人有衛氣.[29]

It was not only naturally occurring watercourses that were matched to the body, but also the waterways and landscapes that defined the imperial unity, the mountains, and rivers of China.

Twelve Standard Channels and the Waters (Rivers) of China in Classical Medical Treatises

Huang Di asked Qi Bo:

> The twelve channels (*jingmai*) link with the twelve channel waters (*jingshui*) on the outside, and on the inside they are connected with the five organs and six bowels.
>
> 黃帝問於岐伯曰: 經脈十二者. 外合於十二經水. 而內屬於五臟六腑.[30]

In the century or so after the evidence of the excavated manuscripts and artifacts discussed earlier, the general observation that water followed courses emerged more systematically in the language of a new structure of body channels through which *qi* flowed, a system that was matched exactly to the watercourses of the territory of empire. These water homologies, as in the *shui* 水 of *jingshui* 經水, refer both to water and to waterways of one kind or another. They were already explicitly defined in chapter 57 of the *Guanzi*, "Duo di" 度地 (Estimating the Earth), which states: "As water emerges from the mountains and flows into the sea, it is called the *jingshui* (channel waters)" (水之出於山, 而流入於海者, 命曰經水).[31] This term becomes deployed in medicine in the *Lingshu* 靈樞 recension of the

Yellow Emperor's corpus, *Lingshu* 12 "Jingshui" 經水 (Channel Waters). The *jing* of this term has a semantic range that encompasses "the warp threads of a loom," "canonical" or "classical texts," and "streams." In combination with *mai*, the old term for body vessels and channels, *jingmai* 經脈 has been frequently translated as "conduit," "channel," and anachronistically as "meridian," although the latter translation is largely to be found as an orthodoxy of modern practitioner texts.

"Jingshui" is one of several treatises that interpret the new science of body channels in distinct but interrelated ways. An adjacent treatise in *Lingshu*, for example, focuses on channels as the muscular and tendinous contours of the body.[32] Another treatise charts the diurnal circuits of *qi* as if *qi* were an astromedical orb in transit.[33] The body-channel-as-river maps a territory bounded by the Yangzi to the south (linked to the Hand Yang Brilliance channel of the large intestine) and the Wei River to the northwest, and it centers on the He, the Yellow River at the traditional heartland of Chinese civilization—a civilization that was being comprehensively invented in these centuries at the beginnings of empire, and that coalesced in the classical textual traditions of Eastern Han (25–220 CE).

There were four rivers known as the Sidu 四瀆 in ancient China. These form part of a ritual set of waterways with the Yangzi and the Yellow Rivers and include the Ji 濟 River and the Huai 淮 River, respectively. From the Qin and Han dynasties to the Ming and Qing dynasties, they were the objects of royal sacrifices to the mountains and the rivers. According to the "Wang zhi" 王制 (Royal Regulations) chapter in the *Liji* 禮記 (Book of Rites), the emperor needed to sacrifice to the significant mountains and rivers in Tianxia (All Under Heaven), including those known as the Five Mountains and Sidu.[34] According to the *Erya* 爾雅, the so-called Sidu refer to China's biggest rivers that have independent sources and eventually flow into the sea.[35] Compared with the Yangzi River and the Yellow River, the Ji River and the Huai River are smaller and, today, the old river channels of the Ji River have been subsumed into the Yellow River.[36] In terms of correspondence with the body channels, the Ji River and the Huai River are the Hand Minor Yin channel of the heart and the Hand Major Yang channel of the small intestine, respectively. These two channels are considered *biaoli xianghe* 表裏相合 (united as surface and interior) in the *Lingshu*, and the two channels corresponding with the Yangzi River and the Yellow River have the same relationship.

Thus, the waterways of the empire are mirrored in the internal Yin and Yang body channels and organs, embracing the depths of every civilized person within the ritual body that was cognate with the imperial sway. Table 2.1 shows the correspondences of each of the twelve channels with the inner

Table 2.1. Twelve Channels and Twelve River-Waters.

Twelve channels	Internal attachment	External link	Geolocation
Foot Major Yang	Urinary Bladder	Waters of Qing 清	Qing River, originating in modern Xiuwu County, Henan
Foot Minor Yang	Gallbladder	Waters of Wei 渭	Wei River, largest tributary of the Yellow River, originating in modern Weiyuan County, Gansu Province
Foot Yang Brilliance	Stomach	Waters of Hai 海	1. The sea 2. Haihe River, flowing into Bohai Sea at modern Tianjin
Foot Major Yin	Spleen	Waters of Hu 湖	Yangping River originating in modern Lingbao County, Henan
Foot Minor Yin	Kidneys	Waters of Ru 汝	A tributary of the Huai River, originating in Mt. Funiu in modern Song County, Henan
Foot Ceasing Yin	Liver	Waters of Sheng 澠	Originating in modern Zibo City, Shandong
Hand Major Yang	Small Intestine	Waters of Huai 淮	Huai River, originating in modern Tongbai, Henan, in ancient times, flowing to the sea through territories now in the modern provinces of Henan, Anhui, and Jiangsu
Hand Minor Yang	Triple Burner	Waters of Ta 漯	1. Also known as the Yongding River 2. In ancient times, a tributary of the Yellow River
Hand Yang Brilliance	Large Intestine	Waters of Jiang 江	Also known as Changjiang (Yangzi River)

Hand Major Yin	Lung	Waters of He 河	Also known as the Yellow River
Hand Minor Yin	Heart	Waters of Ji 濟	Originating in Mt. Wangwu, modern Jiyuan City, Henan, a major river of north China
Hand Heart Ruler	Heart Enclosure	Waters of Zhang 漳	Zhang River, originating in modern Shanxi, divided into two tributaries of clear and turbid waters in ancient times

Source: Created by the author.

body organs and the outer rivers of China, with a modern interpretation of the geolocations taken from Zhu Peng 朱鵬 and Gu Jihong 古繼紅.[37]

From Homology to a Medical *Techne* of Water

Following on from this mapping of China's rivers onto the body comes a passage that demonstrates how the water homology also guided medical practice. Since the channels and the rivers were of unequal depth, one had to insert the needle to different depths and leave it in for certain lengths of time that were counted in number of breaths. This is just one of many ways in which the properties of water were interpreted for medical practice.

Techniques of water control were also applied to managing the directional flow of *qi* through the channels. Clearing stagnant pools of water or *qi*, for example, could not be accomplished when the affected area was frozen or too cold. Warming techniques, including hot compresses and cautery with moxibustion, would be a necessary precondition for reestablishing flow. Anomalies of flow and counterflow that caused surpluses in some areas and deficiencies in others could then be remedied by piercing the body with needles. The framework for choosing specific acupoints was thereafter guided with reference to a complex waterscape that included point categories labeled *jing* 井 (well), *ying* 滎 (creek), *jing* 經 (here referring to "streams" or "channeled waters"), 365 *he* 合 (confluences), and *shu* 俞 or *shuxue* 俞穴 (transport/openings). All of these points became a feature of each of the twelve standard acupuncture channels and were to be attributed to distinct physiological functions.[38]

There were various kinds of channels and vessels, and where they came out on the surface of the body (a place often palpable through the pulse) were the *jing* 井 (well) points at which the doctor could presumably fathom and draw from the depths of the body. A later commentator to these ideas as they were expressed in the *Nanjing* 難經 (Classic of Difficulties), Yang Xuancao 楊玄操 (fl. 7th c. CE), connects the channel water features into an integrated river system. The "well" was explained as an ultimate source, a feature of the "valley spring," rather than a man-made well, and additional terms were given to the water networks as they drained to the sea through *rong* 榮 (brooks) and *jing* 經 (streams and conduits).[39]

The flow of *qi* moved at different speeds through these networks, pouring (*zhu* 注), flowing in swift currents (*liu* 溜), or going steadily (*xing* 行) through these specific categories of water points on the surface of the human body. The *shu* 俞 or *shuxue* 俞穴 (transport/openings) played a critical role in mediating the flow of *qi* to and from the five solid organs and six bowels.[40] These are but a few of the references to fluidity in the body. The Yellow Emperor 黃帝 asked Qi Bo 岐伯 about the functional correspondences between the twelve *jingmai* and *jingshui*. Qi Bo explained:

> Now, the channeled waters receive water and transmit it. The five organs bring together the spirit *qi* with the *hun* 魂 and *po* 魄 souls and store them. The six bowels receive grain and transmit it; they receive the *qi* and disperse it. The channel vessels receive the blood and circulate it.
>
> 夫經水者，受水而行之；五藏者，合神氣魂魄而藏之；六府者，受穀而行之，受氣而揚之；經脈者，受血而營之。[41]

Just as the god Taiyi was immersed in water, so human *qi* and souls and spirits were stored in the organs and fed by bodily streams.

To the Four Seas: Locating the Ravines and the Abyss

A key part of mirroring the hydrological cycle is, of course, the seas and oceans and the network of streams, channels, vessels, and conduits that kept the physiological fluids moving and connected, and converted their resources into bodily nourishment. The functions of the ravines and abysses that we first find mapped onto the Armpit Abyss (*yeyuan* 腋淵) and the popliteal fossa of the Tianhui Laoguanshan figurine were integrated into this system. Qi Bo explains:

> That from which man receives his *qi*, that is the grain. Where the grain flows, that is the stomach. The stomach is the sea where water and grain, the *qi* and the blood gather. The cloud *qi* moving away from the sea, [they cover all] below heaven. The *qi* and the blood leaving the stomach, they follow the conduit-channels. These channels constitute the big network [vessels] linking the five long-term depots and six short-term repositories. When one goes against [the *qi* and the blood] to pillage them, that will end [the patient's life].
>
> 人之所受氣者, 穀也. 穀之所注者, 胃也. 胃者, 水穀氣血之海也. 海之所行雲雨 (氣) 者, 天下也. 胃之所出氣血者, 經隧也. 經隧者, 五藏六府之大絡也, 迎而奪之而已矣.⁴²

The transportation of *qi* and blood from the stomach to the conduit-channels mirrored this hydrological cycle: water of the sea evaporated to the sky and became cloud, then fell on earth as rain. In the opposite direction, the process of *qi* and blood being transported through the conduit-channels to the stomach was like rivers flowing into the sea. The *qi* and blood of the human body achieved a complete hydrological cycle in this way.

> The *qi* of the earth rises and turns into clouds; the *qi* of heaven descends and becomes rain. Rain originates from the *qi* of the earth; clouds originate from the *qi* of heaven.
>
> 地氣上爲雲, 天氣下爲雨. 雨出地氣, 雲出天氣.⁴³

There were four seas that corresponded to body parts and that apparently represented the four directions. Theoretically these were the seas of bone marrow, water/grain, blood, and *qi*, although they are only tenuously located according to the different poles of the body.

Conduits and "On the Seas" ("Hailun" 海論)

Lingshu chapter 33 "On the Seas" begins as follows:

> Huang Di asked Qi Bo: "I have been informed by you of the patterns of piercing. What you told me did not go beyond [the topics of] camp [*qi*] and guard [*qi*], blood and *qi*. Now, the twelve conduit vessels, internally they are tied to the short-term repositories and long-term depots, externally they are connected with the limbs and the joints. And you link them [the twelve conduit channels] up with the four seas?!"

> 黃帝問於岐伯曰:"余聞刺法於夫子,夫子之所言,不離於營衛血氣.夫十二經脈者,內屬於腑臟,外絡於肢節,夫子乃合之於四海乎?"

> Qi Bo replied: "Man, too, has four seas and twelve conduit/stream waters. All these conduit/stream waters pour into the seas. There is an east, a west, a south, and a north sea. Hence one speaks of the four seas."

> 岐伯答曰:"人亦有四海,十二經水.經水者,皆注於海.海有東西南北,命曰四海."

> Huang Di asked: "What do these correspond to in people?"

> 黃帝曰:"以人應之奈何?"

> Qi Bo answered: "People have the Marrow Sea, the Qi Sea, the Water and Grain Sea; there are four of them and they correspond to the four seas."

> 岐伯曰:"人有髓海,有血海,有氣海,有水穀之海,凡此四者,以應四海也."[44]

The "Thoroughfare/Throughway Vessel" as One of the "Four Seas" (*Suwen* Chapter 44)

The thoroughfare vessel, it is the sea of the conduit vessels. It is responsible for pouring [liquid] into the ravines and valleys.

Table 2.2. Physiological Geography of the "Four Seas"

Name	Refers to	Transport		Body area
		Above	Below	
Sea of Water and Grain 水穀之海	Stomach 胃	*Qijie* 氣街	*Sanli* 三裡	Upper Abdomen
Sea of Blood / Twelve Conduits 血海/十二經之海	Throughway Vessel 衝脈	*Dazhu* 大杼	*Shangjuxu* and *Xiajuxu* 巨虛 上、下廉	Lower Abdomen
Sea of *Qi* 氣海	Danzhong 膻中	Above and Below Column Bones 柱骨上下	*Renying* 人迎	Chest
Sea of Bone Marrow 髓海	Brain 腦	Top of Skull 腦蓋	*Fengfu* 風府	Head

Source: Created by the author.

It unites with the yang brilliance [conduit] at the basic sinew. The yin and the yang [conduits] are brought together at the meeting point with the basic sinew, [this meeting takes place at the *qi* street], and the yang brilliance [conduit] is their chief.

衝脈者，經脈之海也，主滲灌谿谷，與陽明合於宗筋，陰陽揔揔宗筋之會，會於氣街，而陽明爲之長。[45]

According to this argument, the function of the thoroughfare vessel is to pour blood into the "ravines and valleys." So what are the "ravines and valleys"? This concept is also repeated in other chapters of the *Neijing*.

[Huang] Di: "Good! I should like to hear about the meeting points of the ravines and valleys."

帝曰: "善! 願聞谿谷之會也。"

Qi Bo: "The large meeting points of the flesh are the valleys; the small meeting points of the flesh are the ravines. In the partings of the flesh, [this is where] the ravines and valley meeting points are located. They serve as passage[ways] of the camp and the guard [*qi*] and they serve to assemble large [quantities of] *qi*."

歧伯曰: "肉之大會爲谷, 肉之小會爲谿, 肉分之間, 谿谷之會, 以行榮衛, 以會大氣."[46]

Huang Di: "I have heard the stomach and the intestines receive grain; the upper burner releases *qi*. It is to them to supply the partings of the flesh with warmth, and to nourish the bones and the joints, as well as to penetrate the skin structures. The *qi* released from the central burner are like dew. They ascend and pour into the mountain gorges and valleys and they provide dampness to the tertiary vessels. When the *jin* and *ye* liquids are balanced, they will transform to red blood. When the blood is balanced, then the tertiary vessels are filled to the extent that they spill over. The spill overflows into the network vessels. As soon as the network vessels are filled, [their contents] will flow into the conduit vessels."

黃帝曰: "余聞腸胃受穀, 上焦出氣, 以溫分肉, 而養骨節, 通腠理. 中焦出氣如露, 上注溪谷, 而滲孫脈, 津液和調, 變化而赤爲血, 血和則孫脈先滿溢, 乃注於絡脈, 【絡脈】皆盈, 乃注於經脈."[47]

Later, Wang Bing's 王冰 (8th c. CE) commentary to *Suwen* chapter 10 gives a detailed explanation to the conception of ravines (*xi* 谿). To the *Suwen* line "This is the morning and the evening of the four limbs and the eight ravines" (此四支八谿之朝夕也), Wang Bing notes:

Xi is the name for the small folds in the flesh. The "eight ravines" are the elbows, the knees, and the wrists/ankle joints [of hands and feet]. Qi and blood, sinews and vessels have alternating states of fullness and weakness here. Hence this is "morning and evening."

谿者, 肉之小會名也. 八谿, 謂肘膝腕也. 如是氣血筋脈, 互有盛衰, 故爲 "朝夕" 矣.[48]

Zhang Zhicong 張志聰 (1616–1674 CE) simply noted that "this is the flesh of the four limbs, legs and arms." But Zhang Jiebin 張介賓 (1563–1642 CE) earlier had explained in more detail:

The hands have elbows and armpits; the feet have the hip and the hollows under the knees. Morning and evening is to say, all the vessels, the marrow, the sinews, the blood, and the *qi* emerge from here and enter here [in the four limbs]; and neither in the morning nor in the evening does their movement leave [the four limbs].

手有肘與腋, 足有髀與膕也, 此四肢之關節, 故稱為谿. 朝夕者, 言人之諸脈髓筋血氣, 無不由此出入, 而朝夕運行不離也.⁴⁹

Lingshu 71 affirms Zhang Jiebin's assessment:

When the lung and the heart are affected by evil *qi*, it settles in the two elbows. When the liver is affected by evil *qi*, it settles in the two armpits. When the spleen is affected by evil *qi*, it settles in the two hips. When the kidneys are affected by evil *qi*, it settles in the two hollows under the knees. All these eight hollows are chambers of motion and juncture, where the true *qi* passes and where the blood network takes its way.

肺心有邪, 其氣留于兩肘; 肝有邪, 其氣流于兩腋; 脾有邪, 其氣留于兩髀; 腎有邪, 其氣留于兩膕. 凡此八虛者, 皆機關之室, 真氣之所過, 血絡之所游.

Nanjing "The Twenty-Seventh Difficult Issue" explains further:

The twenty-seventh difficult issue: Among the vessels are the eight single-conduit vessels which are not touched by the [movement of the influences circulating through the] twelve [main] conduits. What does that mean?

    It like this. . . . There are twelve [main] conduits and fifteen network[-vessels], twenty-seven together. The influences move up and down [through these conduits and network-vessels], following their respective courses. What [does it mean when it is said that] only [the eight single-conduit vessels] are not touched by the [movement of the influences circulating through the main] conduits?

二十七難曰: 脈有奇經八脈者, 不拘於十二經, 何謂也? 然. . . . 經有十二, 絡有十五, 凡二十七氣, 相隨上下. 何獨不拘於經也?

It is like this: The sages [of antiquity] devised and constructed ditches and reservoirs and they kept the waterways open in order to be prepared for any extraordinary [situation]. When rain pours down from heaven, the ditches and the reservoirs became filled. In times like that, when the rain floods rushed wildly, even the sages could not make plans again; [hence, they had to be prepared]. Here [in the organism], when the network-vessels are filled to overflowing, none of the [main] conduits could seize any [of their contents, and it is only then that the surplus contents of these vessels flow into the single-conduit vessels].

然聖人圖設溝渠, 通利水道, 以備不然, 天雨降下, 溝渠溢滿, 當此之時, 蕩霈妄行, 聖人不能復圖也. 此絡脈滿溢, 諸經不能復拘也.[50]

A Mature System of Classical Acupuncture Points

Finally, let us refer to Huangfu Mi's 皇甫謐 (215–282 CE) classic work, *Zhenjiu jiayijing* 針灸甲乙經 (A–B Classic of Acupuncture and Moxibustion), wherein we find a mature system of classical acupuncture points. Section 3 listed a total of 654 *xue* 穴 (acupoints). There are forty-eight single acupoints and 308 bilateral acupoints. Among them, we can find many names of acupoints that draw on the imagination of water. Table 2.3 shows forty-seven such names in ten categories.

Conclusion

In health the *qi* flows downward through the body as water follows streams and rivers within the earth: it gushes in springs, collects in the ponds, seas, and wells of the body. This reflects the eternal Chinese preoccupation with controlling water, whether to mitigate for drought and flood or for crop irrigation. Rising *qi* was almost always related to a pathological condition, often associated with breathing difficulties. Emotions, both normal and abnormal, were also a fullness of *qi*, particularly in relation to martial valor, anger, and belligerence, when uncontrollable sensations welled up in the body. A man who loved to fight was said to *hao qi* 好氣 (be prone to *qi*) and even today when you are *sheng qi* 生氣, literally "generating *qi*," you are angry.

Table 2.3. Acupoints That Relate to Water

Stream 溪	Valley 谷	Spring 泉	Abyss 淵	Pool 池	Lake 澤	Canal 溝/渠	Well 井	Sea 海	Water 水
Heaven Stream 天溪	Shuai Valley 率谷	Lian Spring 廉泉	Abyss Armpit 淵腋	Wind Pool 風池	Chi Lake 尺澤	Water Canal 水溝	Shoulder Well 肩井	Qi Sea 氣海	Water Protrusion 水突
Yang Stream 陽谿	He Valley 合谷	Heaven Spring 天泉	Major Abyss 太淵	Heaven Pool 天池	Curved Lake 曲澤	Branch Canal 支溝	Heaven Well 天井	Minor Sea 少海	Water Bifurcation 水分
Back Stream 後溪	Front Valley 前谷	Supreme Spring 極泉	Cold Abyss 清冷淵	Curved Pool 曲池		Calabash Canal 蠡溝		Small Sea 小海	Water Way 水道
Major Stream 太溪	Yang Valley 陽谷	Yin Ling Spring 陰陵泉		Yang Pool 陽池		Standard Canal 經渠		Blood Sea 血海	
Jie Stream 解溪	Leaked Valley 漏谷	Curved Spring 曲泉				Four Canals 四瀆		Zhao Sea 照海	
Xia stream 俠溪	Ran Valley 然谷	Gushing Spring 湧泉							
	Yin Valley 陰谷	Water Spring 水泉							
	Sunken Valley 陷谷	Yang Ling Spring 陽陵泉							
	Extensive valley 通谷								

Source: Created by the author.

Joseph Needham called the traditional Chinese worldview "organismic"; that is, one in which all the phenomena of the universe are interconnected and each and every level of existence is an exact analogue of every other. Cosmos and body corresponded part to part and function to function. In this description, in fact, he had already rejected a world of metaphor for one of homology, where no one domain was transcendent; where neither of the pairs had the explanatory force. Instead, he described a homology with structural or functional "resonance" between the different elements. But because of his larger project, Needham narrowed his focus to understanding the worlds of proto-science that anticipated the modern project and that did not include deities or spirits-creators, though he also did not specifically exclude them. Donald Harper brought us one stage further as he described the world of Taiyi and the cult to the creator water deity as we find him in the Guodian text *Taiyi sheng shui*.

Most exciting is the qualitative difference between imagining water as an element in natural philosophy and the imagination of a numinous "consciousness," with intent, stored in the water. It animated the world all around and resonated with things of the same nature, filling them with spirit illumination. Understanding that the Han environment was thoroughly infused with spirits that moved within and without helps make sense of the self-cultivation of gentlemen and sages. They sought to master the spirits in order to gain an enhanced state of the senses and sensuality, bodies of *qi* that moved like water.

What we have noted in this chapter is that the earliest references to the water homology refer to natural watercourses. Over the course of the first empire, between the texts and artifacts buried in the Yangzi valley and hinterland tomb sites between 186 BCE and the time of the compilation of the first recensions of the *Huang Di neijing*, the locus classicus of acupuncture, in late Han, there were distinct innovations. There develops for the first time a complex medical discourse about water control and therefore the power of the physician, like Great Yu, to control the essences of the body. We find acupoints named after canals and wells. We find a complete conception of the hydrological cycle applied to the body, along with detailed medical treatments guided by the properties of water. Where the properties of water had guided the deliberations of philosophers and government advisors, we find new evidence of how they came to shape physiological ideas and medical techniques. It is a culture that at this point in time seems to be rooted along the course and hinterland of the Yangzi valley where the newly excavated sources are beginning to permit a geographical texturing of the creation of canonical medicine. This same medical language does not exist in texts discovered or originating in the other great center of medical learning, Shandong. Discovering the association of water with *qi* in the old kingdom of Chu is a subject that demands detailed consideration, and much more research than we have space for in this short essay.

Notes

1. Sarah Allan, *The Way of Water and Sprouts of Virtue* (Albany: State University of New York Press, 1997), 10–18.

2. Angus C. Graham, *Disputers of the Tao: Philosophical Argument in Ancient China* (New York: Open Court, 2015), 232–34.

3. *Daodejing*, chap. 78 (MWD 43). The abbreviation MWD designates the version of the *Daodejing* found in the Mawangdui 馬王堆 silk manuscripts discovered in 1973 in a tomb dating from the second century BCE. The translation here is based on Edmund Ryden, *Daodejing* (Oxford: Oxford University Press, 2008), 161.

4. Classical acumoxa theories are set out in the *Huangdi neijing* 黃帝內經, a corpus now extant in three recensions. Each of these is a compilation of small texts dealing with separate topics that may reflect the thinking in a distinct medical lineage. The oldest texts are thought to have been set down at different times during the first or second centuries BCE. Collectively, they represent the kind of debate through which classical medical concepts matured. See Nathan Sivin, "*Huang ti nei ching* 黃帝內經," in *Early Chinese Texts: A Bibliographical Guide*, ed. Michael Loewe (Berkeley: Society for the Study of Early China and Institute of East Asian Studies, University of California, 1993), 196–215; and Yamada Keiji, "The Formation of the Huang-ti Nei-ching," *Acta Asiatica* 36 (1979): 67–89. The canons of acupuncture must also include Huangfu Mi's *Zhenjiu jiayijing* 針灸甲乙經 and the *Nanjing* 難經 (Canon of Difficulties; 1st or 2nd c. CE), translated in Paul Unschuld, *Nan-ching: The Classic of Difficult Issues; With Commentaries by Chinese and Japanese Authors from the Third through the Twentieth Century* (Berkeley: University of California Press, 1986).

5. *Daodejing*, chap. 8 (MWD 52). Translation based on Ryden, *Daodejing*, 19.

6. Angus C. Graham, *Disputers of the Tao: Philosophical Argument in Ancient China* (New York: Open Court, 2015), 232–34.

7. *Daodejing*, chap. 4 (MWD 48). See also Ryden, *Daode jing*, 11.

8. *Guodian Chu mu zhujian* 郭店楚墓竹簡, ed. Jingmenshi bowuguan 荊門市博物館 (Beijing: Wenwu, 1998).

9. Donald Harper, "The Nature of Taiyi in the Guodian Manuscript *Taiyi sheng shui*: Abstract Principle or Supreme Cosmic Deity?" *Chūgoku shutsudo shiryō kenkyū* 中國出土資料研究 5 (2001): 1–23. For the Chinese text, see *Guodian Chu mu zhujian*, 123–26.

10. *Guodian Chu mu zhujian*, 125. Translation after Harper, "Nature of Taiyi," 4.

11. Harper, "Nature of Taiyi," 5.

12. Gopal Sukhu, "Monkeys, Shamans, Emperors and Poets: Images of Chu during the Han Dynasty," in *Defining Chu: Image and Reality in Ancient China*, ed. Constance A. Cook and John S. Major (Honolulu: University of Hawai'i Press, 1999), 154–57.

13. *Tianxia zhidao tan* 天下至道談, in *Mawangdui Han mu boshu* 馬王堆漢墓帛書, ed. Mawangdui Han mu boshu zhengli xiaozu 馬王堆漢墓帛書整理小組, vol. 4 (Beijing: Wenwu, 1985), 111 (slips 18–24). Titles of this and other Mawangdui texts assigned by modern editors. My translation is modified from Donald J. Harper, *Chinese Medical Literature: The Mawangdui Medical Manuscripts* (London: Kegan Paul, 1998), 426; and Ma Jixing, *Mawangdui guyishu kaoshi* 馬王堆古醫書考釋 (Changsha: Hunan kexue jishu, 1992), 1018–19.

14. *He yin yang* 合陰陽, in *Mawangdui Han mu boshu*, vol. 4, 103 (slips 132–33). Vivienne Lo, "Crossing the *Neiguan* 內關 'Inner Pass': A *Nei/wai* 內外 'Inner/Outer' Distinction in Early Chinese Medicine," *East Asian Science, Technology, and Medicine* 17 (2000): 15–65.

15. *He Yin Yang*, 101–2 (slips 112–115).

16. *Mengzi* 孟子 "Tengwen Gong, shang" 滕文公上; *Shijing* 詩經, ed. Wu Zhenyu 武振玉 (Nanchang: Jiangxi jiaoyu, 2010), 210, 244, 301, 304; Stephen Durrant, Wai-yee Li, and David Schaberg, *Zuo Tradition / Zuozhuan: Commentary on the "Spring and Autumn Annals"* (Seattle: University of Washington Press, 2016); Ian Johnson, *The Mozi: A Complete Translation* (Hong Kong: Chinese University Press, 2010); Paul Fischer, *Shizi: China's First Syncretist* (New York: Columbia University Press, 2012).

17. *Shiji* 史記 (Beijing: Zhonghua, 1959), 29.1408.

18. *Lüshi chunqiu xin jiaoshi* 呂氏春秋新校釋 (Shanghai: Shanghai guji, 2002), 139 ("Jin shu" 盡數 3.2); trans. after John Knoblock and Jeffrey Riegel, *The Annals of Lü Buwei* (Stanford, CA: Stanford University Press, 2000), 100.

19. *Maishu* 脈書, in *Zhangjiashan Han mu zhujian: ersiqihao mu (shiwen xiuding ben)* 張家山漢墓竹簡：二四七號墓 (釋文修訂本), ed. Zhangjiashan ersiqi hao Han mu zhujian zhengli xiaozu 張家山二四七號漢墓竹簡整理小組 (Beijing: Wenwu, 2006), 124–25 (slips 52–53).

20. Vivienne Lo, "Spirit of Stone: Technical Considerations in the Treatment of the Jade Body," *Bulletin of the School of Oriental and African Studies* 65, no. 1 (2002): 99–128.

21. *Mengzi yizhu* 孟子譯注, ed. and trans. Yang Bojun 楊伯峻, 3rd ed. (Beijing: Zhonghua, 2010), 235 (6A.2); see Allan, *Way of Water*, 42.

22. Allan, *Way of Water*, 41.

23. *Yinshu* 引書, in *Zhangjiashan Han mu zhujian*, 176 (slips 36–37). Vivienne Lo, *How to Do the Gibbon Walk: A Translation of the "Pulling Book" (ca. 186 BCE)* (Cambridge: Needham Research Institute Working Papers, 2014), 50.

24. *Maishu*, 125 (slips 56–58).

25. He Zhiguo and Vivienne Lo, "The Channels: A Preliminary Examination of a Lacquered Figurine from the Western Han Period," *Early China* 21 (1996): 81–123.

26. Donald Harper and Marc Kalinowski, eds., *Books of Fate and Popular Culture in Early China: The Daybook Manuscripts of the Warring States, Qin, and Han* (Leiden: Brill, 2017), 169.

27. Gansu sheng bowuguan 甘肅省博物館 and Wuwei xian wenhuaguan 武威縣文化館, *Wuwei Handai yijian* 武威漢代醫簡 (Beijing: Wenwu, 1975), 23.

28. *Wuwei Handai yijian*, 4.

29. *Lingshu* 靈樞 71, "Xieke" 邪客 (Evil Visitors). Translation modified from Paul U. Unschuld, *Huang Di nei jing ling shu: The Ancient Classic on Needle Therapy; The Complete Chinese Text with an Annotated English Translation* (Oakland: University of California Press, 2016), 635.

30. Translation modified from Unschuld, *Huang Di nei jing ling shu*, 215. Here "the channel waters on the outside" may be the same as the *jing shui* 經水 referred to in the *Guanzi* chapter "Duo Di" 度地 cited later.

31. *Guanzi jiaozhu*, 1054.

32. *Lingshu* 13, "Jingjin" 經筋 (The Conduits and Their Sinews).

33. Vivienne Lo, "*Huangdi Hama jing* (Yellow Emperor's Toad Canon)," *Asia Major* 14, no. 2, 3rd ser. (2001): 61–99.

34. *Liji zhushu* 禮記注疏, 12.16a–b, in *Shisanjing zhushu* 十三經注疏, coll. Ruan Yuan 阮元 (1764–1849), 8 vols. (Taipei: Yiwen, 2007), vol. 5, 242.

35. *Erya zhushu* 爾雅注疏, 7.22a, in *Shisanjing zhushu*, vol. 8, 121.

36. Li Ling 李零, "Yue zhen hai du kao: Zhongguo gudai de shanchuan jisi" 嶽鎮海瀆考——中國古代的山川祭祀, in *Women de Zhongguo* 我們的中國, vol. 4 (Beijing: Sanlian, 2016), 125–27.

37. Zhu Peng 朱鵬 and Gu Jihong 古繼紅, "Tantao jingshui pei wu jingmai de yixue jiazhi" 探討經水配伍經脈的醫學價值, *Guangming Zhongyi* 光明中醫 2009.2: 251–52.

38. Unschuld, *Nan-ching*, 46.

39. Yang's commentary to the sixty-third issue of the *Nanjing* reads: "All [the streams associated with] the depots and palaces have a 'well' as their first [hole]. *Jing* 井 (well) refers to "valley spring"; it does not mean a well dug up [by man]. The places in mountain valleys where spring water appears first are called 'wells.' 'Well' carries the meaning of 'ruling the appearance.' After water has come to light in a spring, it stays near [its source]. It winds around and does not yet constitute a major stream. Hence it is called *rong* 滎 (brook). A brook appears as a small [body of] water. Where it stands without moving, it develops depth and there are places where it rushes and shoots, turning here and there like a line. Hence one speaks here of *yu* (*shu*) 俞 (rapids). The rapids are responsible for the accumulation and subsequent moving away [of the water]. Over time, they generate huge tracks. *Jing* 經 (stream, conduit) stands for *jing* 徑 (itineraries). Another meaning is *jingying* 經營

(transaction). The movement in the streams finally reaches its destination; it meets with the sea. Hence [this place] is called *he* 合 (confluence). *He* stands for *hui* 會 (to meet). The meaning implied here is that of water flowing and moving on. [The contents of] man's conduit-vessels reflect this [image], hence the designations [well, brook, etc.] were chosen. The 'wells' constitute 'beginning' and [they reflect the season of] spring because of their inherent meaning of 'generating life.'" Adapted from Unschuld, *Nan-ching*, 552–53.

40. *Lingshu* 1, "Jiuzhen shier yuan" 九鍼十二原 (Nine Needles and the Twelve Origins [Openings]). See Unschuld, *Huang Di nei jing ling shu*, 46.

41. *Lingshu* 12, "Jingshui." See Unschuld, *Huang Di nei jing ling shu*, 216.

42. *Lingshu* 60, "Yuban" 玉版 (The Jade Tablets). See Unschuld, *Huang Di nei jing ling shu*, 555–56.

43. *Suwen* 素問 5, "Yinyang yingxiang dalun" 陰陽應象大論 (Comprehensive Discourse on Phenomena Corresponding to Yin and Yang). See Paul U. Unschuld, Hermann Tessenow, and Jinsheng Zheng, *Huang Di nei jing su wen: An Annotated Translation of Huang Di's Inner Classic—Basic Questions*, 2 vols. (Berkeley: University of California Press, 2011), vol. 1, 97.

44. *Lingshu* 33, "Hailun" 海論; Unschuld, *Huang Di nei jing ling shu*, 361.

45. *Suwen* 44, "Weilun" 痿論 (Discourse on Limpness); Unschuld, *Huang Di nei jing su wen*, vol. 1, 662.

46. *Suwen* 58, "Qixuelun" 氣穴論 (Discourse on *Qi* Holes); Unschuld, *Huang Di nei jing su wen*, vol. 2, 56.

47. *Lingshu* 81, "Yongju" 癰疽; Unschuld, *Huang Di Nei Jing Ling Shu*, 763.

48. *Suwen* 10, "Wuzang shengcheng pian" 五藏生成篇; Unschuld, *Huang Di nei jing su wen*, vol. 1, 191n47.

49. Cheng Shide et al., *Suwen zhushi huicui* 素問注釋匯粹 (Beijing: Renmin weisheng, 1982), vol. 1, 164, cites *Lingshu 71*.

50. Unschuld, *Nan-ching*, 322.

3

Destruction of Temples and Arresting Spirits

Metaphors of War, Illness, and Health in Daoist Conversion Narratives

Gil Raz

Introductory Remarks

Medieval Daoists saw themselves as officials charged with cleansing the world of ghosts and demons who tormented the people. Daoist ritual manuals include numerous instructions for summoning spirit-generals and armies of troops to destroy these offending spirits. One such method states:

> If you wish to destroy the seats in shrines in which ghosts and demonic beings are propitiated, you should summon the Pacifying Heaven Lord and the 120 troops of his palace commander.

若欲破房廟座席禱鬼邪物者, 請平天君官將百二十人。[1]

Commenting on this line, Tao Hongjing 陶弘景 (456–536) wrote:

An early version of this chapter was presented at the conference War as Metaphor: Conflict, Writing, and Living 戰爭隱喻: 衝突, 生命, 書寫, Academia Sinica, Taipei, October 30–31, 2014. All dates are CE unless otherwise noted.

> This refers to a person who had served demonic common spirits and has now rectified and converted to Daoism. He should have destroyed the shrines and extinguished the sacrifices, but after that [the spirits] in retaliation cause him affliction, bringing upon him misfortune and disease. Or it may be that in the vicinity of a person's domicile there are shrines of flesh-feeding spirits that cause misfortune and harm.
>
> 謂人先事妖俗，今稟正化，應毀破廟座，滅除禱請事後，或逆為人患，致凶咎疾病，或所居裡城有諸立食巫壇，為人禍褐害者.²

Tao Hongjing's comment is very important, as it deals with both the relationship between Daoism and local cults and with contemporary ideas about the etiology of disease. It seems that conversion to Daoism from the local religion called for the destruction of the offending shrines. This chapter explores this connection, through the analysis of medieval Daoist conversion narratives and rites of destruction of temples, as well as the notions of illness and warfare in these narratives.

Metaphors of Illness and Warfare

Particularly interesting, and the focus of this chapter, is the use of metaphors of illness and warfare to describe the psychosomatic effects of inner states of the convert. Both metaphors depend on a more basic metaphorical system that describes the movement of *qi* 氣 in terms of "correct" and "unified," or in Daoist terms *zhengyi* 正一, as opposed to "deviant" (*xie* 邪) or "reverse flow" (*ni* 逆). These words were used to express linguistically the abstract and ineffable movement of *qi*. It is important to note that these metaphors and metaphoric schemas did not originate within the Daoist community but were pervasive in early China. Daoists, however, manipulated these metaphors creatively to produce and reinforce their particular teachings.

In using the terms "metaphor" and "metaphoric system" I am following the conceptual metaphor theory introduced by George Lakoff and Mark Johnson in *Metaphors We Live By*.³ This seminal study was followed by numerous publications that further elaborated and nuanced the theory of conceptual metaphor.⁴ More recently, Edward Slingerland, in *What Science Offers the Humanities: Integrating Body and Culture*, combined metaphor theory with new insights from cognitive science. Most pertinent to us here is Slingerland's presentation of conceptual blending theory that emends and augments Lakoff and Johnson's theoretical framework. Among the first attempts to employ Lakoff and Johnson's insight in a sinological context is Sarah Allan's *The Way of Water and Sprouts of Virtue*, which, in turn, informs this chapter.[5]

According to Lakoff and Johnson, metaphors are not merely literary or poetic devices but constitute a primary and ubiquitous aspect of human cognition. Human language and thought are essentially metaphoric and embedded in basic bodily functions. Conceptual metaphors are necessary for humans to consider and discuss an abstract or unstructured domain (target domain) by borrowing or deploying language and structure from a concrete, clearly organized, and conceptualized domain (source domain). The metaphoric system is usually based on bodily metaphors (up/down; front/back; the senses) or on basic and easily understood cultural realms, such as war, illness, agriculture, or cooking. The relationship between the source domain, which provides the metaphors, and the abstract target domain is called a schema. Such schemas are presented formulaically in the form TARGET AS SOURCE.[6] For example, a common conceptual metaphor schema is TIME AS SPACE. From this schema we get the common metaphors of "past is behind, future is ahead." In Chinese, and to a lesser extent in European languages, this schema has the added aspect of "past is above, future is below." A particularly important conceptual metaphor in early Chinese thought (and still current, of course) is the QI AS WATER schema. As shown by Sarah Allan, this schema was pervasive in early China and allowed people to actually think and talk both about the Dao, the invisible process of existence, and about *qi*, the ineffable substance that was the "physical" manifestation of the Dao. This basic schema is indeed the metaphoric basis for the passages from *Master Red Pine's Almanac of Petitions* (*Chisongzi zhangli* 赤松子章歷) and *Secret Instructions for Ascending to Perfection* (*Dengzhen yinjue* 登真隱訣) previously cited.

Emergence and Development of Daoism

Daoism emerged and developed as an institutionalized religion between the second and sixth centuries, which was a tumultuous era of political and social turmoil. The long-lasting Han dynasty (207 BCE–220 CE) declined and collapsed in a long civil war, which was followed by a four-centuries-long period of political disunion (the Three Kingdoms and the Northern and Southern dynasties, 220–589 CE). The political and social crisis was exacerbated by the conquest of northern China, the cultural heartland of the realm, by non-Han peoples, sometimes called the Five Barbarians (*wuhu* 五胡). The nearly constant warfare, invasions, forced migrations, and destruction explain the apocalyptic descriptions we find in many Daoist and Buddhist scriptures of the era. Clearly, Daoist authors viewed their era as a cosmological crisis and they were writing within a complex eschatological context. These apocalyptic and eschatological visions were a major motivation for the rise of Daoism.

Importantly, however, as the lines cited earlier demonstrate, references to war and illness are not limited to apocalyptic texts but pervade medieval Daoist ritual texts, hagiographies, and narratives. The lines are found in two texts, *Master Red Pine's Almanac of Petitions* and *Secret Instructions for Ascending to Perfection*. The former is a compilation by unknown editors of Celestial Master rites, practices, and petitions, which was collated between the fifth and seventh centuries. The latter text is also a compilation of practices and rites, compiled by the great Daoist scholar Tao Hongjing, who also provided commentary to the material he collected, edited, and redacted. Both texts preserve some of the earliest extant materials of Celestial Master Daoism. The fact that the same line is found in both texts is further evidence that it is indeed representative of the early community.

I discuss these passages in detail in this chapter. Suffice it here to say that these passages reveal several of the main concerns and motivations of Daoism, and some of the main themes I discuss in this chapter. First, Daoists were concerned with eradicating the world of the dangerous spirits that dominated the cultic practices of local shrines. Second, these local spirits were responsible for illness. Third, the means to cure such spiritually induced illnesses was by rituals, which were, in fact, military campaigns by spirits that were under the command of the Daoist master. Fourth, in this case, the offending spirits were specifically associated with the family shrines of converts to Daoism.

The texts explicitly state that conversion required the destruction of such shrines, and that Daoists considered certain illnesses to be caused by spirits retaliating to their abandonment by the convert to Daoism. While we are not told what were the symptoms or effects of the illness that was caused by such spirits, we may speculate, based on studies of conversion, that it is caused by inner conflicts as the convert processes his or her decision to abandon one set of beliefs and practices and turn to another. Rites of conversion often involve acts of catharsis, often calling for the actual or symbolic destruction of artifacts that link the convert to her past. The destructions of shrines by Daoist converts may be seen as such cathartic release. This may be one reason that the cure for such illness was not by medical means, but by a ritual summoning of spirit troops who would carry out a pacification campaign, modeled on the military campaigns of the state against offending bandits and rebels. These notions are pervasive in Daoist writing and practice.

Exploration

To start our exploration, we turn to the opening lines of *Demon Statutes of Lady Blue* (*Nüqing guilü* 女青鬼律). Among the earliest preserved records of Celestial Master Daoism, this text describes the sociopolitical situation in early medieval China as a cosmological crisis in which ghosts and demons ran amok, freely killing the people.[7] The Dao, here personified as the Most High Great Way, feels the necessity to intervene and bestows upon Zhang Daoling 張道陵, the first Celestial Master, this very text with which to command and control the rampaging spirits.

> When heaven and earth were first generated the primordial *qi* was bestowed and flowed. The myriad spirits spread their *qi*, and there were no repulsive, rebellious, demonic, deviant, and improper ghosts. Men were filial and women were chaste; princes were respectful, and ministers loyal. The six directions were as one, and there was no harm or pain. Later, since the first year of the Celestial Sovereign, through repeated rebirths and hundred artifices, as there was no belief in the Great Way, throughout the five directions there was rebellious killing, and noxious *qi* gradually increased. Tigers, wolves, and the hundred beasts accumulated *qi* and grew larger, the hundred insects, snakes, and demons were daily more fecund. In heaven, there are sixty days, and each day has a spirit, and each spirit directs a day. But now the days had a thousand ghosts flying and roaming, and they cannot be controlled and stopped. The Great Way did not issue restrictions and the Celestial Master did not issue commands, so the ghosts ran amok throughout the world, competing in their ferocity. They freely killed the people, and the dead numbered in the millions. The Most High Great Way

could not bear to see this, and in the second year, seventh month, seventh day, at noon it sent down the *Demon Statutes*, in eight *juan*, as a record of all the names of the ghosts in the world and the methods of fortune and misfortune, and bestowed it upon Zhang Daoling, entrusting him to command the ghosts and spirits so that they would not roam wildly in all directions. Later, were male and female students of the Way to look at my secret scripture, they would know the names of the ghosts and all will be well, the myriad ghosts would not offend, and the thousand spirits will submit.

天地初生，元氣施行，萬神布氣，無有醜逆袄邪不正之鬼，男孝女貞，君禮臣忠，六合如一，無有患害．自後天皇元年以來，轉生百巧，不信大道，五方逆殺，疫氣漸興，虎狼萬獸，受氣長大，百蟲蛇魅，與日滋甚．天有六十日，日有一神，神直一日．日有千鬼飛行，不可禁止．大道不禁，天師不勅，放縱天下，凶凶相逐．唯任殺中民，死者千億．太上大道不忍見之，二年七月七日日中時下此鬼律八卷，紀天下鬼神姓名吉凶之術，以勅天師張道陵，使勅鬼神，不得妄轉東西南北．後有道男女生，見吾祕經，知鬼姓名皆吉，萬鬼不幹，千神賓伏．[8]

Of particular interest for us here is the metaphoric language used to describe the various actions of the Way and *qi*, and of the contravening actions of the demons. The first sentence presents a clear dichotomy between the "primordial *qi*" (*yuanqi* 元氣) that is "bestowed" (*shi* 施), "flows" (*xing* 行), and "spreads" (*bu* 布) to the proper spirits. Like water, *qi* is morally neutral and can flow into the beasts and demons who grow (*chang* 長) and flourish (*zi* 滋). Demons are described as "repulsive, rebellious, demonic, deviant" (*chou ni yao xie* 醜逆袄邪), or more simply as "improper" (*buzheng* 不正) ghosts. When the world is harmonious, it is "as one" (*ru yi* 如一), but when artifice (*qiao* 巧) appears, it is followed by "rebellious killing" (*nisha* 逆殺) and "noxious *qi*" (*yiqi* 疫氣). We should especially note that the word translated as "rebellious" here is *ni* 逆, which literally means "reverse flow." It is this "reverse flow" of *qi* that defines the improper actions of the demons, which are "undisciplined" (*fangzong* 放縱), "have free rein to kill" (*ren sha* 任殺), and are "ferocious" (*xiongxiong* 凶凶). At this point in the text, the conceptual metaphor of "reverse flow" (*ni* 逆) has shifted to the broader meaning of *ni* 逆 as "rebellious" and "unrestricted by law." As the text explains, it is precisely because of the lack of restrictions (*jin* 禁) and commands (*chi* 勅) that the demons flourish. The legalistic terminology thus overlaps with the water metaphor, as it is the uncontrolled flow of *qi* that produces the demons. Much of the text of *Demon Statutes of Lady Blue* consists of long lists of names of spirits and demons by which the Daoist can control them.

This Daoist narrative of decline and its basic metaphor of water resonates, perhaps surprisingly, with a passage in *Mencius* 孟子 (3B.9) describing the deluge that was eventually cleared by Yu. This passage is fully translated and analyzed by Sarah Allan, so I will only refer to the opening and final lines:

> The world was generated long ago. Sometimes there is order and sometimes disorder. At the time of Yao, the water flowed in reverse (*nixing* 逆行) and inundated the central states. Snakes and dragons dwelt there, and humans had no place to settle. . . . [After Yu channeled the waters] the birds and beasts that harmed the people disappeared. Then the people obtained flat land and dwelt there.
>
> 天下之生久矣, 一治一亂. 當堯之時, 水逆行, 氾濫於中國. 蛇龍居之, 民無所定. . . . 鳥獸之害人者消, 然後人得平土而居之.[9]

In this pre-Qin Confucian classic, it is the reverse flow of water that leads to the disorder (*luan* 亂) of the deluge. It is by proper channeling (*zhu* 注) that Yu clears up the flood. Proper government is therefore good water management. Both passages show how the basic metaphor of the QI AS WATER schema is easily transformed into the schema GOVERNMENT AS WATER MANAGEMENT.

In the *Mencius* passage we find that dragons and snakes, watery beasts nourished by the flooding waters, take over the place of humans. In the end of the passage these mythical creatures are replaced by more mundane "birds and beasts." In the *Demon Statutes* we similarly find the human realm overrun by beasts and demons nourished by the overflowing *qi*. Importantly, the clearing of the flood obtains "flat land" (*pingtu* 平土), but we should remember that in this case *ping* 平 actually refers to "extinguishing" (*xiao* 消) the beasts, and thus perhaps "pacifying" would be a better understanding of this line. This would resonate with the Pacifying Heaven Lord 平天君 summoned to pacify the offending spirits by the Daoists according to the *Secret Instructions* and *Master Red Pine's Almanac*. The water-management metaphor has now shifted to the military metaphor of "pacification" through destruction of offending creatures.

In the passages from *Mencius* and *Demon Statutes* we find that beasts and snakes are a metaphoric symptom of disorder, illness, and bad government. Keeping this metaphor in mind, we may look at two brief narratives describing Daoists providing healing by nonmedical means. The *Traditions of Students of the Dao* (*Daoxue zhuan* 道學傳), a no-longer-extant collection of hagiographies compiled in the sixth century, includes hagiographic notices depicting Gu Huan 顧歡 (420–483), a well-known Daoist of the fifth century:[10]

> There were many demonic illnesses at Baishan Village. The villagers reported this seeking succor. Gu entered the village and recited the *Laozi* and cordoned off an earth prison. Momentarily, hordes of foxes, turtles, and alligators were seen entering the prison. The ill were thus all healed.
>
> 白山村多邪病. 村人告訴求哀. 歡往村中為講老子, 算地獄. 有頃見狐狸黿鼉, 自入獄中者甚衆. 病者皆愈也.[11]

We are not told here what illnesses afflicted the people of Baishan, except that these were defined as "demonic" illnesses (*xiebing* 邪病), or, more precisely, illnesses caused by "deviant" (*xie*) *qi*. These agents of illness are finally manifested as foxes and watery beasts. Such illnesses could not be treated medically. Gu Huan provides healing by reciting the text of the *Laozi* and then creating a prison for the demons. We are not told whether he performed other ritual actions. This brief narrative clearly shares the same metaphoric complex as both the Confucian classic and the Daoist scripture. A passage with a similar method of healing demonic illness is included among the *Shenxianzhuan* 神仙傳 hagiographies:

> Wang Yao was from Poyang. He was quite good at healing, and no illness would be uncured. He could heal without using sacrifices, talismanic water, acupuncture, or drugs. Instead, he simply rolled out an eight-foot-square cloth on the floor on which he would sit without eating or drinking. Soon the illness would be cured and the patient would depart. In the case of a corrupt demon causing harm, Yao would draw a prison on the ground and summon it for investigation. The demon's shape

would always appear within the prison, whether a fox, turtle, or snake. He would then behead and burn it and the patient would be healed.

王遙字伯遼都陽人也. 頗行治病, 病無不愈. 亦不祭祀, 不用符水, 鍼藥. 其行治病, 但以一八尺布帕敷地坐, 不飲不食, 須臾病愈便去. 其有邪魅作禍者, 遙但晝地作獄囚, 口召呼之, 皆見其形在獄中, 或狐貍龍蛇, 乃斬而焚燒之, 病者尋愈也.¹²

Like Gu Huan, Wang Yao 王遙 cures demonic illness by inscribing a prison on the ground and summoning the offending spirits. These spirits are manifested as foxes and aquatic beasts. As with Gu Huan, the metaphor has shifted from destruction to imprisonment, or from a military campaign to a juridical process.¹³ We should note that both the military and juridical metaphors are based on the more basic conceptual metaphor QI AS WATER. This metaphoric complex conceptualizes social and individual disorder as caused by deviant or backward-flowing *qi*. This disruption is presented metaphorically as demons that cause illness. Such illness can only be managed by reinstating the correct flow of *qi*, which is metaphorically presented as arresting or punishing the agents of disruption.

So far, we have looked at narratives that refer to the agents of disorder as beasts or vaguely defined spirits. Other Daoist texts, including the *Demon Statutes*, present far more detailed demonologies with the names, titles, and jurisdictions of innumerable demons and spirits. While it is not clear how these inchoate demonic beings are related to the disease-causing spirits in shrines referred to in the passages from *Secret Instructions* and the *Almanac*, they are all metaphorically associated with uncontrolled or improper flow of *qi*.

Another contemporary text, *Master Lu's Abridged Codes for the Daoist Community* (*Lu xiansheng daomen kelüe* 陸先生道門科略) by the well-known liturgist Lu Xiujing 陸修靜 (406–477), presents a succinct Daoist vision of history. As in the opening lines of the *Demon Statutes*, this passage too provides the reason for the creation of Celestial Master Daoism, here named *Covenantal Authority of Correct Unity* (*Zhengyi mengwei* 正一盟威), as a response to the current social and political situation, which is depicted as a cosmological crisis.

> The Most High Lord Lao saw that in recent antiquity there was a decline into violence, purity was diffused, and simplicity

was scattered. The cosmic order lost its balance, and men and demons mingled chaotically. The stale vapors of the Six Heavens took on official titles and appellations and brought together the hundred sprites and the demons of the five kinds of wounding, dead generals of defeated armies, and dead troops of rebellious armies. The men called themselves "General"; the women called themselves "Lady." Leading ghostly troops, they traveled and camped as armies and divisions. Roaming through the world they arrogated to themselves authority and the power to dispense blessings. They took over people's temples and sought their sacrificial offerings. They caused anxiety and disorder among the people who killed the three kinds of sacrificial animals, used up all their resources, cast away all their goods, and exhausted their produce. They were not blessed with good fortune, but on the contrary received disaster, so that those who died violently and before their time could not be counted. The Most High was distressed this was so and bestowed upon the Celestial Master the Way of *Covenantal Authority of Correct Unity* . . . [providing the precepts, codes, organization, and the Petitions and Writs of the 1,200 Officials] and the Execution Talismans for Attacking Shrines, to kill ghosts and [save] the living, to cleanse and purify the universe, brightly correct the cosmic order, so that throughout heaven and earth there will no longer be excessive and deviant ghosts.

太上老君以下古委黟，淳澆樸散，三五失統，人鬼錯亂，六天故氣稱官上號，搆合百精及五傷之鬼，敗軍死將亂軍死兵. 男稱將軍，女稱夫人. 導從鬼兵軍行師止，遊放天地，擅行威福. 責人廟舍，求人饗祠，擾亂人民宰殺三牲費用萬計傾財竭產. 不蒙其祐反受其患. 柱死橫夭不可稱數. 太上患其若此，故授天師正一盟威之道 . . . 誅符伐廟，殺鬼生人，蕩滌宇宙，明正三五，周天匝地，不得復有淫邪之鬼.[14]

As has been noted and discussed by many scholars, the ritual system of the early Celestial Master community was established in direct contrast to the prevailing sacrificial system of the imperial and ancestral rites. The Celestial Master community defined itself in opposition to the traditional local religious practices and saw its mission as the eradication of the false practices pervading the realm. Chief among these practices were the blood sacrifices offered at the various local shrines, ancestral shrines, temples to local deities, and on the imperial altars. Gods who demanded flesh and blood offerings were deemed false. Not only were these gods not efficacious, but their rapacious demands brought more harm on the populace. Of particular importance, however, is that Lu Xiujing defines the origins of these false gods in the "stale or stagnant *qi* of the Six Heavens" (*liutian guqi* 六天故氣).

Conceptual Metaphors

Qi as Water ↔ Government as Water Management

The term "stale *qi* of the Six Heavens" appears in several fifth-century Daoist texts. While there is still debate regarding the exact referent for the term Six Heavens, scholars agree that it refers to the traditional cosmic ritual order.[15] This ancient order had recently, that is, since the Han, fallen into disarray. Here, the metaphoric system informing the passage is made explicit, as Lu tells us that the cause for the current chaos is the stagnant *qi* that accumulated in the world due to the collapse of the former order. The basic conceptual metaphor here is QI AS WATER. The original "pure" (*chun* 淳) fluid has "leaked out" or "dispersed" (*jiao* 澆) leading to the mixing of the living and the ghosts. The noxious *qi* of the ghosts took on physical form and took over the temples of the people, demanding blood sacrifice. We should stress that this is a Daoist view of traditional local religion. We should also note that the noxious *qi* that was depicted as "dragon and snakes, birds and beasts" in the *Mencius* and the Daoist *Almanac* is here described in terms of ghostly generals leading armies of ghostly troops. This shift in metaphor explains why the shrines of these marauding agents of disorder need to be destroyed (*fa miao* 伐廟) using the Execution Talismans (*zhufu* 誅符).

While this imagery may be mapped onto the conceptual metaphor of KEEPING ORDER AS WAR, these ghostly armies of disorder should also be understood as a Daoist interpretation of the actual historical situation during the late Han and through the succeeding centuries. Indeed, we find the same set of terms and metaphors encapsulated in Zhuge Liang's 諸葛亮 famous maxim "execute the violent and punish the rebellious" (*zhu bao tao ni* 誅暴討逆).[16]

Zhengyi

I return to discuss the ritual destruction of shrines later, but first we should examine the metaphoric sense of *zhengyi* 正一, the preferred label of Celestial Master Daoism for its own teaching. Translatable as "orthodox unity," this term reflects the vision of the Celestial Master as representing the correct teaching of the Dao, the ultimate one. However, for our purposes this translation is too interpretive and may occlude the more basic and metaphoric meaning of the term. First, it is important to note that the term *zhengyi* does not in fact designate the community but the *qi* of the Dao. This is evident when we look at the earliest extant record of the Celestial Master community, a fragmentary inscription dating to 173 CE:

> Second year of the Xiping era (173 CE), third month, first day. Hu Jiu [lacunae], demon soldier of the Celestial Elder, [announces]: "you have followed the path to transcendence and your Dao is complete. The dark spread has extended your lives. The correct and unitary *qi* of the Dao has been distributed to your *qi*. It has been decided to summon the libationers Zhang Pu, Meng Sheng, Zhao Guang, Wang Sheng, Huang Chang, and Yang Feng to come and receive twelve scrolls of subtle scriptures. The libationers pledge to spread the teachings of the Way of the Celestial Master without limit!"
>
> 熹平二年三月一日，天老鬼兵胡九□□：「仙歷道成，玄施延命，道正一元（炁），布于伯氣．定召祭酒張普、萌生、趙廣、王盛、黃長、揚奉等，詣受微經十二卷．祭酒約施天師道法無極才（哉）．」[17]

This inscription presents many problems, but we will focus on the words *shi* 施 and *bu* 布, which were also used in the opening lines of the *Demon Statutes* to describe the proper movement of *qi* (元氣施行，萬神布氣).[18] Here, we find the somewhat enigmatic "dark spread" (*xuanshi* 玄施), which Terry Kleeman translates as Mystic Dispensation, explaining neither the concept he uses nor his terminological choice. I suggest we understand the term *xuan* as a synonym for Dao,[19] with the word *shi* 施 referring to the flowing of *qi* that is bestowed upon the libationers, granting them longevity. Note also that *xuan* and *yuan* are sometimes interchangeable, so that *xuanshi* may indeed have the same meaning as the phrase *yuanqi shixing* 元氣施行 in *Demon Statutes*. Furthermore, 施 is also used in the final line to define the action of the libationers in spreading the teachings of the Celestial Master. Most importantly, it is clear that *zheng* and *yi* are used as descriptive terms applied to aspects or qualities of the *qi* emanating from the Dao.

In his analysis of the word *zheng*, Chen Chi-yun noted that the graph was explicated by the Han philologist Xu Shen 許慎 as "to stop, to stand firm." In Shang oracle bones the graph signified "successful targeted action." By the Han dynasty the word acquired the connotation of "aligned," "upright," and "correct" in a moral sense.[20] In this sense, the word "orthodoxy" that etymologically means "correct belief" does overlap to some extent with *zheng*. But *zheng* does not itself carry the sense of belief. This is clearer when the metaphor of uprightness or alignment is compared with words used to define improper or illicit teachings or practices, such as "deviant" (*xie* 邪), "overflowing" (*yin* 淫), and "bent" (*qu* 曲).[21] In Daoist contexts, a better translation would be "correct"—as adjective or verb. In understanding how the correct and deviant *qi* interact it is critical to remember the basic conceptual metaphor of QI AS WATER. For example, one of the Shangqing 上清 (Highest Clarity) scriptures includes the following explanation for the departure of correct *qi* from the body and its replacement by stale and deviant *qi*:

> Hence, when the Three Ones depart, then the correct *qi* leaves. As one loses correct *qi*, stale *qi* advances. As stale *qi* advances, death comes nearer daily. When common people study the Way, many seek ostentatious words and do not believe that the True One is the most valuable. Beginning with this intention, they cannot but later turn to worse. As their intention is not unified, corrupt *qi* enters as before. As to the precepts of Preserving Oneness, if one is not focused on these precepts or does not practice them long enough, then the Three Ones depart, the body becomes an empty house with no lord and misfortune dwells within for long.

> 故三一去則正炁離, 夫失正炁者則故氣前, 故氣前則死日近也. 俗人學道, 多尋浮華, 不以真一為貴. 初雖有其志, 後必變敗, 皆由用志不一, 邪氣來入故也. 守一之戒, 戒於不專, 專復不久, 久不見精, 則三一去矣, 身為空宅耳. 空宅無主, 其禍安久.[22]

Celestial Master ritual instructions also show that *zhengyi* should be understood as the *qi* emanating from the Dao rather than as a reference

64 | Gil Raz

to the ecclesia of the Celestial Master. The *Instructions for Entering the Oratory* (*Rujingfa* 入靜法)—preserved in Tao Hongjing's *Secret Instructions*—incorporates a version of the most basic Celestial Master rite, reformulated within a Shangqing context.[23] Upon entering the Oratory, the adept begins by invoking the Most High Lord Lao and spirit officers and officials. The adept proceeds to request the "correct *qi* of the eight directions" (*bafang zhengqi* 八方正氣) to enter the body. Next, the adept announces:

> Solemnly I call upon the three Masters, the Celestial Master, the Consort Master, and Successor Master, and the officers and clerks of their institution. I wish to receive the three *qi* of correct oneness, to wash over and nourish my form and spirits, so that my five viscera sprout flowers, and my six storehouses freely communicate, that this would extinguish the calamities and troubles in the four directions, release my seven ancestors of seven generations from disaster and harm, that I would obtain longevity, and become a flying transcendent.
>
> 謹關啟天師, 女師系師三師, 門下典者君吏, 願得正一三炁, 灌養形神, 使五藏生華, 六府宣通, 為消四方之災禍, 解七世之殃患, 長生久視, 得為飛仙.[24]

The rhetoric of this invocation is clearly based on the QI AS WATER metaphor. The adept summons the three *qi* of the correct unity (*zhengyi sanqi* 正一三炁) to irrigate and nourish the body, causing flowers to bloom in the viscera and open communication among the organs.[25]

Protocol of the Early Celestial Master Rite

According to *Master Lu's Abridged Codes* the most important function of the Celestial Master, and the only ritual actually mentioned in the opening passage of the text, was the destruction of local shrines. This impression is supported by the protocol of the earliest Celestial Master rite, preserved in the *Secret Instructions* as the "Hanzhong Method for Entering the Parish and Holding Audience at the Oratory" (Hanzhong ruzhi chaojing fa 漢中入治朝靜法).

The rite begins with directional invocations, as the adept turns to the east, north, west, and south, summoning the specific spirit of each direction and requesting the appropriate benefits. These requests reveal the main concerns and motivations of Daoists. These benefits, concerns, and motivations would also draw in converts to the religion, as we will see in the next section of the ritual.

Thus, facing east the adept summons all Lords and Elders (*zhujun zhangren* 諸君丈人) and requests longevity, to become a seed person (*zhongmin* 種民), dissolution of calamity, healing of all illness, and finally the Daoist notion of salvation and enlightenment, that the "spirit luminaries will attach to the body, my heart will open, and my mind awaken" (神明附身, 心開意悟).

Turning to the north, the adept would summon the Supreme Unitary Lord of Great Darkness (Taixuan Shangyi Jun 太玄上一君) and request pardon for sins, fording of troubles, and avoiding of trials. The adept would also request that all threats of metal and stone, water and fire be dispelled (金石為開, 水火為滅), and that "evil, backward [*qi* demons] submit and sprites and deviant [*qi* demons] be eradicated" (惡逆賓伏, 精邪消散).

To the west, the adept summons the Celestial Master (Tianshi 天師) requesting that all one's wishes be fulfilled, and all tasks completed. The adept seeks perspicacity and acuity, and also asks for the expulsion of all illness and that the body become both light and strong.

Facing south, the adept summons the Lord of the Way and Power (Daode Jun 道德君) and requests that he allow his "beneficent and pervasive *qi* to spread and wash over my bones and form and allow the *qi* of the Way to flow through my body" (恩潤之氣佈施骨體, 使道氣流行甲身) to remove disease and bring fortune.

At this point we need not belabor the obvious watery metaphors and the use of the words *bu* 布 and *shi* 施 in this last invocation. We note that the most common request is the eradication of illness. Indeed, healing seems to be a central concern in this ritual as it is in Daoist conversion stories, a few of which we will turn to at the end of the chapter.

The directional invocations, summons, and requests serve to prepare the ritual space. The next stage in the rite is the presentation of petitions and talismans (*zhangfu* 章符). This is the central phase of the rite. The instructions present four cases for petitioning. All of them are about illness due to demons, revealing the extreme concern of the early Celestial Master community with this issue.

The first case is simply named "urgent" (*jishi* 急事). This is explained as "a case of violent illness or extreme misfortune" (有暴疾病, 及禍難憂懼). In this case, the libationer should use vermilion ink to write the petition and mark it with Red-Marker Tallies (*chibiao fu* 赤標符) to ensure haste. We should note that in writing his name and title, the libationer also includes the source of his authority, which is "Correct and Unitary Pacifying *Qi* of the Mystic Capital of Great Purity" (太清玄都正一平炁係天師某治炁祭酒臣某).

Following the general instruction for "urgent" cases, the text turns to listing petitions for specific cases.

1. Petition for Expulsion of Ghosts ("Suiguizhang" 遂鬼章). This is explained as a case of a home infested by evil and strong ghosts causing trouble and illness (謂家有惡強之鬼為禍祟).

2. Petition for Healing Demonic Illness ("Zhi xiebing zhang" 治邪病章). This is explained as a case when "one is beset by overflowing and deviant *qi*, or by harm caused by deviant ghosts of local shrines" (人有淫邪之氣, 及諸廟座邪鬼為患). In this case one should summon the Pacifying Heaven Lords to destroy and control these ghosts (平天君等消制之).

3. In the case of demonic illness caused by infusion of *qi* (*zhuqi guibing* 注氣鬼病), one should present the Petition for Attacking Ghosts ("Dangzuo ji gui zhang" 當作擊鬼章). This refers to cases of sepulchral interrogations and plaints in which the dead send their *qi* back and infuse the living to cause illness and harm (家有五墓考訟死喪逆注之鬼來為病害).

Having listed the instructions for these three petitions, the text turns to more general instructions for summoning officials (*qing guan* 請官). Here the text lists various scenarios with specific illnesses and ailments, provides explanations for these problems, and names the spirit officials that should be invoked and which petitions should be used. Again, the most important concern in these cases are ailments caused by backward-flowing *qi*, noxious *qi*, ghosts, and goblins, such as the "five epidemics of toxic poisons, and six types of drought ghosts" (五瘟蠱毒六魃之鬼). It is in this context that we find the lines cited at the very start of this chapter, namely those on summoning the Pacifying Heavenly Lord and the 120 troops of his palace commander, to which Tao Hongjing comments.

It should by now be clear that Daoists saw themselves as fighters in a cosmic battle against hordes of ghosts and demons. These ghosts and demons come into existence and are nourished by backward-flowing, stale, or old *qi*, or improper control of *qi*. On a metaphoric level these ghosts and demons are manifestations of chaos, due to the lack of proper governance in the world. The illnesses caused by these ghosts and demons are therefore metaphors for the absence of good government. This is why such illnesses cannot be cured by medical means but through rites modeled on military and juridical interventions.

Individual Healing in Tales of Conversion

Interestingly, the same metaphors of illness and war are also found in narratives depicting individuals being healed. While not always stated explicitly, many of the narratives in Daoist hagiographic contexts may also be seen as tales of conversion as they functioned as proofs of the efficacy of Daoist masters.

A particularly good example is a narrative of individual healing incorporating much of the cosmological and ritual rhetoric of "stale *qi*" and "correct and unitary *qi*" found in the hagiography of Du Jiong 杜炅, of Qiantang 錢唐 in Wu 吳. Active in the late third century, Du Jiong was an important Daoist practitioner.[26] According to a passage from the *Daoxuezhuan* 道學傳:

> Du Jiong was styled Zi Gong. When he reached adulthood, his knowledge and fidelity were profound and diligent. He devotedly served correct unity. [Already] when he was young, he was enrolled on a register for a parish of the Celestial Masters. With it he transformed and guided people, providing aid to all. Through practice he became concentrated and pure, emptying his heart and aiding beings, without seeking pledges and payment. Later he established a parish oratory and widely broadcast salvation and protection [for the people]. In all cases he was efficacious.
>
> 杜炅, 字子恭, 及壯識信精勤, 宗事正一, 少參天師治籙, 以之化導, 接濟周普, 行已精潔, 虛心拯物, 不求信施, 遂立治靜, 廣宣救護, 莫不立驗也.[27]

Before proceeding further, we should note the emphasis in this passage on Du Jiong's converting people (*yi zhi hua dao* 以之化導) by his conduct and efficacy.

In another version of the hagiography Du states his motivation for joining the Celestial Masters: "Now ghosts and men are mixing wildly, but without the correct and unitary *qi*, there is no way to guard against this" (方當人鬼殽亂, 非正一之炁, 無以鎮之). He then serves Chen Wenzi of Yuhang 餘杭陳文子, receives a parish, and becomes a Disciple of Correct Unity (受治為正一弟子).²⁸

The narrative then turns to several tales of healing. The most interesting for our purposes is the extended tale of Du Jiong's defeat of two local mediums.

> [Du] was skilled at healing and could foresee the good and evil [fate] of people. Long Zhi of Shangyu and Si Shen of Qiantang were both spirit mediums. They envied the flourishing of Jiong's way and constantly spoke ill of him. Someone told Jiong of this. Jiong said, "To slander the Correct Rituals is to invite otherworldly inquisition." Shortly thereafter Zhi's wife died suddenly, and Shen contracted a mysterious illness. Both gave thought to their trespasses and repented. Jiong [conducted a ritual of] release and penitence for them, and right away they were both healed.
>
> 杜炅, 字子恭, 為人善治病, 人間善惡皆能預睹. 上虞龍稚, 錢唐斯神, 並為巫覡. 嫉炅道王, 常相誘毀, 人以告炅, 炅曰: "非毀正法, 尋招冥考." 俄而稚妻暴卒, 神抱隱疾, 並思過歸誠, 炅為解謝, 應時皆愈.
>
> Later, Shen was ill again. Jiong said to him, "You are harboring demonic things, and your illness is simply an affliction of stagnant vapors." Shen then confessed, saying: "In truth I am hiding a chest of good clothes." He brought the clothes to the parish and burned them, and suddenly he was fully cured.
>
> 神晚更病, 炅語曰: "汝藏鬼物, 故氣祟耳." 神即首謝曰: "實藏好衣一箱." 登取於治燒之, 豁然都差.²⁹

We find here a Daoist master bettering his competitors, who after besmirching the Correct Teaching (*zhengfa* 正法) were struck by mysterious illness and death. The Daoist cures them by a ritual of penitence. When one of them falls ill again, Du diagnoses the cause as an "affliction of stagnant vapors" (*guqisui* 故氣祟). The medium confesses that he continues to hide a chest of good clothes and proceeds to burn these at Du's parish temple. It is not quite clear what these clothes were, but we may speculate that they are connected to the medium's vocation, perhaps his ritual vestments. In order to be cured he needs to burn them at the parish center. We may further speculate that the first ritual of "release and penitence" (*jiexie*) was perhaps considered a conversion. This would explain why the medium was obliged to burn his hidden "old *qi*." I suggest that this narrative resonates with the passage in *Secret Instructions* with which we began this essay.

Another narrative, explicitly referring to conversion, is preserved in the *Declarations of the Perfected* (*Zhen'gao* 真誥):

> Fan Boci of Guiyang came from a family that worshiped popular cults. Suddenly he became mad, fell ill with a deviant debilitating illness, and stayed in bed for a year. He approached a healer seeking a cure. The demands of the healer were so high that he almost used up his family's fortune. But the illness was not cured. Hearing that the "Great Way of Pure Covenant" did not involve expenditure, his intention shifted toward it. He heard that Daoist master Chen Jing was powerful and his healing powers were extremely efficacious. Fan therefore abandoned the vulgar cult and served him. After fifty days the illness was completely cured.
>
> 范伯慈者, 桂陽人也. 家本事俗, 而忽得狂邪, 因成邪勞病, 頓臥床席經年, 迎師解事費用, 家資漸盡, 病故不愈. 聞"大道清約"無所用, 於是意變, 聞沈敬作道士精進, 理病多驗, 乃棄俗事之, 得五十日, 病疾都愈.[30]

Here we find the worshiper of local gods becoming infected with mysterious ailments, both psychological and physical. He cannot be cured by common means but is soon cured when he turns to Celestial Master Daoism.

We find a similar theme in another narrative, that of Hua Qiao:

> The magistrate of Jiangsheng, Hua Qiao of Jinling, had for years venerated vulgar spirits. Once he had a sudden dream in which he traveled together with a horde of spirits, eating and drinking with them. After returning home drunk, he vomited all that he had eaten and drunk. For several years afterward

the spirits demanded that Qiao recommend talented people [to serve at the infernal bureaus]. Qiao could not refuse. He pointed out some dozen people, all of whom died. Using Qiao's recommendations the spirits thus gained talented recruits and acquired the knowledge of the sages. The demands became heavier, and Qiao was severely punished for even minor infractions. Qiao became terrified that he himself would become a target for the spirits. He therefore turned his back on the vulgar and entered the Dao. He approached the libationer of Danyang parish and received methods for revering the Dao. The multitude of spirits vanished and never reappeared.

江乘令晉陵華僑，世奉俗神，忽夢見群鬼神與之遊行飲食．群鬼所與僑共飲酒，僑亦至醉，還家輒吐所飲噉之物．數年諸鬼遂課限僑舉才，僑不得已，先後所舉十餘人，皆至死亡．鬼以僑所舉得才，有知人之識，限課轉多．若小稽違，便彈治之．僑自懼必為諸鬼所困，於是背俗入道，詣祭酒丹陽許治，受奉道之法．群鬼各便消散，不復來往．[31]

Following his conversion to Celestial Master Daoism, Hua Qiao begins to receive visitations from two perfected persons who instruct him in the secret teachings of Shangqing Daoism. This aspect of the narrative and its sad denouement are beyond the scope of this chapter. What is important for our purposes here is that Hua Qiao, like Fan Boci, was afflicted by the spirits of his own family shrine. These are precisely the type of uncontrolled deviant spirits that *Master Lu's Abridged Codes* asserts are the cause of chaos in the world and for which the *Secret Instructions* provides various ritual remedies.

Conclusion

Daoist narratives of conversion and instructions for destroying shrines by converts to Daoism include similar motifs of incurable illness attributed to demons and healing by Daoists through ritual means. Less clear in the conversion stories, but made explicit in the ritual instructions, these rites involve destruction of the shrines that are modeled on military and juridical procedures. These same motifs are found in the grand eschatological narratives that describe the emergence of Celestial Master Daoism as a response to the chaos of the current age, caused by the invasion of the realm by demons and ghosts. This in turn is said to be a result of the collapse of the cosmic order. We may ask how is it that the individual process of conversion—acceptance of the new religious beliefs, faith, and practices—is described in the same terms as the apocalyptic visions of medieval Daoist texts?

By investigating the conceptual metaphors that pervade these narratives and instructions we find that both illness and war are metaphors for social and political crisis as well as for individual crisis. Both metaphors are based on a more basic set of metaphorical schemata, primarily QI AS WATER and GOVERNMENT AS WATER MANAGEMENT. These basic metaphors allow people to discuss the abstract workings of invisible *qi* in terms of proper channeling and flowing or, conversely, in terms of backward flow or deviance. While these metaphors were found in ancient texts, they took on added significance after the fall of the Han, as the social and political situation became increasingly chaotic.

Reading the flood narrative in the *Mencius* alongside the opening passage of the *Demon Statutes of Lady Blue* reveals how medieval authors elaborated ancient metaphors to explain and interpret current events. Daoist apocalyptic and eschatological descriptions are thus expressions of religious creative imaginations interpreting historical reality. That is, religious texts are interpretive and not descriptive; they interpret reality from particular exegetical perspectives and use these interpretations to further bolster and refine these very perspectives. Religious texts of this kind should be understood, therefore, as both participating in and creating particular symbolic universes. Accordingly, they may or may not cohere with other texts describing and interpreting the same events. Our task is therefore to understand the hermeneutic keys of the texts before us and try to understand the symbolic universe in which their authors operated.

These texts were both transformative and performative. On the one hand, they called for the transformation of individuals and communities through particular practices. On the other hand, they transformed the mental or symbolic universe of their audience (whether readers or hearers) by the language they deploy. Most importantly, by actually writing these metaphors into ritual manuals and into narratives of conversion, Daoists literally attempted to transform the world around them, to cleanse it of the offending demons, and to rectify and unify the realm. This then is what Celestial Master Daoism was all about—to "correct and unify" (正一).

Notes

1. *Chisongzi zhangli* 赤松子章歷 (DZ 615), 2.21a; *Dengzhen yinjue* 登真隱訣 (DZ 421), 3.21b3. Daoist texts are cited from the *Zhengtong daozang* 正統道藏, Hanfenlou facsimile ed., 60 vols. (1926; rpt. Taipei: Xinwenfang, 1985), hereafter DZ. Numbers after DZ in parentheses refer to the numbers assigned in *The Taoist Canon: A Historical Companion to the Daozang*, ed. Kristofer Schipper and Franciscus Verellen (Chicago: University of Chicago Press, 2004).

2. *Dengzhen yinjue* (DZ 421), 3.21b3.

3. George Lakoff and Mark Johnson, *Metaphors We Live By* (Chicago: University of Chicago Press, 1980).

4. The number of relevant studies is enormous and beyond the scope of this chapter. Most useful is the bibliography in Edward G. Slingerland, *What Science Offers the Humanities: Integrating Body and Culture* (Cambridge: Cambridge University Press, 2008), 161–218.

5. Sarah Allan, *The Way of Water and Sprouts of Virtue* (Albany: State University of New York Press, 1997).

6. Conventionally, the metaphoric schema is set in small caps to distinguish this formulaic phrasing from regular semantic phrases.

7. Terry Kleeman dates the text "no later than the end of the third century"; Terry F. Kleeman, *Celestial Masters: History and Ritual in Early Daoist Communities* (Cambridge, MA: Harvard University Asia Center, 2016), 81. Lai Chi-tim accepts that the text may contain very early passages but prefers a slightly later date of compilation in the fourth century; Lai Chi-tim 黎志添, "*Nüqing guilü* yu zaoqi Tianshidao dixia shijie de guanliaohua wenti" "女青鬼律"與早期天師道地下世界的官僚化問題, in *Daojiao yanjiu yu Zhongguo zongjiao wenhua* 道教研究與中國宗教文化, ed. Lai Chi-tim (Hong Kong: Zhonghua, 2002), 2–36.

8. *Nüqing guilü* 女青鬼律 (DZ 790), 1.1a.

9. *Mengzi yizhu* 孟子譯注, ed. and trans. Yang Bojun 楊伯峻, 3rd ed. (Beijing: Zhonghua, 2010), 141; for an analysis of the full passage, see Allan, *Way of Water*, 40.

10. Biography in the recluse chapters of the *Nanshi* 南史 (Beijing: Zhonghua, 1975), 75.1874–80 ("Yinyi" 隱逸), and *Nan Qi shu* 南齊書 (Beijing: Zhonghua, 1972), 54.928–35 ("Gaoyi" 高逸). Gu Huan is best known for his "Treatise on Chinese and Barbarians" ("Yixia lun" 夷夏論), he also compiled the *Zhenjijing* 真跡經 and *Daojijing* 道跡經, two anthologies of Shangqing materials.

11. Wang Yan 王延, *Sandong zhunang* 三洞珠囊 (DZ 1139), 1.16a7–10, where the "Jiudaopin" 救道品 cites *juan* 7 of the no-longer-extant *Daoxuezhuan* 道學傳.

12. *Shenxianzhuan* quoted in *Sandong zhunang*. For a full translation of the hagiography, see Robert Ford Campany, *To Live as Long as Heaven and Earth: A Translation and Study of Ge Hong's "Traditions of Divine Transcendents"* (Berkeley: University of California Press, 2002), 342.

13. On the juridical metaphor and its importance in Chinese religious culture, see Paul R Katz, *Divine Justice: Religion and the Development of Chinese Legal Culture* (London: Routledge, 2009), 24–47.

14. *Lu xiansheng daomen kelüe* 陸先生道門科略, DZ 1127.1a; translation based on Peter Nickerson, "Abridged Codes of Master Lu for the Daoist Community," in *Religions of China in Practice*, ed. Donald S. Lopez Jr. (Princeton, NJ: Princeton University, 1996), 352; also see Terry F. Kleeman, "Exorcising the Six Heavens: The Role of Traditional State Deities in the Demon Statutes of Lady Blue," in *Exorcism in Daoism: A Berlin Symposium*, ed. Florian C. Reiter (Wiesbaden: Harrassowitz, 2011), 89–104.

15. Wang Zongyu 王宗昱, "Daojiao de liutian shuo" 道教的六天說, *Daojiao wenhua yanjiu* 道教文化研究 16 (1999): 22–49; Kleeman, "Exorcising the Six Heavens"; Gil Raz, *The Emergence of Daoism: Creation of Tradition* (New York: Routledge, 2012), 236–38.

16. Found in the "Managing Armies" 治軍 section of Zhuge Liang's 諸葛亮 *Sixteen Stratagems* 便宜十六策.

17. Preserved in *Lixu* 隸續, vol. 3, 309 (3/8a-b), which states that the inscription was originally located in Shu, but no specific location is given. Chen Yuan 陳垣, *Daojia jinshilüe* 道家金石略 (Beijing: Wenwu, 1988), 4; Long Xianzhao 龍顯昭 and Huang Haide 黃海德, eds., *Bashu daojiao beiwen jicheng* 巴蜀道教碑文集成 (Chengdu: Sichuan daxue, 1997), 1. I follow Kleeman's suggestions for reading the inscription; see Kleeman, *Celestial Masters*, 48–53.

18. *Nüqing guilü* (DZ 790), 1.1a.

19. As, for example, in "Penetrating the Dark" ("Changxuan" 暢玄), the opening chapter of Ge Hong's 葛洪 (283–343) *Baopuzi neipian* 抱朴子內篇; see Gil Raz, "Ge Hong and the Darkness," in *Dao Companion to Xuanxue* 玄學 (*Neo-Daoism*), ed. David Chai (Cham, Switzerland: Springer International, 2020), 411–26.

20. Chi-yun Chen, "Orthodoxy as a Mode of Statecraft: The Ancient Concept of *Cheng*," in *Orthodoxy in Late Imperial China*, ed. Liu Kwang-Ching (Berkeley: University of California Press, 1990).

21. John B. Henderson, *Construction of Orthodoxy and Heresy: Neo-Confucian, Islamic, Jewish, and Early Christian Patterns* (Albany: State University of New York Press, 1998), 21.

22. *Dongzhen taishang suling dongyuan dayou miaojing* 洞真太上素靈洞元大有妙經 (DZ 1314), 27a–38b. This passage appears with variants in two other recensions: (1) *Jinque dijun sanyuan zhenyi jing* 金闕帝君三元真一經 (DZ 253), 3b8–4a3, and (2) *Yunji qiqian* 雲笈七籤 (DZ 1032), 50.14b1–8.

23. This rite is said to be the version of the rite taught by Zhang Daoling to Wei Huacun. The complexities of this section have been studied in detail by Cedzich, Lü Pengzhi, and others, and need not be rehearsed here. See Lü Pengzhi, "Daoist rituals," in *Early Chinese Religion, Part Two*, vol. 2, ed. John Lagerwey

and Lü Pengzhi (Leiden: Brill, 2010), 1275–76; Ursula-Angelika Cedzich, "The Organon of the Twelve Hundred Officials and Its Gods," *Daoism: Religion, History and Society* 1 (2009): 1–93.

24. *Dengzhen yinjue* (DZ 421), 3.8b.

25. Tao Hongjing explains that one must first summon the master in order to obtain the correct and unitary *qi* (正一之氣, 以師為本).

26. Miyakawa Hisayuki 宮川尚志, *Chūgoku shūkyoshi kenkyū* 中國宗教史研究 (Kyoto: Dōhōsha, 1983), 227–43.

27. Originally cited in *Sandong zhunang* (DZ 1139), 1.1a8–1b1; Chen Guofu 陳國符, *Daozang yuanliukao* 道藏源流考 (Beijing: Zhonghua, 1963; rpt. 1989), vol. 2, 461; Stephan Peter Bumbacher, *Empowered Writing: Exorcistic and Apotropaic Rituals in Medieval China* (St. Petersburg, FL: Three Pines, 2016), 161–69.

28. *Dongxianzhuan* 洞仙傳, cited in *Yunji qiqian* 雲笈七籤 (DZ 1032), 111.7a.

29. *Dongxianzhuan* 洞仙傳, cited in *Yunji qiqian* 雲笈七籤 (DZ 1032), 111.7a.

30. *Zhen'gao* (DZ 1016), 14.11b10–12a10.

31. *Zhen'gao* (DZ 1016), 14.11b10–12a10.

4

Patterns in Stone

The Third Metaphor of Chinese Philosophy

EDMUND RYDEN

Introduction

Sarah Allan's *The Way of Water and Sprouts of Virtue* was a groundbreaking study in which she argued that two metaphors—water and plants—are fundamental to the way in which the Chinese think and are the root of all Chinese philosophy in the classical period, pre-Qin to early Han.[1] The goal of this essay is very simple: to expand Sarah Allan's insight and argue the case for *li* 理 (principle, pattern) as the third basic metaphor of Chinese philosophy, thus allowing the full development of Chinese thought.

My own work has been greatly influenced by Sarah Allan, who mentored me during my studies at SOAS. I have reflected deeply and at length upon her groundbreaking insight that these metaphors provide the rationality and structure of Chinese thought. I then looked at how these two Chinese metaphors functioned in works not explicitly discussed in Allan's book, notably the philosophy of war and peace in the *Huainanzi* 淮南子; then, further, into the Song-Qing philosophy of *qi* 氣 (steam being a form of water). As explained in what follows, the new evidence reinforced the correctness of Allan's reasoning.

Metaphors and Chinese Philosophy

Sarah Allan made her great contribution in 1997. However, I have found that there are a number of scholars of early China who have failed to appreciate the full impact of Sarah's insight or have simply not understood it. It should be noted from the outset that the metaphors under discussion are not simply food for thought, or for aesthetic inspiration; nor are they confined to one "school" of philosophy rather than another. Instead, they describe the basic methodology and scope of thought for anyone who constructs an intellectual edifice using the Chinese language. They function in every school of Chinese philosophy and in all works: "The systems which I have described represent a root metaphor for Chinese thought not only of the ancient period but throughout the ages."[2] It is a common error in this field to start with the later classifications into schools and to read these as independent entities, failing to appreciate the commonality of their background. Sarah Allan's work undermines all such errors by restoring the integral nature of the whole of Chinese thought. Moreover, it is very important to grasp that the root metaphors of water and plants are unique and essential to Chinese thinking and that they reflect the "patterns of reality" in the Chinese mind. Once this is understood, it is easy to grasp that, in a similar way, the root metaphors of the thought of other civilizations are unique and specific to the thought of those civilizations.

WATER AS A METAPHOR OF THE DAO

Water—flowing water in particular—is the first image we meet. The Chinese notion of the Dao 道, which is beyond language, draws on images. Sarah has shown quite convincingly that the basic image is that of a river, flowing from a source down to the sea. In an article on the Guodian 郭店 text *Taiyi sheng shui* 太一生水, she suggests that the cosmic river is the Silver River in the sky, coming out of the Pole Star and flowing throughout the universe.[3] This river is interpreted as a cosmic reflection of the humble rivers and streams of our earth. The true Dao is beyond all images, yet it is based on this great image. Meditating on this watercourse Way leads us to see how Chinese thinkers can dispute whether water will naturally flow down (*Mencius*) or is indifferent to the direction of flow ("Gaozi" 告子) or needs dikes and ditches to ensure that it does not flood.[4] The arguments make sense because they all draw on the same metaphor. Likewise, the *Daodejing* may seek to take us back to the pure source and thus go against the natural flow of the river, but this rethink depends on the original metaphor for it to make sense.⁵ Essentially, though, the metaphor of water is constrained in direction from its source in the mountains to its reaching down to the sea.

The image of a river leads to the image of a pool. A pool may be choked with weeds, which need to be removed for the water to return to its pristine clarity. Likewise, in texts not discussed by Allan but clearly compatible with her thesis, the removal of the weeds is the point of military expeditions that meet the exacting criteria of *yi* 義 (ethical conduct), just as the army intervenes to remove the bad ruler, as one uproots weeds, removes otters, or even combs one's hair.⁶ The still pool is not stagnant though. The winds of ignorance may not disturb it (Zong Mi 宗密, 740–841), but, even when still, it is living water.⁷

Philosophically, the image of the Dao as a river enables us to construct space. As the cosmic river, it is the greatest thing we can see in the sky. As a drop of water, it is the smallest indivisible thing. It is both the ocean of the sea turtle and the well of the frog (*Zhuangzi*). Stretched across heaven, running across the earth, it is also the way of moral conduct in the human person. In Chinese thought, nature and morality are part of one continuum. Looking at nature enables us to discern the correct path we must choose in order to be true to society and ourselves.

Plants as a Metaphor of Relationships

While water flows down, shoots sprout up. Allan has pointed out that the Chinese word *sheng* 生, which so often describes the relationship between ideas—between *wu* 無 and *you* 有, for instance—is a metaphor of plant growth, not animal birth. Thus, *sheng* is the best way to describe relationships between things, whether between moral virtues or between invisible and visible realities. This does not mean that Chinese has no way of distinguishing between one thing and another. The roots are not the branches; the branches are not the roots. Yet, perhaps, we should translate *sheng* not as "generate" or "produce" but as "grow into." When we say *Dao sheng Fa* 道生法 (the Way grows into the Law), we mean that the Law is the visible aspect and the Dao, the invisible.⁸ The Law bears the same sense of absolute uniqueness that is peculiar to the Dao. There can only be one Dao; likewise, only one Law. No wonder the legalist Han Fei 韓非 (ca. 280–233 BCE) wrote the first commentary on the *Daodejing*.

Plants not only grow up; they do so according to the sequence of the seasons. Hence, plant growth naturally leads to our thinking in terms of day and night, the cycles of the moon, the four—sometimes with an extra fifth in late summer—seasons and the year. While water goes down, plants go up. These directions are inbuilt. True, water can become steam and go up, but, so, too, can plants wither in winter and die, falling back to the soil. Just as water and steam set up a cycle of *qi*, so too can plants set up a cycle of time, corresponding to the notion of space provided by the Dao. The pattern of the seasons and the events of the natural year are the model for human conduct. Perhaps, this association is natural because the word for virtue and the word for *plant* share both a common graphic element (*zhi* 直) and, originally, a similar sound.[9]

One can argue that the way of water is particularly oriented toward space, in that water flows from A to B, while the growth of plants provides a metaphor for time, developed as the cycle of the four seasons, which influences much later Chinese thought.

A Logic of Nature

What Allan means by saying that flowing water and growing plants provide the basic metaphors for all Chinese thought can be expressed both positively and negatively. Positively, it means that all Chinese thinkers will think about ultimate reality, the Dao for instance, in language drawn from the flow of water and from the growth of plants. To think in Chinese implies thinking according to these metaphors. The logic of water and of plants is the logic of Chinese philosophy. Negatively, it means that Chinese philosophy does not use the Greek reflection on linguistic elements such as interrogative words—What, How Many, Why . . . —to speak of the categories of reality: substance, number, cause . . . This is not to say that Chinese philosophers were unable to think of the latter questions. It is merely to say that the dominant ways of thinking throughout classical Chinese philosophy were determined by the root metaphors of water and how it behaves, and of plants and how they behave.

Continuity in the Use of the Root Metaphors

While Allan concentrated on pre-Han Chinese philosophy, by the Song-Ming period historians of Chinese philosophy generally identify three key concepts: *xin* 心, *qi* 氣, and *li* 理. It is worth asking how these concepts can be understood in terms of the metaphors of water and plants.

Xin

The concept of *xin* is often associated with Wang Yangming 王陽明 (1472–1529). Although this is a simplification, it is quite clear that *xin* is understood then as it was in the *Mencius*. It is the clear pool of water, an image used in Buddhist thought as well. *Xin* can be explained in two images that derive from water. For Cheng Hao 程顥 (1032–1085), it is necessary to remove the mud from the river and return to the purity of the source.[10] For Cheng Yi 程頤 (1033–1107), we need to become still, not stirred by surface winds or formed into eddies by underlying pebbles.[11] Wang Yangming also talks about a quiet and inactive original substance of the mind (*xin*). *Xin* is clearly understood according to the water metaphor.

Qi

Zhang Zai 張載 (1020–1077) uses the notion of *qi* to rethink the relationship of *wu* 無 and *you* 有, such that there is no pure *wu*, no complete void. *Wu* is but a diffuse form of what is solidified in *you*. Both are *qi*. Fang Yizhi 方以智 (1611–1671) reinterprets the original *qi* in terms of light and sound because it is dynamic.[12] This metaphor, though, is not at variance with that of water as steam or breath on a cold day. In today's science, we know that matter—coagulated *qi*—and energy—diffuse *qi*—are in fact convertible.

The concept of *qi* is developed by Zhang Zai and is understood according to the natural behavior of water: ice turns into liquid water and then into vapor: a water image. Again, this confirms Allan's insight.

Moreover, philosophers who used the terms *qi* and *xin* also testify to use of the plant metaphor. Wang Tingxiang 王廷相 (1474–1544) talks about *qi* as both the origin—a water metaphor—and as the root—a plant metaphor.[13] Wang Yangming also reflected on the *ben* 本 and *mo* 末 of the *Great Learning* 大學. This is a plant image: roots and top of tree. The plant metaphor is also found in the work of Wang Fuzhi 王夫之 (1619–1692), who also used the concept of *qi*. Wang Fuzhi writes that supreme harmony is the ultimate form of harmony (*taihe, he zhi zhi ye* 太和, 和之至也) since it gathers difference within itself, though the differences arose within the context of an initial harmony.[14] The logic at work here is that of plant growth, in which the integrity of the seed is preserved in the fully grown tree. The virtue of "sincerity" (*cheng* 誠) is that of a "becoming" (*cheng* 成), which remains true to itself.

These examples serve to corroborate Allan's thesis about the key role played by water and plant metaphors. Given, then, that the metaphors of water and plants can work together so that the course of a river becomes the growth of a plant from roots to branches, it might seem that, since it already had an internal consistency, Chinese philosophy had no need of any further metaphor.

The Third Term: *Li* 理

The third concept, which is associated with Zhu Xi 朱熹 (1130–1200), is *li*. This term does not seem to permit being understood in terms of either water or plants. Hence, I will suggest that it is a third metaphor.

Li in Chinese Philosophical History

Of course, like all philosophical terms, this one has a long history. Zhang Dainian 張岱年 (1901–2004) gives the first use of the word in a philosophical text as coming from the Mencius. He explains it, first, as standards of moral conduct, the common norms everyone agrees on. Because of this, it is like the blending of instruments to produce harmony in an orchestra.[15] In the *Zhuangzi* 莊子, it is the *li* of the meat carved by the butcher. Cheng Xuanying's 成玄英 (fl. 631–655) commentary here refers to the natural lines or principles of the meat.[16]

Graham notes early uses of *li* in what he terms the Great Man sections of the *Zhuangzi*, where the myriad things have "patterns."[17] In the *Zapian* 雜篇 (Miscellaneous Chapters), he lists a text in which he translates *li* as "arranging": "The 'Way' is the Power's arranging in a layout."[18] Graham's comments on *li* 理—in *Later Mohist Logic*—provide an excellent introduction. He writes: "*Li* is the patterned arrangement of parts in a structured whole, of things in an ordered cosmos, of thought in rational discourse, and . . . of words in a completed sentence."[19] He notes several uses in the *Mozi* 墨子, which I list as follows:

- the organization of names in the sentence
- the interrelations of the objects to which it refers
- the structure common to parallel sentences, comparable to the articulation of the human body

- the ordered relations of rational thought
- the objective pattern of logical relations between claims

Graham further refers to the *Han Feizi* 韓非子, where *li* is the "specific configuration of properties in each kind of thing."[20] In the *Xunzi* 荀子, these patterns are imposed by human beings, yet not quite in a Kantian sense. For Xunzi, "thinking is inferring from the regularities of 'patterns.'" He sees thinking as "correlation rather than analysis." In his discussion of the *Han Feizi*, Graham notes: "The term *li* has sometimes been translated (by this author, among others) as 'principle.' This might suggest that the thinking here is primarily deductive and inductive. But it is rather a matter of correlating affairs through which the same pattern is said to run."[21] In the *Lüshi chunqiu* 呂氏春秋 (Master Lü's Spring and Autumn Annals), *li* is the orderly relations of thought and the ultimate source of judgments of right and wrong.[22] In the *Han Feizi*, the *li* is proper to things, while the Way is what includes all the *li*, but is not itself a *li*.[23]

A key text for the later development of the term is the *Dazhuan* 大傳 (Great Appendix) to the *Yijing* 易經 (Book of Changes). Zhang Dainian notes that "principle is the rule of simplicity underlying the complications of all things." He also quotes from the *Renwu zhi* 人物志 (Gazette of Human Nature) by Liu Shao 劉劭 (3rd c. CE):

> The changes of *qi* in heaven and earth, its decrease and increase are the *li* of the Dao. Correcting actions through legal institutions is the *li* of (political) activity. The correct and appropriate application of ritual and teaching are the *li* of just relationships. The hinge of human affections is the *li* of emotions. That these four *li* are not the same lies in their matter (*cai* 財).
>
> 若夫天地氣化, 盈氣損益, 道之理也. 法制正事, 事之理也. 禮教宜適, 義之理也. 人情樞機, 情之理也. 四理不同, 其於財也.[24]

Here there are four kinds of *li*, which may not be combined into one. The first deals with climatic changes, the second with politics, the third with ethical conduct, and the fourth with human relations. Though different, the various uses help to identify certain common traits of the term *li*. The fourth kind uses the term "hinge" to define *li*, suggesting that it is both the key and a point of change. The third usage is defined as "what is appropriate or suitable" for governing conduct. In the second, the emphasis is on "correcting" affairs, while in the first there is a dynamism of growth and decline. From this we may say that the word *li* carries connotations of importance, normative guidance, and regularity in the face of change. These uses overlap with those of arrangement, ordered relations, and interrelation highlighted by Graham.

In his exegesis of the *Daodejing*, Wang Bi 王弼 (226–249 CE) uses the term *li* eleven times, of which I highlight two. In chapter 5, commenting that the line that heaven and earth have no special preference for any particular thing, he notes that each of them puts itself in order: "Each of the myriad things orders (*zhi-li*) itself" (*wanwu zixiang zhili* 萬物自相治理).[25] In chapter 47, commenting that the consistency of the Dao is such that even in the confines of one's own home one can know the past, he uses Dao and *li* in a parallel construction: "The Dao is possessed of great constancy; *li* of great penetration" (*Dao you dachang, li you dazhi* 道有大常, 理有大致).[26] This line does not yet make Dao and *li* equivalent in meaning, but at least it establishes a certain similarity. Hence, from these two instances, we can see that he retains the use of *li* as applicable to individual things. In Wang Bi's *Zhouyi lüeli* 周易略例 (Simple Exemplifications of the Principles of the Book of Changes), the term occurs only once: "Things never err; they always follow their principle" (*wu wu wangran, bi you qi li* 物無妄然, 必由其理).[27] In his commentary on the *Analects*, Wang Bi uses *li* to refer to that which gathers all the various *shi* 事 (doings, realities) into one: "Doings have that to which they turn back; *li* has that which gathers together" (*shi you gui, li you hui* 事有歸, 理有會).[28] Zhang Dainian's comment on this is that "what is universal yet gathers all to one" is a good definition of *li*.[29] Unlike Beinglessness and the Dao, *li* crosses the metaphysical divide because *li* is by definition embedded in realities (*shi*). Already, then, it has the capacity to apply both to the one reality beyond form and to the myriad realities below form. It is a short step from here to reunderstanding *li* as the term that applies to the Dao or *benwu* 本無 (original Beinglessness), the *Yi* 易 (Change) of the *Book of Changes* and the root (*ben* 本) of the Great Learning, while at the same time being applied also to phenomenal realities—*wanwu* 萬物 (myriad things), *shi* 事 (doings/realities), *mo* 末 (branches).

It is less clear, though, why the term should suddenly emerge in the Song dynasty as a key concept. Perhaps, it is the *Jinshizi* 金獅子 (Golden Lion) of the Buddhist monk Fazang 法藏 (643–712) that enables Chinese philosophy to fully utilize this term.[30] In the *Golden Lion*, the gold is the *shifajie* 事法界 (dharma realm of appearances); while the lion is the dharma realm of *li*. The ears of the lion are different from its eyes, but each is composed of gold and is an ear or an eye only because the gold is shaped that way. The total shape of the gold as a lion is what determines each specific part of it. So, if each *shi* 事 (appearance) has a *li*—it is the *li* of the whole lion, which ensures that each *shi* also has its own proper *li* as an ear or an eye. Each hair of the lion, therefore, contains the whole lion. In modern terms, we can say that the DNA present in each hair is the same as the DNA of the whole lion. In this example, we can see how the *li* of the lion determines the whole and also determines the different *li* of each part. The word *li* combines both multiplicity and unity.

The Function of *Li* in Song Philosophy

What was implicit in the writings of Wang Bi is made explicit in Fazang's essay. The term *li* is able to relate individual items to the whole in a way that neither water nor plants seem to have done. Referring to the Supreme Ultimate (*taiji* 太極) from the *Book of Changes*, Zhu Xi writes:

> The supreme ultimate is but the principle of heaven, earth and the myriad things. . . . Before there was yet heaven and earth there must have been this principle. Only once there was this principle was there heaven and earth. If there was not this principle there would be no heaven and earth, no human beings, no things; nothing would be.
>
> 太極只是天地萬物之理. . . . 未有天地之先, 畢竟也只是理. 有此理, 便有此天地; 若無此理, 便亦無天地, 無人無物, 都無該載了![31]

Here *li* becomes the unifying principle for Neo-Confucian metaphysics that combines the idea of Heaven with that of the Supreme Ultimate.

In striking continuity with the example of the *Golden Lion*, Zhu Xi understands all things to have their *li*. In his commentary on the *Great Learning*, he writes: "If we seek to extend our knowledge, we must investigate the *li* of things we encounter."[32] Furthermore, *li* is also a moral norm: "*Li* then becomes benevolence, justice, rites, and wisdom." Cheng Yi, in his commentary on the *Book of Changes*, had already associated the four terms *yuan* 元, *heng* 亨, *li* 利, and *zhen* 貞 with the four virtues,[33] such that the first term in each series (*ren* 仁 and *yuan* respectively) includes the whole set.[34] *Li* "principle" is the term for the set or the cycle of the four.

Zhu Xi's writings abound with the term *li*. What is striking, though, is that it is not a term found in the original texts on which he is commenting. An exegete is normally expected to keep close to the text being studied.

Zhu Xi clearly felt justified in using a "new" term—"new" with respect to the texts he is studying—to clarify the meaning of those texts. He does not explain why he must do this, nor does he analyze the properties of *li* such that it can serve the wide range of contexts in which he places it. In what follows, I will analyze it as a metaphor in a way similar to those of water and plants identified by Allan.

Li as a Metaphor

The idea of *li* does not do away with the previous metaphors. Zhu Xi still uses the terminology of the seasons to talk about moral virtues. He still understands there to be one Dao. Rivers flow downward and plants grow upward, but *li* is a pattern that can go in any direction. It is not bound to the metaphorical embedding of rivers or plants. It is thus freer than the previous metaphors. Of course, this very freedom can lead to misunderstanding by those who fail to grasp that a metaphysical principle is not one thing among many.

Let us reexamine the metaphors discussed earlier from the point of view of *li*. The first metaphor is that of the *Dao* as a river. This metaphor uses terms such as source or origin. The name *Dao* itself is always greater than anything that can be seen, even than the whole universe. In this sense it is transcendent. As a river, its most valuable part lies in its source. As water more generally, its most valuable part lies in its being a still but not stagnant pool. The metaphor tends to imply that not all parts of water are good: the lower reaches of the river or the disturbed waters of a pool. It is not neutral. The metaphor of the plant also gives priority to the roots or the seed as containing the whole. Development may go wrong; it is only correct when it remains true to its origin. The metaphor of *qi*, likewise, puts the emphasis on the purity of the original.

Li, however, does not reduce the individuality of each thing that exists into a deformed copy of an original. It can be the original in the sense of the *li* of heaven and can be an equivalent of the *Dao*, but it can also be the principle that each thing possesses; each thing has its pattern, but the individual patterns of each thing are part of a whole pattern of the universe. Since the pattern can be read in any direction, the word does not stress the origin or the root at the expense of the full river and the branches. It does not need to negate the many in order to return to the one.

Furthermore, it is not bound to the clock of the seasons, though Zhu Xi does believe that benevolence is the substance of the mind that is the *li* of heaven. In other words, he can speak of *li* in a way that conforms to the aforementioned valuation of the origin. Yet, the word itself no longer carries such a sense within it.[35]

The metaphor of *li* is also always embedded. Of course, rivers are confined by riverbeds and plants grow on the land, but one has the impression that these metaphors can exist outside their own context, as if the context did not exist. We can talk about the purity of the source without thinking about the surrounding rock, about the roots and branches of actions without thinking about what they are rooted in. *Li*, though, makes no sense by itself. It is always the *li* of something, from the Dao, to Heaven, to each bird and beast. Many philosophers use the word *qi* to describe what it is embedded in. It thus requires the other terms of Chinese philosophy. It does not displace them or negate them. It does not even challenge their priority as the fundamental metaphors of Chinese thought.

RETHINKING *LI*

What *li* does is bring unity to the whole. Moreover, this unity involves a higher degree of abstraction such that the earthiness of the previous two metaphors is overcome. When we use the term *li*, we no longer need to be confined to plants that grow up according to the seasons of the year or rivers that flow down from a pure source to a polluted sea. The earthiness of the metaphors is raised to a great level of abstraction, more fitting to the Dao. Since ultimate reality is always beyond language, no one metaphor can ever be a complete expression of reality. The Dao is like a river yet it is not a river. Hence, we will now consider how best to translate the word *li* and what role it performs in Chinese thought.

Traditionally, we translate *li* as "principle," meaning "what is foremost,"[36] but that takes us off into a different philosophical world. Etymologically, it is the pattern in a piece of jadeite.[37] The value of jade, its presence in the tombs, and its overall significance surely suggest that the natural patterns in it were studied and gave rise to thinking about the patterns (*li*) of veins that run through each object (each little nugget of stone) and, by extension, through the whole universe, in which the *li* of all things is contained. Just as water and plants are concrete things, so, too, is *li* a concrete thing: the pattern formed by the veins running through the precious stone jadeite.

Jadeite, because of the veins in it, can break, and these veins are called "cleaving veins." Therefore, *li* is a vein in stone, the wave of combed hair, the line of a dress, the fold in clothing. In *Disputers of the Tao*, Graham uses the translation "pattern" in the index,[38] while, in his translation of the *Zhuangzi*, he writes "pattern, arrangement."[39] The pattern of the piece can become part of the pattern of the whole, as when tiles are laid on the floor. However, the word "pattern" can also be used to translate the Chinese term *wen* 文. "Configuration" may be better than "pattern" since it suggests a structure. In older computer terminology, the *li* is perhaps the format of a floppy disk. It is the format of a thing that makes it what it is. However, the word "format" has a drawback in that it is imposed from outside.[40] Hopkins coined the word "inscape" to talk about the unique nature of something that makes it what it is, but this word would seem to be bound to the specific uniqueness of each thing and not to the common unity Zhu Xi ascribes to *li*.[41]

Li is connected to life; it is growing and not dead. One must assume that, in the Chinese world, even stone is not dead. It is alive. Wood provides two words that could serve as possible translations. "Grain refers to the orientation of wood-cell fibers."[42] "The grain of wood refers to the alignment of the wood elements in relation to the timber's longitudinal axis."[43] But the term is used in a more general way too, such that it can be described as a "confusingly versatile term."[44] The second term, "figure," "refers to the appearance of wood, as seen on a longitudinal surface."[45] Furthermore, "the term figure refers to the characteristic, special or unusual markings that may be found on the surface of wood—typically on side-grain surfaces."[46] Strictly speaking, then, the pattern that we can see is best described as "figure," while the "grain" is what is given by the cell structure of the wood and what also determines the strength of the wood. Given the way *li* is used in Chinese philosophy, the term "grain" would seem to be the more appropriate translation.

However, in choosing this word, we must be aware that we need to include the aforementioned senses: vein, fold, configuration. The word must be applied in a general sense and should not be interpreted too closely to the usage of the word "grain" in English-speaking carpentry. Thus, we find that the Cheng brothers' saying that everything has its "grain" (a particular use, more like "inscape"), that horses have the "grain" of "horse" (a universal use, more like "format"), and that there is only one "grain" in the whole world (a unique, but all-encompassing use like "pattern" or "figure"). Perhaps, the "confusing versatility" of the term is a bonus, in that it can be made to serve in so many ways. Moreover, we already noted that Liu Shao commented on the diverse references to the term *li*.

What the word *li* does is resolve the dichotomies that early Chinese philosophy produced. In the Confucian tradition, there is the dichotomy of heaven and earth; in the *Book of Changes* that of yin and yang; in the *Daodejing*, *wu* (Beinglessness) and *you* (Being). The metaphor of the river gives rise to a dichotomy between "beginning" and "end," while that of plants divides into "roots" and "branches." In the sequence of the year, there is "spring" and "autumn." The Song philosophers attempted to use the Supreme Ultimate as the point of reconciliation, but this is simply a statement of the difference and mutual relationship between yin and yang. The heaven-earth pair also functions in a similar way. The two items are correlative to each other and have no single term that reconciles them.

The use of a word such as *qi* tends to be reductionist, in that it denies one half of the pair. Thus, *qi* stresses *you* 有 by denying that there is any absolute *wu* 無: what appears to be *wu* is actually a diffuse form of *you*. In Wang Yangming's idealism, *xin* 心 could be read as a similar, though contrary, form of monism.

What all these terms lack is a word that can encompass the uniqueness of the whole and yet allow different realities to exist as fully real entities. *Li* expresses the one point that gathers all of reality together and also the individuality of each thing. What the Cheng brothers and Zhu Xi do is to value both these uses of the word and so forge an instrument that can bring unity to the field of Chinese metaphysics.

In Chinese metaphysics, there is a dichotomy between the invisible realm (*Dao*, etc.) and the visible, between the source (concealed) and the river (flowing), between the roots (hidden) and the branches (visible). *Li* serves to overcome this gap by drawing the "grain" embedded in each thing into the larger single grain that pervades the universe. The "grain" of each thing forms part of the "grain" of the whole universe.

Conclusion

In this chapter, I have compared *li* with the two fundamental metaphors that Sarah Allan identified in her groundbreaking work on Chinese metaphors: flowing water and growing plants. Both of those two metaphors have an implied directionality ("down" and "up" respectively). *Li* is not so bound. I have also argued that the water metaphor prioritizes the source and the plant metaphor the root. *Li* is free from any such value judgment. Because of this, I have argued that *li* has certain properties that make it better able to express the kind of abstract notion Zhu Xi and many subsequent philosophers have required. Was Zhu Xi himself aware of this? There is no evidence for any such awareness. Indeed, Chinese philosophy seemed to get on quite happily for centuries without the metaphor of *li*; and Zhu Xi's understanding is, moreover, indebted to Buddhist influences as well, as I have indicated by citing the example of Fazang. Yet these historical circumstances are, in certain respects, beside the point. The facts are that the metaphor of *li* fits neither that of water alone nor of plants alone and that, since the Song dynasty, it has played a major role in Chinese philosophy. By highlighting its metaphorical background, I hope I have shown the value of Allan's approach to Chinese philosophy. This essay is a rough sketch of a few ideas that others can refine and develop. I have tried to show that the metaphors of water and plants leave a dichotomy at the heart of Chinese philosophy that can only be solved by the use of the metaphor of the "grain" of jadeite. Its higher level of abstraction enables it to overcome the limitations of direction in the other metaphors. Its suitability—both to the whole and to the individual piece—resolves the dichotomy of "above and below form" (*xing er shang* 形而上 and *xing er xia* 形而下) and joins all in one, while not reducing all to one or seeing all merely as the one.

If I were to select a painting to illustrate this essay, it would, perhaps, be Su Dongpo's 蘇東坡 (1036–1101) "Withered Tree and Strange Rock" 枯木怪石圖 (*Kumu guaishi tu*) (see fig. 4.1).

Figure 4.1. Su Shi (1037–1101), "Withered Tree and Strange Rock." The whirling grain of the rock becomes the grain of the tree. Both are united by *li*.[47] *Source:* Fu Xinian, ed., Zhongguo meishu quanji, *Huihua bian 3: Liang Song huihua, shang* (Beijing: Wenwu chubanshe, 1988), plate 25, 51. Album leaf, ink on paper; location unknown, no dimensions given. Public domain.

Notes

1. Sarah Allan, *The Way of Water and Sprouts of Virtue*, SUNY series in Chinese Philosophy and Culture (Albany: State University of New York Press, 1997). Allan based her discussion of metaphors on: George Lakoff and Mark Johnson, *Metaphors We Live By* (Chicago: Chicago University Press, 1980).

2. Allan, *Way of Water*, 148.

3. Sarah Allan, "The Great One, Water, and the *Laozi*: New Light from Guodian," *T'oung Pao* 89 (2003): 237–85, especially 283: "Indeed, we can now see that the *dao* was not simply modeled on a river that flows continuously from a natural spring, but that it was taken as *the* celestial river that flows unceasingly from the womb of the Great One."

4. "In ruling the world, the early kings had to clarify laws and norms so as to put a stop to the people's desires, to erect dykes to prevent flooding" (先王之御世也, 必明法度以閉民欲, 崇堤防以御水害). Cui Shi 崔寔 (d. ca. 170 CE), *Zhenglun* 政論 (On administration), in *Liang Han quanshu* 兩漢全書, ed. Dong Zhi'an 董治安, 36 vols. (Jinan: Shandong daxue, 2009), vol. 22, 12869.

5. The first two lines of chapter 6 of the *Daodejing* are all about a river flowing through a valley. In the third line, the metaphor moves to that of weaving: *mian-mian* 綿綿, in which the woven cloth emerges from the "abstruse cleft" of the woman (*xuanpin* 玄牝) who sits on the ground with her wooden footloom. The weaving metaphor is construed in terms of the flow of water from a source.

6. These metaphors are all found in the opening section of Liu An's 劉安 (179–122 BCE) "Binglüe xun" 兵略訓 (An Overview of the Military), chap. 15 in *Huainanzi* 淮南子. For discussion, see Edmund Ryden, *Philosophy of Peace in Han China: A Study of the Huainanzi Ch. 15 on Military Strategy* (Taibei: Ricci Institute, 1998); Liu An 劉安, *The Huainanzi: A Guide to the Theory and Practice of Government in Early Han China*, trans. John S. Major et al. (New York: Columbia University Press, 2010). See also Liu An, *The Dao of the Military: Liu An's Art of War*, trans. Andrew Seth Meyer (New York: Columbia University Press, 2012).

7. See Peter N. Gregory, *Tsung-mi and the Sinification of Buddhism* (Honolulu: University of Hawai'i Press, 2002), 205.

8. *Huangdi sijing* 黃帝四經 (The Yellow Emperor's Four Canons), revised, annotated, and translated into modern Chinese by Yu Mingguang 余明光, English trans. Leo S. Chang and Feng Yu (Changsha: Yuelu shushe, 2006), "Jingfa" 經法, 1a. For an earlier edition, see Mawangdui Hanmu boshu zhengli xiaozu 馬王堆漢墓帛書整理小組, ed., *Huangdi sijing: Jingfa* (The Four Canons of the Yellow Emperor: The Constancy of Laws) (Beijing: Wenwu, 1976).

9. In the *Dictionnaire Ricci de caractères chinois*, ed. Les Instituts Ricci (Paris: Institut Ricci de Paris, 1999), *chih* [*zhi*] 直 is listed with the phonetic *d'iək; *te* [*de*] 德 as tək. The closeness of the two sounds is evident in various southern Chinese

languages, illustrated by the case of Vietnamese, for example, which has the advantage of having a standard well-known phonetic transcription.

10. Angus C. Graham, *Two Chinese Philosophers: The Metaphysics of the Brothers Ch'êng* (La Salle, IL: Open Court, 1992), 132.

11. Graham, *Two Chinese Philosophers*, 53.

12. "*Qi* coagulates into visible shapes; it develops into light and sound" (氣凝為形, 發為光聲). Fang Yizhi 方以智, *Wuli xiaoshi* 物理小識 (A Little Understanding of the Principles of Things) (*Qinding siku quanshu* 欽定四庫全書 ed.), 1.8a "Guanglun" 光論.

13. Wang Tingxiang ("Ya shu" 雅述): "original *qi* is the root of the Way"; quoted in "Wang Tingxiang's 'Elegant Description,'" in *Key Concepts in Chinese Philosophy*, ed. Zhang Dainian 張岱年, trans. Edmund Ryden (New Haven: Yale University Press, 2002), 61.

14. "Supreme harmony is the ultimate in harmony. The Dao is the common principle of heaven and earth, human beings and material things, what is called the *taiji*. Yin and yang are different but in their interweaving in supreme emptiness they unite together and do not harm each other. They roll into one with no gaps. This is the ultimate in harmony. Originally, before there were shapes or objects, there was no disharmony. Now that there are shapes and objects, harmony is not lost. This therefore is supreme harmony" (太和, 和之至也. 道者, 天地人物之通理, 即所謂太極也. 陰陽異撰, 而其絪縕於太虛之中, 合同而不相悖害, 渾淪無間, 和之至矣. 未有形器之先, 本無不和, 既有形器之後, 其和不失, 故曰太和). Wang Fuzhi, *Zhangzi zhengmeng zhu*, in *Chuanshan quanshu* 船山全書, vol. 12 (Changsha: Yuelu, 2000), 5 (*Taihe pian* 太和篇).

15. Zhang Dainian, *Key Concepts*, 27.

16. Zhang Dainian, *Key Concepts*, 29.

17. A. C. Graham, *Chuang-tzŭ: The Seven Inner Chapters and Other Writings from the Book Chuang-tzŭ* (London: Allen & Unwin, 1981), 148.

18. Graham, *Chuang-tzŭ*, 149.

19. A. C. Graham, *Later Mohist Logic, Ethics, and Science* (Hong Kong: Chinese University Press, 1978), 191.

20. Graham, *Later Mohist Logic*, 192.

21. A. C. Graham, *Disputers of the Tao: Philosophical Argument in Ancient China* (La Salle, IL: Open Court, 1989), 287.

22. Graham, *Later Mohist Logic*, 191–92.

23. Graham, *Disputers of the Tao*, 286–87.

24. Liu Shao 劉劭, *Renwuzhi* 人物志, *Sibu congkan* 四部叢刊 ed., 1.15b ("Cai li" 財理).

25. *Laozi Daodejing zhujiaoshi* 老子道德經注校釋, commentary by Wang Bi, ed. Lou Yulie 樓宇烈 (Beijing: Zhonghua, 2008), 13 (chap. 5).

26. *Laozi Daodejing zhujiaoshi*, 126 (chap. 47). Here I translate *zhi* 致 as "penetration," which may not be a good translation. The idea is that *li* is able to attain to the utmost within things.

27. *Wang Bi ji jiaoshi* 王弼集校釋, ed. Lou Yulie (Beijing: Zhonghua, 1980), 591 ("Ming tuan" 明彖). Chan, *Source Book*, 318. Note that Chan uses the English word "principle" to translate other Chinese terms in the same text.

28. *Lunyu shiyi* 論語釋義, in *Wang Bi ji jiaoshi*, 622 (comment on *Lunyu* 4.15).

29. Zhang Dainian, *Key Concepts*, 230.

30. Zhang Dainian refers to this text in his section on *shi* 事 and *li* 理 (*Key Concepts*, 227). Fung Yu-lan (Feng Youlan 馮友蘭), *A History of Chinese Philosophy*, trans. Derk Bodde (Princeton, NJ: Princeton University Press, 1952), 339–59, has a longer discussion. Chan provides a translation of the text in *Source Book*, 409–14. Fazang discusses the lion in his essay *Jinshizi zhang* 金獅子章, see *Taishō shinshū Daizōkyō* 大正新修大藏經 (Tokyo: Taishō Issaikyō Kankōkai, 1922–1933), vol. 45, 663–67.

31. Zhu Xi, *Zhuzi yulei* 朱子語類, punct. Wang Xingxian 王星賢, 8 vols. (Beijing: Zhonghua, 1986), 1.1. Quoted in Zhang Dainian, *Key Concepts*, 36–37.

32. Zhu Xi, *Remarks on the Great Learning* (*Daxue zhangju* 大學章句), quoted in Chan, *Source Book*, 89.

33. Tu Weiming translates the four terms as "origination, flourishing, facility, and firmness." See Tu Weiming, "Chinese Philosophy: A Synoptic View," in *A Companion to World Philosophies*, ed. Eliot Deutsch and Ron Bontekoe (Malden, MA: Blackwell, 1991), 20.

34. Zhu Xi, *A Treatise on Benevolence*, quoted in Chan, *Source Book*, 594.

35. See Feng Youlan 馮友蘭, *Xinlixue* 新理學 (New Rational Philosophy) (1939; rpt. Shanghai: Changsha shangwu, 1996). Feng understands "principles" as absolute and eternal. They are metaphysical and also social. The social principles determine the nature of a society.

36. Derk Bodde, in his translation of Fung Yu-lan, *History of Chinese Philosophy* (vol. 2, 444n1), quotes Needham as rejecting the translation of *li* as "law" or "laws" in favor of "principle," which Needham defines as "the 'principle of organization' in the universe . . . the order and pattern in Nature . . . a dynamic pattern as embodied in all living things, and in human relationships and in the highest human values."

37. Bodde (*History of Chinese Philosophy*, vol. 2, 444n1) gives the original sense of *li* as the "veins or markings in a block of jade." Historically, jade was of great value in Chinese culture, more valuable than either gold or silver. The presence of certain metals—copper, chromium, and iron—produces patterns in the "jade" and colors ranging from subtle gray-greens to brilliant yellows and reds (https://www.khanacademy.org/humanities/art-asia/imperial-china/neolithic-art-china/a/chinese-jade-an-introduction).

38. Graham, *Disputers of the Tao*, 487.

39. Graham, *Chuang-tzŭ*, 287.

40. Graham notes that Xunzi would seem to see "pattern" as imposed by human beings: "It arises from man [*sic*] as the third, patterning things from his own point of view" (*Disputers of the Tao*, 242).

41. In his *Journal*, Gerard Manly Hopkins wrote: "There is one notable dead tree . . . the inscape markedly holding its most simple and beautiful oneness up from the ground through a graceful swerve below (I think) the spring of the branches up to the tops of the timber. I saw the inscape freshly, as if my mind were still growing, though with a companion the eye and the ear are for the most part shut and instress cannot come." *The Journals and Papers of Gerard Manley Hopkins*, ed. Humphry House and Graham Story (Oxford: Oxford University Press, 1959), 215, 228.

42. "Understanding Wood Grain," *Wood Magazine*, November 2, 2018, https://www.woodmagazine.com/materials-guide/lumber/understanding-wood-grain.

43. "Figure in Wood," *Wooduchoose Blog*, June 26, 2017, https://www.wooduchoose.com/blog/figure-in-wood/.

44. R. Bruce Hoadley, "Glossary," in *Understanding Wood: A Craftsman Guide to Wood Technology* (Newtown, CT: Taunton, 1980), 265.

45. Hoadley, "Glossary," 265.

46. "Figure in Wood."

47. You may also enjoy a lecture on this painting on https://www.youtube.com/watch?v=J4YeoSSglv4.

5

Humans Can Broaden the Way, Sages Can Continue and Carry Out the Workings of *Tian*

人能弘道, 聖人能繼天立極

Roger T. Ames

Setting the Problem

Most every one of us has been properly inspired by the career and the many accomplishments of our distinguished colleague, Sarah Allan. Indeed, in writing this essay, my starting point has been the sustained work she has undertaken in promoting a nuanced understanding of early Chinese cosmology, and, in particular, her correlation between the sages and the celestial order (*tianming* 天命). In a recent publication, Allan interprets the earlier expression *xingming* 性命 that describes the relationship between the human experience and the natural order (*ming* 命) as a probable precursor to the later cosmological theory of resonance between sky and earth captured in the language of *ganying* 感應.[1] In this discussion, she has occasion to cite a passage from a lost document: "The *Royal Record of Yú* (*Shun*) says: 'If the sun and moon do not rise, the myriad living things will all be in darkness. If the sage is not in authority, all-under-heaven will inevitably deteriorate.' When order is at its highest, the unworthy are cared for; when disorder is at its zenith, men of worth are destroyed. The humane, because of this, come forward."[2] In what follows, I want to press Sarah on how we are to understand this perceived collaterality between *tian* and the human experience within the natural order of things, and to see if she would be willing to go as far as I want to go on the cosmic consequence of human sages.

To set the problem, we must begin from our own Gadamerian prejudices—the assumptions we uncritically bring to the discussion. When Christian missionaries such as Jesuit Matteo Ricci and Protestant James Legge introduced Chinese culture into the Western academy, they were motivated to close the distance between these two traditions by interpreting the Chinese world through a heavily Christianized language.[3] Indeed, over the last four centuries of cultural encounter, the vocabulary established for the translation of classical Chinese texts into Western languages has been freighted by a patently Christian framework, and the effects of this "Christianization" of Chinese texts are still very much with us.

I will argue here it is *li* 禮 as an achieved propriety in roles and relations rather than the always abstruse notion of *tian* 天 that is perhaps the most important term in giving voice to the distinctively Confucian family-centered religiousness. And it is within this context of *li* that the ancestral/numinous/cultural/natural conception of *tian* has its role. The familiar mantra invoked to describe Confucian religiousness, *tianren heyi* 天人合一, describes the inseparability of the relationship between the numinous and the human experience, the inseparability of the relationship between the cultural and natural context and human thinking and living.

Like the heavens and the earth (*tiandi* 天地), the numinous and the human (*tianren* 天人) are aspectual, that is, one and two at the same time. These terms describe a relationship rather than two discrete entities. We are concerned about the "depth of coalescence" (*du* 度) that can be cultivated and achieved in their first order relationality. It is thus that such correlative expressions are not simply descriptive but are also prescriptive. The relationship is fecund and generative, with *tian* and *ren* working together collaboratively to build the connector for their own time and place, and, in so doing, to extend the cosmic order (*hongdao* 弘道). And *tian* and *ren* in their relationship are to be understood as doing and undergoing, shaping and being shaped, in this dyadic yet resolutely constitutive relationship.

Here then is the question. It is clear that human beings in this *tianren* relationship derive much benefit from the ancestral/numinous/cultural/natural resources denoted by *tian*. *Tian* certainly provides human beings with a context for flourishing and serves us as a model to emulate and revere.

And Allan does insist that the sage is a necessary complement to *tian* in this natural order. But since the relationship between *tian* and human beings is irreducibly collateral, we have to ask: What through personal cultivation can be made of this *tianren* relationship on the human side? And importantly, what does *tian* get in this relationship from human beings? It is here I want to query the seemingly too passive language where the sage "correctly aligns himself with *tian* and the cosmic forces under its aegis" in order "to act in concert."[4] I want to argue that if "correlative" and "resonance" (*ganying*) in fact mean to be mutually shaping and being shaped, we must challenge a familiar unilaterality as defining of a dualistic *tianren* relationship in which human beings are affected by it but *tian* is not. This would be the strict transcendence we find in the notion of an independent and self-sufficient Abrahamic God that I would argue has little relevance for explaining Confucian religiousness.

My argument will be that, in these classical Confucian canons, human sagacity not only introduces epochal transformations in the human experience but also has a transformative effect on the configuration of *tian* and the natural order broadly, especially its moral content. Said another way, it is my claim that the relatively vague notion of *tian* as it is expressed in these texts is amplified and made explicit through the specific lives of our human sages. I want to suggest that not only can "human beings broaden the way" (*ren neng hong dao* 人能弘道), but "sagacious human beings can broaden *tian*" (*shengren neng hong tian* 聖人能弘天).

Emerson's "Transcendentalism"

Ralph Waldo Emerson's pantheistic "transcendentalism" with its inseparability of God and man can be useful in taking us one step in the direction of an early Chinese, nondualistic religiousness, and in providing us with a familiar example that might serve us further in de-exoticizing early Confucian assumptions about a human- rather than God-centered religiousness. A young Emerson, having graduated from Harvard Divinity School in 1834, is invited back by the class of 1838 to give the commencement speech. In what is called the "Divinity School Address," Emerson unleashes an assault on historical Christianity that in its own time is so scandalous that this increasingly famous orator, in spite of living his whole life within the proximity of Cambridge, is not invited back to his alma mater until after the Civil War. In this address, Emerson accuses historical Christianity of having two faults that have immediate association with his own rejection of the doctrine of strict transcendence and its assumptions about a world-independent source of meaning.

The first defect for Emerson is the false assertion of the established Church that Jesus is a God rather than a man. In advancing this claim, the clerics have sought to empower themselves by making Jesus into a deity detached from human life and a remote object of worship by supplicating Christians. For Emerson, Jesus, in being the historical person he was, stands as a source of inspiration for every man with a soul to aspire to the magnitude of this human exemplar. The Church in thus co-opting Jesus has robbed human beings of their own divinity. In Emerson's words:

> Jesus Christ belonged to the true race of prophets. He saw with open eye the mystery of the soul. Drawn by its severe harmony, ravished with its beauty, he lived in it, and had his being there. Alone in all history, he estimated the greatness of man. One man was true to what is in you and me. He saw that God incarnates himself in man, and evermore goes forth anew to take possession of his world. He said, in this jubilee of sublime emotion, "I am divine. Through me, God acts; through me, speaks. Would you see God, see me; or, see thee, when thou also thinkest as I now think."[5]

The second defect of historical Christianity for Emerson is corollary to the first, with the Church making the idea of God into something that is distant, past, and finished rather than being alive in the moment and available for each person as a vital source of their own divinity. In his words: "The second defect of the traditionary and limited way of using the mind of Christ is a consequence of the first; this, namely; that the Moral Nature, that Law of laws, whose revelations introduce greatness,—yea, God himself, into the open soul, is not explored as the fountain of the established teaching in society. Men have come to speak of the revelation as somewhat long ago given and done, as if God were dead."[6]

What seems patently clear for us is that Emerson is first a theist—a person who believes in a creator God as the ultimate reality—and secondly is a pantheist—someone who identifies God with this world, and who understands the world and human beings too as a manifestation of God. What is much less clear is the status of the human being for Emerson. The question that we are left with in trying to understand Emerson's monistic transcendentalism is, with human beings standing in the shadow of a God closely identified with the forces of nature and the natural world itself, what is the value of individual human effort? Do the lives of persons as individuals make their own unique contribution to the world, or are they ultimately nothing, absorbed wholly into an all-encompassing One, the Universal Being, the Over-Soul? Sometimes Emerson's language seems to suggest this kind of self-abnegation and capitulation to the One: "Historical Christianity . . . has dwelt, it dwells, with noxious exaggeration about the *person* of Jesus. The soul knows no persons. It invites every man to expand to the full circle of the universe and will have no preferences but those of spontaneous love."[7] Indeed, Emerson even at times describes his religiousness as a kind of personal renunciation:

> The intuition of the moral sentiment is an insight of the perfection of the laws of the soul. These laws execute themselves. They are out of time, out of space, and not subject to circumstance. Thus; in the soul of man there is a justice whose retributions are instant and entire. . . . If a man is at heart just, then in so far is he God; the safety of God, the immortality of God, the majesty of God do enter into that man with justice. . . . A man in the view of absolute goodness, adores, with total humility. Every step so downward, is a step upward. The man who renounces himself, comes to himself.[8]

And yet there are other times when Emerson, who famously says "trust thyself: every heart vibrates to that iron string,"[9] seems to celebrate the kind of "individuality" that John Dewey celebrates as "the realization of what we specifically are as distinct from others."[10] Indeed, it is particularly in the example of the singular person of Emerson himself that we have the strongest sense of the inimitable worth of each person:

> Be yourself; no base imitator of another, but your best self. There is something which you can do better than another. Listen to the inward voice and bravely obey that. Do the things at which you are great, not what you were never made for. . . . The energetic action of the times develops individualism, and the religious appear isolated. I esteem this a step in the right direction. Heaven deals with us on no representative system. Souls are not saved in bundles.[11]

Is Emersonian religiousness, then, a Vedantic assimilationism that reveals the illusionary nature of particularity in its being subsumed into the one Over-Soul. Or, on the contrary, is the one also many in Emerson's religiousness? It is precisely this ambiguity, then—What is the status and significance of the particular person?—that I want to address in exploring Confucian human-centered religiousness. I want to argue that for Confucianism, human lives in their uniqueness are not only celebrated as a source of cosmic meaning, but that human religiousness comes with the aspiration to be co-creators with the heavens and the earth.

This relationship between the one and the many for me becomes a vitally important religious question because it is in this respect that Confucian religiousness stands in greatest contrast to the asymmetry between human beings and their God as it is commonly understood in the Abrahamic religions. The aseity or self-sufficiency of a perfect and thus unchanging Abrahamic God means that human morality at the end of the day is entirely derivative of God, and that human beings do not make a difference in themselves. God is everything; human beings are nothing. The role of the human being is simply to worship and to obey the superordinate One. The theologian Friedrich Schleiermacher describes such religiousness as a doctrine of absolute dependence: "The feeling of absolute dependence, accordingly, is not to be explained as an awareness of the world's existence, but only as an awareness of the existence of God, as the absolute undivided unity."[12] Contrary to Schleiermacher who finds great solace in this reassuring claim, I regard such a doctrine of self-abnegation and absolute dependence irresponsible and morally repugnant. My understanding of the liberating humanism of the European renaissance is that it was a direct challenge to such a hegemonic and oppressive religiousness by insisting upon the intrinsic worth and responsibility of human beings in themselves without reference to a transcendent and thus independent God.

At issue here is what William James calls, as a term of abject criticism, a "block universe"—a world devoid of individuality and particularity. Dewey, in explaining this term as it is used by his visionary mentor, states:

> Mechanism and idealism were abhorrent to him [William James] because they both hold to a closed universe in which there is no room for novelty and adventure. Both sacrifice individuality and all the values, moral and aesthetic, which hang upon individuality, for according to absolute idealism, as to mechanistic materialism, the individual is simply a part determined by the

whole of which he is a part. Only a philosophy of pluralism, of genuine indetermination, and of change that is real and intrinsic gives significance to individuality. It alone justifies struggle in creative activity and gives opportunity for the emergence of the genuinely new.[13]

Getting Past Transcendence: Distinguishing Chinese Cosmology from Greek Ontology

What then, in pursuing this question of the relationship between the one and the many—between divinity and human beings—is the nature of Confucian religiousness? First, given the misinterpretation of Confucianism prevailing within a Western academy that shelves the Confucian philosophical canons in its libraries in a section called "Eastern Religions," we might first want to say what Confucian religiousness is *not*. After all, the distinguished French sinologist Marcel Granet observes rather starkly that "Chinese wisdom has no need of the idea of God."[14] Granet in this succinct assertion is rejecting the relevance of the Abrahamic One-behind-the-many model of religiousness that follows from the doctrine of strict transcendence. Albeit in different formulations, Granet's characterization of classical Chinese philosophy has had many iterations by many of our most prominent sinologists. Tang Junyi (1909–1978) for example states unequivocally: "The Chinese as a people have not embraced a concept of 'Heaven' (*tian* 天) that has transcendent meaning. The pervasive idea that Chinese have with respect to *tian* is that it is inseparable from the world."[15] Joseph Needham (1900–1995) would also disassociate Chinese cosmology from assumptions about some underlying permanent structure when he claims: "Chinese ideals involved neither God nor Law. . . . Thus the mechanical and the quantitative, the forced and the externally imposed, were all absent. The notion of Order excluded the notion of Law."[16] Indeed, our best interpreters of classical Chinese philosophy, Chinese and Western alike, are explicit in rejecting the idea that Chinese cosmology begins from some independent, transcendent principle.[17]

It behooves us to be clear at the outset as to what is being meant here by transcendence—that is, strict philosophical transcendence. Strict philosophical or theological transcendence is to assert that an independent and superordinate principle A originates, determines, and sustains B, where the reverse is not the case. This is the definition David Hall and I first stated in *Thinking Through Confucius* in 1987, and we have not wavered from it in any subsequent publications.[18] The notion of *eidos* that is found and that is foundational in both Plato and Aristotle as "ideals" and "immutable species" respectively, or the notion of an independent, perfect, and hence unchanging creator God that emerges in mainstream Christian theology, would be familiar examples of such strict transcendence. If, as the dominant classical Greek views would have it, unity and permanence are fundamental, then the phenomenal world experienced as unbounded change cannot be finally real and cannot be the object of knowledge. In this classical Greek worldview of which Whitehead's understanding of the abstract formist Plato is a fair representative, "Reality" must refer to that which *grounds* the world of appearances, while changing phenomena as mere appearances are at best misleading and illusory.[19] Metaphysical realism (Plato) and substance ontology (Aristotle) both entail this strict sense of transcendence by postulating principles that exist in themselves as the ultimate objects of knowledge and of predication.

The notion of the real as the *objective* ground of apodictic knowledge is an immediate implication of the reality/appearance distinction and the dualistic worldview it entails. It is this ability to make an object of the world—a world or *the* world—that allows philosophers to think they can assume a view from nowhere, thereby decontextualizing themselves and stepping outside of the human experience. And it is indeed this "view from nowhere" that stands as guarantor for the possibility of objective description, the truth that would attend it, and the quality of certainty such description would provide.

A corollary to the privileging of a formal, unchanging, and substantial reality over the flux of appearances in the dominant classical Greek worldview is the tendency to give priority to the discrete and quantitative over the qualitative and continuous. The identity of "things" tends to be discrete and atomistic: a function of quantitative discreteness that parses identity in terms of essential and accidental properties and thus external rather than internal relations. Wholes are constructed out of discrete yet coherent parts. Communities are a collection of individual persons, each of whom has their own integrity, like spoons in a drawer, like pennies in a jar. This priority of discreteness and quantity follows from the priority of permanence and stasis, of the substantial over the processual. Each person in the community defined by some selfsame identical characteristic has some presocial, precultural, and enduring warrant for membership. Further, this priority given to discreteness and quantity in turn disposes toward a concern for the clarity of formally defined concepts and the necessity of unchanging truths—both of which are more congenial to a quantitatively discrete and measurable world.[20]

One important outcome of taking Granet's insight into Chinese cosmology seriously is that it will enable us to disambiguate some of the central philosophical vocabulary of classical Chinese philosophy by identifying equivocations that emerge when we elide the distinction between classical Greek ontological assumptions and those cosmological presuppositions indigenous to the classical Chinese worldview. Angus Graham cautions us about such equivocations: "In the Chinese cosmos all things are interdependent, without transcendent principles by which to explain them or a transcendent origin from which they derive. . . . A novelty in this position which greatly impresses me is that it exposes a preconception of Western interpreters that such concepts as *Tian* 'Heaven' and *Dao* 'Way' must have the transcendence of our own ultimate principles; it is hard for us to grasp that even the Way is interdependent with man."[21]

The philosophical implications of Granet's seemingly offhand observation that China did not need the idea of a transcendent God are fundamental and pervasive, entailing as transcendence does the plethora of dualistic categories that follow from such a reality/appearance distinction. The familiar dualisms of subject/object, agent/action, mind/body, and nature/nurture that arise from this kind of substance ontology have little relevance for the Confucian notion of the relationally constituted person. Indeed, this Confucian conception of *person* makes no appeal to superordinate, substantive categories such as "soul," "self," "will," "faculties," "human nature," "mind," "character," and so on, but instead locates *person* gerundively as the embodied, social activity of thinking and feeling within one's environments of family, community, and nature. Persons so understood are complex events rather than discrete "things," processes of "becoming" rather than essential "beings," ongoing "doings" rather than autonomous "is's," configurations of concrete, dynamic, constitutive relations rather than individuated substances defined by some subsisting agency.

When we turn to Confucian religiousness, we find that it does not appeal to an independent, retrospective, and substantive Divine Agency as the reality behind appearance and as the source of all cosmic significance. The world is an autogenerative, "self-so-ing" process—*ziran er ran* 自然而然—that has the energy of its ongoing self-transformation resident within it. It is an inside without an outside. And human religious feelings themselves are a motor of religious meaning, understood prospectively as an unfolding and inclusive spirituality achieved within the qualitatively inspired activities of the family, the community, and the natural world. Human beings are both a source of and contributors to the numinosity that inspires the world in which we live.

In the absence of a concept of "God," there seems to be some general agreement that there is little recourse to anything like a "two-world," reality/appearance distinction in classical Chinese thought.²² There is little evidence that early Chinese thinkers were interested in the search for and the articulation of an ontological ground for phenomena—some Being behind the beings, some One-behind-the-many, some ideal world behind the world of change. As Tang Junyi, insists: "When Chinese philosophers speak of the world, they are thinking of the world that we are living in. There is no world beyond or outside of the one we are experiencing. . . . They are not referencing '*a* world' or '*the* world,' but are simply saying 'world as such' without putting any indefinite or definite article in front of it."²³

It seems that the early Chinese thinkers were preoccupied with making the most of the phenomenal world of process and change construed simply as *dao* 道: "the unfolding field of experience," or *wanwu* 萬物: "the ten thousand processes and events," or perhaps more simply put, "everything that is happening." These philosophers were less inclined to ask *what* makes something real or *why* things exist, and more interested in *how* the complex relationships among the changing phenomena of their surroundings could be coordinated to achieve optimum productivity. It is this achieved personal, social, and ultimately cosmic harmony, rather than any theological or teleological assumptions about origins or design, that is their fundamental guiding value.

Whence Is Confucian Religiousness?

There are numerous examples of grossly inappropriate terms having become the standard equivalents in the Chinese/English dictionaries that we use to perpetuate our understanding of Chinese culture: "the Way" (*dao* 道), "Heaven" (*tian* 天), "benevolence" (*ren* 仁), "righteousness" (*yi* 義), "rites" (*li* 禮), "virtue" (*de* 德), "substance" (*ti* 體), "principle" (*li* 理), "material substance" (*qi* 氣)," and so on. Such translations raise fundamental questions of interpretation. Can a Western student read the capitalized "Heaven" as anything other than a metonym for the familiar notion of the spiritual home of a transcendent God? Is living a life as this Dad's son or daughter a "rite"? Should we reduce what is quite literally the image of cultivated, consummate human beings in all their aspects—cognitive, moral, aesthetic, religious, somatic—to a single psychological disposition: "benevolence"? When and in what context would a native English speaker ever utter the word "righteousness"?

The definition of "religion" in our best English-language dictionaries begins from the concept of God. The *OED*, for example, defines religion as "the belief in and worship of a superhuman controlling power, especially a personal God or gods." With this uncritical assumption in mind, most scholars begin their exploration of Confucian religiousness from the Chinese equivalencies they have used to translate this Abrahamic idea of God: usually the Shang and Zhou dynasty ancestral notions of *shangdi* 上帝 and *tian* respectively. Although, as we will see, *tian*, in denoting something much different from "God," does have an important role to play in the way in which the human-centered religiousness comes to be articulated and expressed, a strong and compelling argument can be made that the key term needed to explain Confucian religiousness is not this attempt to insinuate "God" in Confucian cosmology, but it is in fact the socioreligious idea of "rites" (*li*): "an achieved propriety in one's roles and relations."

We find that many of the terms that become important in Confucianism date back to the earliest practices of ancestral sacrifices. Going back to the Shang dynasty, formally prescribed rites and rituals were performed at stipulated times to reinforce the political and religious status of the participants and to punctuate the seasons of the life at court. For that group of officials responsible for casting the bronzes and for the choreography of court functions, "ritual propriety" (*li*) meant knowing one's place and thus knowing where to stand. The graph for "rites" (*li*) is found on the oracle bones 豊 and on the bronzes 豊 as a pictograph depicting an offering of two pieces of jade in a ritual vessel that was set out to seek blessings and good fortune for the court.²⁴ If the phenomenon of bronze production can tell the story of the Shang dynasty, it is the evolution of this notion of "ritual propriety" or *li* as the "aestheticization" of the human experience that provides a window on the narrative of the Zhou dynasty that followed.²⁵

First, the increasingly broader, societal aspect of ritual propriety is an important consideration. Originally, ritual performances were narrowly defined and were formal religious procedures enacted by the ruler and his elite entourage to fortify their relationship with nature and with the ancestors of the other world. These rituals were often constituted in imitation of perceptible cosmic rhythms as a means of strengthening the coordination of the human, natural, and spiritual environments. They were used to reinforce a sense of human participation and context in the regular operations of the cosmos. Gradually over the centuries these ritual activities were extended outward from the ruler himself to the community more broadly, developing an increasingly social and communal significance. In these ritual observances, participants would have their proper status and place, their *wei* 位. If persons did not understand the details of the ritual procedures, they would quite literally not know where to stand (*li* 立). The term "stance" (*li*) found on the oracle bones 𗧉 and in the bamboo-strip manuscripts 𗧉 is on occasion read as "rank, position, status" (*wei*) 𗧉.²⁶

In Confucius's account of his own personal growth, he states that "by fifteen I had set my purposes on learning, and by thirty I had taken my stance (*li*)," referring thereby to the general posture he had assumed and the assiduous resolution he was directing at his continuing project of personal cultivation.²⁷ Throughout the *Analects*, it is repeatedly stated that it is "ritual propriety" (*li*)—also frequently translated as "rites," "ceremony," "etiquette," "decorum," "manners"—that enables persons to determine, consolidate, and display virtuosity in the relational transactions of their daily lives:

> Chen Gang asked the son of Confucius, Boyu: "Have you been given any kind of special instruction?"
>
> "No." he replied. "Once when my father was standing alone and as I hastened quickly and deferentially across the courtyard, he asked me . . . 'Have you studied the *Book of Rituals*?' I replied, 'Not yet,' to which he remarked, 'If you do not study the *Rituals*, you will be at a loss as to where to stand.' I deferentially took my leave and am studying the *Rituals*."²⁸

It is only consummate persons who are able to express the meaning and the musicality of the ritually aestheticized life: "The Master said: 'What have persons who are not consummate in their conduct to do with achieving ritual propriety in their roles and relations? What have persons who are not consummate in their conduct to do with the playing of music?'"²⁹ Such passages in the *Analects* can be used as a heuristic from which to glean several insights into what "ritual propriety" had become by the time of Confucius, some five hundred years after the fall of the Shang dynasty.

Although clearly having a formal, ceremonial dimension, the preponderant weight of significance of *li* in defining family and communal life still lies in those personal, informal, and particular aspects that conduce to and are necessary for religious experience. *Li* as cognate with the character *ti* 體 (body, embodiment) also have a profoundly somatic dimension in which body is often as effective as language in communicating the deference necessary to strengthen the bonds among those participating in the various life forms. The *li* have an affective aspect wherein feelings suffuse and fortify all of our relational activities, providing the communal fabric with a tensile strength that resists the inevitable tensions and rupture that attend associated living. Refinement through the performance of *li* must be understood in light of the uniqueness of each participant engaged in the profoundly aesthetic project of becoming this exceptional and always inimitable person. *Li* is a process of personal articulation in the roles and relations one lives—the growth and disclosure of an elegant disposition, an attitude, a posture, a signature style, and ultimately, a persistent identity.

What Is the Role of *tian* 天 in Confucian Religiousness?

It is within the context of *li* as an achieved propriety in roles and relations that the ancestral/numinous/cultural/natural notion of *tian* has its role. And since the relationship between *tian* and human beings is irreducibly collateral, we have to ask: How and to what extent is *tian* itself different because of the human contribution made to cosmic order? How does *tian* benefit from human beings in its relationship with them?

In our response to these questions, we might appeal to the extensive work of the contemporary philosopher Tang Yijie on this notion of *tianren heyi*. Tang begins by citing Confucius, who says: "It is human beings who broaden the way, not the way that broadens human beings." With respect to *tian* specifically, he goes on to say: "It is only the capacities of human beings that are able to advance and promote the magnificence of the way of *tian*."[30] Tang then observes further that "human beings cannot separate from *tian* because if they did, they could not continue to exist, and *tian* cannot separate from humans because if it did, there would be no way for its verve and vitality to be made manifest."[31]

Given the doctrine of constitutive, internal, organic relations Tang assigns to this worldview, we must allow that, just as humans are importantly shaped by *tian*, *tian* is also shaped by human beings. Tang allows that *tian* and human beings share the same "heartminding" (*xin*), where "true" (*zhen* 真) is "truing" as the deepening congruence that assiduous personal cultivation is able to effect in the relationship between the two. But how is the *tian* aspect of this shared heartminding itself changed and made deeper because of the human role in the extension of cosmic order, and how is this human transformation of *tian* itself expressed in the canonical texts? Remembering Granet's assertion that the notion of a transcendent God has little relevance for Confucian religiousness, it is the collaborative, mutually generative relationship between *tian* and human beings that provides such a stark contrast with the Abrahamic traditions. Indeed, it is the need to cultivate a "depth of coalescence" (*du* 度) in this *tianren* relationship that can be brought to bear on how we might want to think about *tianren heyi* and the human transformation of *tian*.

The *Five Modes of Virtuosic Conduct* (*Wuxingpian* 五行篇) is an ancient but only recently recovered document that might help us think through the human effects on *tian*. Over the past generation, two different versions of this text have been found buried at different times in two separate archaeological sites.[32] This important document is in the same lineage as *Focusing the Familiar*—the *Zhongyong* 中庸—that takes as its central argument its claim that human beings through personal cultivation have both the capacity and the responsibility to serve as co-creators with the heavens and the earth.

The opening chapter of *Five Modes of Virtuosic Conduct* explains how personal conduct becomes habituated as characteristic, identity-forming patterns of moral virtuosity, and how this continuing cultivation first produces efficacy (*shan* 善) in human relations and then culminates in a world-changing moral virtuosity (*de* 德):

> Consummatory conduct in roles and relations (*ren* 仁) taking shape within is called moral virtuosity (*de*); where it does not take shape within, it is called merely doing what is deemed consummate. Appropriate acting (*yi* 義) taking shape within is called moral virtuosity (*de*); where it does not take shape within, it is called merely doing what is deemed appropriate. An achieved ritual propriety in roles and relations (*li* 禮) taking shape within is called moral virtuosity (*de*); where it does not take shape within, it is called merely doing what is deemed proper. Wisdom (*zhi* 智) taking shape within is called moral virtuosity (*de*); where it does not take shape within, it is called merely doing what is deemed wise. Sagacity (*sheng* 聖) taking shape within is called moral virtuosity (*de*); where it does not take shape within, it is called merely doing what is deemed sagacious.[33]

This passage makes the same distinction as the Mencius between just doing something that is prompted by the approbation of others and, by contrast, acting consistently and instinctively out of a cultivated moral virtuosity (*de*) that, having been habituated, has become who you are: "Mencius said:

'What distinguishes people from the brutes is ever so slight, and while the common run of people might lose this difference, exemplary persons preserve and develop it. Shun was wise to the way of all things and had real insight into human roles and relationships. He acted upon his moral habit of being consummatory and optimally appropriate in his conduct rather than merely doing what was deemed consummatory and appropriate by others.'"[34] There is a vital distinction being made here between persons who are merely able to follow conventional values in acting in a way deemed proper by the community and sages who through an assiduous personal regimen are able to establish consummatory habits of conduct in their roles and relations, and to act out of this moral virtuosity. Indeed, it is such persons who have an influence on an evolving natural order.

How then does this cultivated moral virtuosity "take shape within" to become habituated conduct? In interpreting this passage, we can appeal to the Confucian expression *shenqidu* 慎其獨 to shed light on the way in which this habituated conduct is set and is consolidated "within." The interlinear commentary included in the Mawangdui version of this *Five Modes of Virtuosic Conduct* document offers its explanation of this same expression *shenqidu* and is explicit in referencing *xin* or "heartminding" as the personal identity that is produced when these five patterns are consolidated and set as the root of virtuosic conduct. The commentary reads: "The expression *shenqidu* means accommodating these five modes of virtuosic conduct within and focusing them carefully in one's heartminding. Having consolidated these five modes of conduct, they become one. And this 'one' then refers to the five modes of virtuosic conduct that, having been consolidated as the [one] heartminding, is then taken as their personal identity."[35] The meaning of this expression *shenqidu* as we find it in the *Expansive Learning* (*Daxue* 大學) has much the same import as when it occurs here in *Five Modes of Virtuosic Conduct*. It is defined as "becoming resolute in one's thoughts and feelings" (*cheng qi yi* 誠其意): that is, to internalize and consolidate a habitual disposition of conduct to be expressed consistently as moral virtuosity.

Having made this important distinction between mere conduct and moral virtuosity, this opening passage of *Five Modes of Virtuosic Conduct* then concludes by offering the reader a distinction between efficacy (*shan* 善) as "the way-making of the human being" and moral virtuosity (*de* 德) as "the way-making of *tian*": "When harmony (*he* 和) is achieved among these five modes of virtuosic conduct, it is called moral virtuosity (*de* 德), while achieving harmony only among the first four is called efficacy (*shan*

善). Efficacy is human way-making (*rendao* 人道), while moral virtuosity is the way-making of *tian* (*tiandao* 天道)."³⁶ This distinction between human way-making and the way-making of *tian* that assigns "moral virtuosity" (*de*) to *tian* is made curious by the fact that the text has up to this point used the same term "moral virtuosity" (*de*) to describe the quality of human conduct achieved when it has been internalized as a habitual way of behaving. In this first chapter, then, moral virtuosity (*de*) is described both as the way-making of *tian* and, at the same time, as the way-making of consummate human beings.

To understand what is meant here by the distinction between "human way-making" and "the way-making of *tian*," we need first to suspend our default Abrahamic theological assumptions and thus resist the temptation to think this distinction is referencing two exclusive domains. As Tang Yijie has repeatedly averred, the human-*tian* collaboration in way-making is an emergent, increasingly inspired way of being in the world that always has both a human and a cosmic aspect. Here the text states that a harmonious integration of the first four modes of virtuosic conduct as moral virtuosity (*de*) produces human efficacy (*shan* 善). But when the fifth mode of virtuosic conduct is added to this harmony—that is, the sagacity of the human sages (*sheng* 聖)—it produces a moral virtuosity (*de*) that then becomes integral to the enhanced meaning of *tian*.

Sagacity as the Depth of Coalescence in the First Order *tianren* Relationship

In this text then, moral virtuosity (*de*), far from being described as the exclusive way-making of *tian*, stands and is expressed as a collaboration between *tian* and the way-making of the highest order of humanity, the sages. Given that the sages are the utmost exemplars of what is humanly possible, this moral virtuosity is manifested in the world as the consummate expression of the operations of both sagacious human beings and the contextualizing *tian* as they deepen their relationship in their collaborative activities. Not only is such sagacity in human conduct to be understood as the human being achieving the reach and the influence of *tian* itself, but moreover we must allow that *tian* itself is deepened and extended by this accumulating human sagacity. This shared virtuosic conduct not only underscores the primacy of the *tianren* relationship over the secondary distinction between *tian* and human beings, but it also makes the important point that human beings in their role as sages can continue the work of *tian*.

This insight into the mutuality of the way-making of the human and *tian* expressed through sagacious conduct is further strengthened when we reflect on the four inclinations (*siduan* 四端) of "heartminding" (*xin* 心) that for Mencius are defining of the native conditions that locate the human being within family and community, and that are thus available for personal cultivation. Of course, as we have seen in this *Five Modes of Virtuosic Conduct* chapter, these first four modes of virtuosic conduct *ren yi li zhi* 仁義禮智 are identical to the "four inclinations" (*siduan*) of the Mencian heartminding. As we have also found in Mencius, "those who make the most of their 'heartminding' (*xin*) realize their natural propensities (*xing*). And again, those who realize their natural propensities then realize the world around them (*tian*)."³⁷ What is clear here is that such moral virtuosity is a collaboration between persons and their worlds rather than some characteristic pattern of behavior derived either from external, antecedent principles, or from the reduplication of an erstwhile internal and innate human nature. Again, these four inclinations are not only productive of a cultivated human efficacy (*shan*) but also provide the ground for the Mencian claim that everyone, given these initial conditions, can aspire to behave sagaciously in our conduct.

But we need clarification here. The claim is not that each human being has some innate potential that can be actualized to make every one of us a sage, but rather that the evolving collaboration between our initial inclinations and world can produce sagacious conduct. There is an important difference between saying that everyone has some inherent potential of becoming a sage, and that everyone who behaves like a sage is a sage. The potential for becoming a sage only emerges pari passu in the transactional events that constitute the substance of a human life. Mencius makes this point explicitly:

> Cao Jiao inquired: "Is it the case that we can all become Yaos and Shuns?"
> Mencius replied: ". . . The way-making of Yao and Shun was nothing but family reverence and fraternal deference. If you wear Yao's clothes, speak his words, and do what he does, then you *are* a Yao."³⁸

Mencius's point here is that it is sagacious conduct that makes someone a sage. Indeed, it is sagacity that lies as the ultimate "depth of coalescence" (*du* 度) in the first-order *tianren* relationship. Sagacity is a quality of human virtuosity that allows for our full collaboration in guiding the workings of a flourishing cosmos.

Human Sagacity as the Face of *tian*

And there is considerable textual evidence that sagacity is the ultimate coalescence in the first-order *tianren* relationship. As we witness throughout the canonical Confucian texts, the vague notion of *tian* takes on the lines and visage of a particular human face as the canonical texts repeatedly characterize these always unique sages metaphorically in grand, celestial terms. In the Guodian version of *Five Modes of Virtuosic Conduct*, for example, the same celestial vocabulary is used to correlate the excellence of the sage-king Wen, the paragon of human culture, and the way of *tian*: "Sagacity and wisdom are whence propriety and music arise, [and are what bring harmony to the five modes of virtuosic conduct]. When the five modes of virtuosic conduct are in harmony there is happiness; where there is happiness, there is moral virtuosity; where there is moral virtuosity, the state will flourish. Such was the insight of King Wen. '[King Wen presiding above; he shines] in the heavens (*tian*).'[39] This is what this passage from the *Book of Songs* means."[40] And again, it states quite explicitly in *Focusing the Familiar* that if everyone can conduct themselves as sages, then everyone can also have a transformative effect on *tian*:

> Only those in the world of utmost resolution are able to separate out and braid together the many threads on the great loom of the world. Only they set the great root of the world and realize the transforming and nourishing processes of heaven and earth.
> How could there be anything on which they depend?
>
> So earnest, they are consummate (*ren*);
> So profound, they are a bottomless abyss (*yuan*);
> So pervasive, they are *tian*.
>
> And only those whose own capacities of discernment and sagely wisdom extend to the powers of *tian* could possibly understand them.[41]

In the *Analects*, the same kind of celestial hyperbole is used to describe Confucius specifically: "Shusun Wushu spoke disparagingly of Confucius. Zigong responded, 'Do not do this! Confucius cannot be disparaged. The superior character of other people is like a mound or a hill that can still be scaled, but Confucius is the sun and moon that no one can climb beyond.

Were persons to cut themselves off from such illumination, what damage would this do to the sun and moon? It would only demonstrate that such persons do not know their own limits.'"[42] Indeed, in this same chapter of the *Analects*, there are several such passages that would associate Confucius directly with *tian*:

> Chen Ziqin said to Zigong, "You are only being deferential—how could Confucius be superior in character to you?" Zigong replied, "Exemplary persons must be ever so careful about what they say. On the strength of a word others can deem him either wise or foolish. The Master cannot be matched just as a ladder cannot be used to climb the sky (*tian*). Were Confucius to have become a head of state or of a clan, he would have confirmed the saying:
>
> He gave them a place and they took a stand,
> He led them forward and they followed,
> He brought peace and they flocked to him,
> He aroused them and they achieved harmony.
> In life he was glorious, and in death he was mourned.
> How could anyone be his peer?[43]

Again, in *Focusing the Familiar*, Confucius takes on full cosmic proportions in being identified with the seasonal operations of the natural order itself:

> Confucius revered Yao and Shun as his ancestors and carried on their ways; he emulated and made illustrious the way of Kings Wen and Wu. He modeled himself above on the rhythm of the turning seasons (*tian*), and below he was attuned to the patterns of water and earth. He is comparable to the heavens and the earth (*tiandi*), sheltering and supporting everything that is. He is comparable to the progress of the four seasons, and the alternating brightness of the sun and the moon.[44]

Tang Yijie, drawing upon the cosmology made explicit in the *Book of Changes* has argued that it is in this sense that human "becomings" with their production of human culture are inseparable from the flourishing of nature's sublimities. That is, human beings are nothing less than a co-creative and transformative moral force in the cosmos. My argument here, inspired by Tang's work on the *tianren* relationship, is that in these classical Confucian canons, human sagacity is understood not only as having the capacity to introduce epochal transformations in the human experience but also to have a transformative effect on the cosmos broadly. Said another way, the relatively vague notion of *tian* as it is expressed in these early texts is amplified and made explicit through the specific lives of our human sages. Of course, there is metaphor here, but the cosmic morality represented by *tian* in substance too is a collaboration with this highest order of humanity. If Confucius can elevate the worth of human "becomings" by insisting that they "are able to broaden the way" (*ren neng hong dao* 人能弘道), we can extend this celebration of humanity by joining Zhu Xi 朱熹 in proclaiming that the sages, as the highest among these human "becomings," "are able to continue and carry out the workings of *tian*" (聖人能繼天立極).[45]

I am not sure if Sarah Allan would agree with my argument about the collaterality and mutual shaping within the *tianren* relationship here, but what I do know is that she would have something important to say in responding to it. In her own explanation of the early cosmology, she has drawn upon the early canons and emphasized the function of the sagely ruler to gain the cosmological center and thereby bring harmony to the cosmos. As she notes, such a function has been familiar in world religions as a sacred center or axis mundi that, in providing a line of communication among the horizontal tiers of the cosmic forces, sustains a center of cosmic order. The natural center for *tian* is the pole star around which the other stars move. And Allan has argued that the concept of *shangdi* 上帝 as "Supreme Thearch" for the Shang people is best understood as the spirit of this North Star.[46]

The idea of sagacity as a centering force in the *tianren* relationship defined in terms of political "virtuosity" (*de*) recalls a familiar passage in the *Analects*: "The Master said: 'Governing with virtuosity (*de*) can be compared with the North Star; the North Star dwells in its place, and the multitude of stars circumambulate to pay it tribute.' "[47] This *Analects* passage draws an analogy between virtuosity (*de*) in the human political realm as sagacious rule, with the governance of *tian* and the pole star. And as we saw earlier, the *Wuxingpian* described this same virtuosity (*de*) as both the human habituation of proper conduct and "the way of *tian*." *Tian*, far from requiring what Schleiermacher describes as "absolute dependence"—a self-abnegating deference to a self-sufficient, independent Deity—is instead an invitation for human collaboration with and contribution to the numinous aspect of our experience.[48]

Indeed, *tianren heyi* 天人合一 describes "the mutuality of the relationship between the human and the cosmic order." Importantly then, given the resolutely inseparable *heyi* relation between humans and their context, we must resist reading this expression as a "putting together" of what were two originally separate things and read it in terms of their mutuality in difference. The concern is with the "depth of coalescence" (*du* 度) that can be cultivated and achieved in their first order relationality. It announces the continuity between the drama of human thinking and living, and the cultural and natural context within which this spectacle takes place. The *heyi* relation is a *yinyang* contrastive yet mutually entailing first order relationship of two inseparable, "aspectual" features of experience that can only be understood in terms of each other. Just as with dyadic pairs such as "up and down" (*shangxia* 上下) and "the heavens and the earth" (*tiandi*), the expression "the cosmic and the human" (*tianren*) denotes a relationship that is one and two at the same time: two complementary aspects of the same phenomenon that cannot be fairly understood or acted upon without reference to each other.

Notes

1. Sarah Allan, *Buried Ideas: Legends of Abdication and Ideal Government in Early Chinese Bamboo-Slip Manuscripts* (Albany: State University of New York Press, 2015), 104–10, esp. 108.

2. 《虞志》曰: 大明不出, 萬物皆暗。聖者不在上, 天下必壞。治之至, 養部肖; 亂之至, 滅賢。仁者爲此進也。Allan, *Buried Ideas*, 106.

3. James Legge (1815–1897), the great Scottish translator of the Chinese classics on whose broad shoulders twentieth-century sinology has been built, was a missionary in the field and, as such, appealed self-consciously to the theology of Joseph Butler (1692–1752) in the vocabulary he selected as equivalencies for Chinese terms and in his interpretation of the tradition broadly. See James Legge, *The Notions of the Chinese concerning God and Spirits* (Taipei: Chengwen, 1971). In translating *tian* 天 as "Heaven," *dao* 道 as "the Way," *yi* 義 as "Righteousness," *li* 禮 as "Ritual," *ren* 仁 as "Benevolence," and so on, Legge's Confucianism became increasingly familiar to his Christian audience. In his interpretation of Mencius, for example, he wondered aloud about why Mencius did not just use "God" instead of the ambiguous term *tian* and concluded that Mencius's understanding of a benevolent human nature was almost precisely the same as that of the anti-Hobbesian theologian Joseph Butler in his *Sermons on Human Nature*.

4. Allan, *Buried Ideas*, 107.

5. Ralph Waldo Emerson, "The Divinity School Address" (Harvard Divinity School, Cambridge, MA, July 15, 1838), www.age-of-the-sage.org/transcendentalism/emerson.

6. Emerson, "Divinity School Address."
7. Emerson, "Divinity School Address."
8. Emerson, "Divinity School Address."
9. Ralph Waldo Emerson, *Self-Reliance and Other Essays* (Dover, 2012), https://archive.vcu.edu/english/engweb/transcendentalism/authors/emerson/essays/selfreliance.html.
10. John Dewey, *Early Works, 1882–98*, ed. Jo Ann Boydston (Carbondale: Southern Illinois University, 1969–1972), vol. 3, 304.
11. Emerson, *Self-Reliance and Other Essays*.
12. Friedrich D. E. Schleiermacher, *The Christian Faith*, ed. H. R. Mackintosh and J. S. Stewart (London: T & T Clark, 1999), 132.
13. John Dewey, *The Moral Writings of John Dewey*, ed. James Gouinlock (New York: Prometheus Books, 1994), 35.
14. Marcel Granet, *La pensée Chinoise* (Paris: Editions Albin Michel, 1934), 478.
15. 中國民族無含超絕意義的天的觀念. 中國人對天有個普遍的觀念, 就是天與地是分不開的. Tang Junyi 唐君毅, *Tang Junyi quanji* 唐君毅全集, vol. 11 (Taipei: Xuesheng, 1991), 241.
16. Joseph Needham et al., *Science and Civilisation in China*, vol. 2 (Cambridge: Cambridge University Press, 1956), 290.
17. For similar characterizations of early Chinese cosmology, see Granet, *La pensée Chinoise*, 279; Xiong Shili 熊十力, *Xin weishi lun* 新唯識論 (Beijing: Zhonghua, 1985), 297 and 554; Zhang Dongsun 張東蓀, *Zhishi yu wenhua: Zhang Dongsun wenhua lunzhu jiyao* 知識與文化: 張東蓀文化論著輯要, ed. Zhang Yaonan 張耀南 (Beijing: Zhongguo guangbo dianshi, 1995), 271, and *Lixing yu liangzhi: Zhang Dongsun wenxuan* 理性與良知: 張東蓀文選, ed. Zhang Rulun 張汝倫 (Shanghai: Shanghai yuandong, 1995), 285–90; A. C. Graham, *Disputers of the Tao* (La Salle, IL: Open Court, 1989), 222; Nathan Sivin, *Medicine, Philosophy and Religion in Ancient China: Researches and Reflections* (Aldershot, UK: Variorum, 1995), 3; Chad Hansen, *A Taoist Theory of Chinese Thought* (Hong Kong: Oxford University, 1992), 215; Joel Kupperman, "Confucius and the Nature of Religious Ethics," *Philosophy East and West* 21, no. 2 (1971): 189; Norman Girardot, *Myth and Meaning in Early Taoism: The Theme of Chaos (Hun-tun)* (Berkeley: University of California Press, 1983), 64.
18. David L. Hall and Roger T. Ames, *Thinking Through Confucius* (Albany: State University of New York Press, 1987), 13. See also Hall and Ames, *Thinking from the Han: Self, Truth, and Transcendence in Chinese and Western Culture* (Albany: State University of New York Press, 1998), 190.
19. It is important to stipulate whose Plato. Much good research is being done to rescue the more interesting artist and ironist Plato from the received abstract formist, idealist, rationalist Plato, dominated as this latter interpretation has been by systematic metaphysics. But it is this received Plato filtered through Augustine and the Church fathers, and through twentieth-century scientism, promoting him

as a metaphysical realist, that has exercised a defining influence on the evolution of the Western cultural narrative.

20. This priority of the quantitatively discrete is the target of William James when, in the *Principles of Psychology*, he argues for the reality of "conjunctions and transitions" in the stream of consciousness. See *William James: The Essential Writings*, ed. Bruce W. Wilshire (Albany: State University of New York Press, 1984), 47–81.

21. A. C. Graham, *Studies in Chinese Philosophy and Philosophical Literature* (Albany: State University of New York Press, 1990), 287.

22. For a discussion of this issue in some detail, see Hall and Ames, "Cultural Requisites for a Theory of Truth in China," chap. 6 in *Thinking from the Han*, 123–46.

23. Tang Junyi, *Tang Junyi quanji*, 101–03.

24. Images and interpretation taken from Kwan Tze-wan, "Hanyu duogongneng ziku" 漢語多功能字庫 [Multi-function Chinese Character Database], Research Institute for the Humanities, CUHK, 2014, http://humanum.arts.cuhk.edu.hk/Lexis/lexi-mf/.

25. See my "Re-iconizing Artifacts: Using the Curriculum to Recontextualize Asian Art," in *Reading Asian Art and Artifacts: Windows to Asia on American College Campuses*, ed. Joan O'Mara and Paul Nietupski (Lanham, MD: Rowman & Littlefield, 2011).

26. For a fuller description of this radial extension of *li*, see Robert M. Gimello, "The Civil Status of *li* in Classical Confucianism," *Philosophy East and West* 22 (1972): 203–11.

27. *Analects* 2.4: 吾十有五而志於學, 三十而立.

28. *Analects* 16.13: 陳亢問於伯魚曰: "子亦有異聞乎?" 對曰: "未也. 嘗獨立, 鯉趨而過庭." 曰: . . . "學禮乎?" 對曰: "未也. 不學禮, 無以立." 鯉退而學禮.

29. *Analects* 3.3: 子曰: "人而不仁, 如禮何? 人而不仁, 如樂何?"

30. 孔子說: "人能弘道, 非道弘人." 只有人才可以使天道發揚光大. Tang Yijie, *Tang Junyi quanji*, 420.

31. 人離不開天, 離開天則人無法生存; 天離不開人, 離開人則天的活潑潑的氣象無法彰顯. Tang Yijie, *Tang Junyi quanji*, 424.

32. Two versions of this text belonging to the Zisizi-Mengzi lineage (Si-Meng pai 思孟派) have been recovered in archaeological finds, first on a silk text at Mawangdui (1973) dating to 168 BCE, and then the Guodian text (1993) on bamboo slips dating from ca. 300 BCE. The fact that redactions of the same text have been found at such a temporal and physical distance from each other speaks to the perceived importance of the document in its own time.

33. 仁形於內謂之德之行, 不形於內謂之行. 義形於內謂之德之行, 不形於內謂之行. 禮形於內謂之德之行, 不形於內謂之行. 智形於內謂之德之行, 不形於內謂之行. 聖形於內謂之德之行, 不形於內謂之行. 德之行五, 和謂之德, 四行和謂之善. 善人道也, 德天道也.

34. *Mencius* 4B19: 孟子曰: 人之所以異於禽獸者希. 庶民去之, 君子存之. 舜明於庶物, 察於人倫, 由仁義行, 非行仁義也. See also 6A8.

35. 慎其獨也者, 言舍夫五而慎其心之謂也. 獨然後一, 一也者, 夫五為囗 (一) 心也, 然後得之.

36. 德之行五, 和謂之德, 四行和謂之善. 善人道也, 德天道也.

37. *Mencius* 7A1: 盡其心者知其性也. 知其性則知天矣.

38. *Mencius* 6B2: 曹交問曰: "人皆可以為堯舜, 有諸?" 曰: . . . "堯舜之道, 孝弟而已矣. 子服堯之服, 誦堯之言, 行堯之行, 是堯而已矣."

39. *Book of Songs*, no. 235; compare Bernhard Karlgren, *The Book of Odes: Text, Transcription, and Translation* (Stockholm: Far Eastern Antiquities, 1950), 185–86.

40. *Wuxingpian* 15: 聖知, 禮樂之所由生, 五【行之所和】也. 和則樂, 樂則有德, 有德則邦家興. 文【王之示也如此. 文王在上, 于昭】於天. 此之謂也.

41. *Zhongyong* 32: 唯天下至誠, 為能經綸天下之大經, 立天下之大本, 知天地之化育. 夫焉有所倚? 肫肫其仁! 淵淵其淵! 浩浩其天! 苟不固聰明聖知達天德者, 其孰能知之?

42. *Analects* 19.24: 叔孫武叔毀仲尼. 子貢曰: "無以為也, 仲尼不可毀也. 他人之賢者, 丘陵也, 猶可逾也; 仲尼, 日月也, 無得而逾焉. 人雖欲自絕, 其何傷於日月乎? 多見其不知量也!" See also *Analects* 19.21 and 25.

43. *Analects* 19.25: 陳子禽謂子貢曰: "子為恭也, 仲尼豈賢於子乎?" 子貢曰: "君子一言以為知, 一言以為不知, 言不可不慎也. 夫子之不可及也, 猶天之不可階而升也. 夫子之得邦家者, 所謂立之斯立, 道之斯行, 綏之斯來, 動之斯和. 其生也榮, 其死也哀, 如之何其可及也."

44. *Zhongyong* 30: 仲尼祖述堯, 舜, 憲章文, 武; 上律天時, 下襲水土. 辟如天地之無不持載, 無不覆幬, 辟如四時之錯行, 如日月之代明.

45. See Zhu Xi's preface to his commentary on the *Zhongyong* (*Zhongyong zhangju jizhu* 中庸章句集注) in his commentary on the *Four Books* (*Sishu jizhu* 四書集注).

46. Allan, *Buried Ideas*, 289–95.

47. *Analects* 2.1: 子曰: "為政以德, 譬如北辰, 居其所而眾星共之."

48. Schleiermacher, *The Christian Faith*, 132.

6

Exorcism and the Spirit Turtle

Constance A. Cook

This essay examines the concepts and vocabulary of Shang era healing technology as preserved in the oracle-bone inscriptions of the Huayuanzhuang dongdi 花園莊東地 (HD) burial ground in Anyang, Henan, and which date to the late thirteenth and early twelfth centuries BCE. Information is preserved on turtle bones, in inscriptions on bone, and in the archaic script itself. To unlock undeciphered or cryptic materials and words, the author looks at similar magico-religious practices preserved on fourth-, third-, and second-century BCE manuscripts for inspiration, much in the way that twentieth-century oracle bone scholars turned to the first-century CE etymological dictionary, the *Shuowen jiezi* 說文解字, to crack the code of the Shang oracle-bone inscriptions (OBI). Over the millennia, knowledge and understanding clearly shifted but the continuous use of the sexagenary ritual calendar to organize time and of exorcism and sacrifice rituals as primary modes of treatment suggest some threads we can follow backward to help us crack the mysteries.

One shift is in the nature of turtle divination itself. After the Shang, turtle divination continued but inscriptions on the bones did not.[1] The symbolism of the turtle as a divine instrument associated with the cosmos and with kings, as described by Sarah Allan, helps to explain its evolution into a god.[2] The role of the turtle in healing is a key context in which to unpack the vocabulary of healing preserved in the inscriptions. It is significant that healing often involved attention to time.

Turtles and Kings

By the early medieval period in China, the Spirit Turtle (Shen Gui 神龜 or Ling Gui 靈龜) was one member of a varying pantheon of indigenous and transnational supernatural identities that had the power to obstruct people's careers or affect their health. As an indigenous spirit, the Spirit Turtle originated as a bone media used to interpret the will of human and nature spirits in the Shang pantheon. As an animal bone it could also represent a sacrificed victim, which perhaps took on supernatural agency in the spirit world and hence played a role in the diagnostic and healing process. Han texts mention a Spirit of the Water (Shui Shen), which in early medieval texts is described as a giant turtle that must be forced to the surface by a magician.[3]

Divination required bones and was controlled by diviners, priests, and members of the royal family, who determined the diagnosis and healing rituals. OBIs record their efforts to identify the prevailing spirits and how to appease them to heal the perceived affliction. King Wu Ding 武丁 and his sons provide us with an invaluable if cryptic record of bodily afflictions and the consequent healing techniques. Notably, the majority of the records concerning royal affliction required searing specific points of turtle plastrons with hot pokers, the treatment given at different times of the ritual calendar. The movement around the symbolic turtle body is paralleled in medieval times with movement of the "spirit" (shen 神) around the body as determined by the calendar.[4] Medieval healers avoided treating those areas when treating patients with heat or with needles. Scholars have long connected the Shang divination process conceptually with the late Han practice of acupuncture, the use of needles to regulate the yin and yang flows of inner "cosmic vapor" or "spirit of breath" (qi 氣) in the channels and organs of the body.[5] It is likely that the earlier predominate use of cauterization and lancet stones or other objects was also determined by the calendar.

Piercing the outer shell or skin of the body, physically or merely symbolically, is suggested in OBI graphs that may depict treatments pictographically. These images, examined later in the chapter, suggest a potential conceptual alignment between the treated body and the divine turtle. The application of fire to the body of a water animal to produce mantic patterns may have had metaphorical links to the later practice of cauterizing yin and yang "vessels" (mai 脈) in the human body.[6] The question then is whether the Shang priests viewed the cauterizing of different parts of the turtle body as an aspect of healing the king's body. Connected to this question is the definition of the king's body. This author considers the king's body to extend in layers from the physical to the sociopolitical, as defined by the Shang-held territory and notion of the cosmos.

Sarah Allan links the revolving concept of time and the design of the Shang calendar to royal lineage origin myths, and she links the cycle of the Ten Suns to the ten categories of royal ancestral signs. She shows how the blueprint of the royal tomb and the graph representing the social status of Ya 亞 officers reflected the imagined cosmic body or space: a cruciform with four quadrates around a center—much like the shape of a turtle plastron. She was the first to note that the five sections of the static, "four quadrate" (*sifang* 四方) cosmos (including the four directions and the center) would evolve into the dynamic pattern of "Five Agents" (*wuxing* 五行, which was keyed during the third and second centuries BCE to the change of seasons, to powers of *yin* and *yang*, and to other cosmic points in space and time). During the Han, the Five Agents were understood as modes of *qi* that could influence the body. There is no proof that the concept of *qi* existed before the fourth century BCE, but the turtle's body as a metaphor for the cosmos can be traced back a millennium.

Allan notes that the turtle's round back easily represented the Sky (Tian) and that the cruciform plastron represented the Earth (Di); she further argues that its longevity represents time itself. The ancient diagram of the cruciform of five spaces has four corner spaces, which in toto produce a large square comprising eight squares located around the center square. According to legend, each corner had a sacred tree that held up a circular sky. The application of fire (an element later identified as *yang*) to the bone of a creature from the water (an element later identified as *yin*) in the process of divination represented the joining of cosmic oppositions.[7] Hu Houxuan 胡厚宣 (1911–1995) was among the first to notice the similarity between applying hot pokers to the oracle bone and later practices of acumoxa (acupuncture and moxibustion).[8] Jao Tsung-I highlighted the symbolism of using a water divinity.[9] Donald Harper explained that the word used for applying heat therapy to an afflicted area in Han times (*jiu* 灸) also denoted "the act of thrusting the firebrand against the turtle shell to make it crack." Fire, he noted, is "transformational, exorcistic, and prophylactic."[10]

The *Huangdi neijing* 黃帝內經 (Inner Canon of the Yellow Emperor), was a medical classic that was edited in the medieval era, but which preserved some early material; it defines illness as an imbalance in the various modes of *qi*, which causes "a dysfunction of the human organism within the system of vessels and internal organs."[11] The imbalances allowed "perverse" or "evil qi" (*xieqi* 邪氣) to penetrate the body, causing malady (*bing* 病). In Shang OBI, the site of the affliction was *tuo* 蠱 (commonly read as "harm," *hai* 害, but, in fact, more likely: "toxin," *du* 毒).[12] In fourth-century BCE bamboo manuscripts, "affliction" was caused by "harmful supernatural influences that inflicted calamity, curses" (*sui* 祟), a term that also occurs in OBI as a condition requiring exorcism.[13] Fourth-century BCE manuscripts often name specific pathogenic intruders. These named supernatural identities included human and nonhuman spirits and demons. They included ancestral spirits as well as gods of climatic, spatial, temporal, astral, and terrestrial domains. The Shang pantheon, although not so clearly defined, included the same categories of spirits. In both Shang and Warring States eras, the most virulent categories of spirits were recently deceased ancestors and anonymous ghosts.

Healing the afflicted body during the Shang era, whether it was the king's physical body or the political body or state, required sacrifices as well as ritual choreographies to "ward off" harm. Words for these sacrifices, discussed later, are difficult to interpret, but warding off and exorcism rituals from better documented later sources provide clues. The name of the primary Shang warding off ritual was *yu* 禦 (anciently pronounced something like *mqʰraʔ; hereafter "*yu*-exorcism"), defined by David Keightley as "to ward off, protect against (enemies)" and "to perform an exorcism ritual (on somebody's behalf or to invoke the aid of a certain Power)."[14]

Exorcism, Harper explains, was the "logical treatment" for illness believed to be the result of an invasive agent.[15] Some healing rituals for dealing with harm described in later texts may have derived from Shang *yu*-exorcism practices. These may involve symbolic beating, piercing, and binding, accompanied by invocation and perhaps by dance. By the Warring States period, specific mental or verbal motions (*si* 思 and *ming* 命), along with manual actions of "beating, attacking" (*gong* 攻) and "sending off" (*shi* 使) demonic afflictions, resulted in "releasing" (*jie* 解) the body from the supernatural trouble (*sui*).[16] Han medical texts from the second century BCE document an exorcist performance (the Pace of Yu 禹步), along with invocations to the powers of Sun and Moon as well as those of Mother and Father, threats (to the harmful spirits) of beating (*ji* 擊) with a hammering stone (*duanshi* 鍛石). In some cases, healers actually hammered with an iron mallet (*tiechui* 鐵椎).[17] Physical twisting of the body and actions that tied up or bound the harmful presences, combined with oral pronouncements (*gao* 告), are documented by Harper in the third-century BCE exorcist rituals of "spellbinding, accusing" (*jie* 詰). He notes that knotted bound forms, such as topknots, could also repel demons.[18] Similar concepts in which instruments are used in exorcism are suggested in some Shang OBI graphs.

Marta Hanson explores the idea that the instrument of healing (including the divination medium) represented a proxy for, or an extended part of, the healer's body. She notes that even the healer's body, especially the hands, functioned as a type of instrument of diagnostic and healing technology.[19] From this we can see that the turtle plastron in shape and function might serve as a proxy for the king's extended body. The ills of his personal body and his activities—along with those of his family and those of other members of the Shang elite, and extended to those of the political body or state—were all diagnosed through the same bone medium, suggesting that they represented layers of the king's socially constructed body. Any part of the extended body (the king's physical body or the lands he governed) could be "afflicted" (*ji* 疾) by the incursion of a perceived pathogen, such as non-Shang peoples, nature spirits, and climatic influences, the Shang equivalents of the Han idea of "perverse *qi*." Royal ancestral spirits, associated with different day signs of the ten-day week, controlled healing and had to be bribed through sacrifices on particular days of the ten-day week or cycle. Diviners used the bone to determine the ritual parameters of the sacrifice: to whom, when, how much of what kind of animal or human captive, and what method of preparation—whether burnt, sliced, or chopped—should be offered. Often the day of sacrifice was the name day of the ancestor, suggesting a fluctuation in spiritual influence in the web of space-time that covered the king and his kin ordered, or at least prescribed, by the calendar. In other words, all squares of the cosmic spatial pattern intersected to a cosmic temporal pattern and all were empowered and perhaps connected to the royal bodies of the past, present, and future. Exorcism and sacrifice were tools for human manipulation of the system.

The Turtle Proxy Body and the Nature of Affliction

Nathan Sivin has shown how early Chinese medical theory assumed that the human body was simply a microcosmic representation of the macrocosmic pattern.[20] In both Allan's and Sivin's work, the political hierarchy, like the human or turtle's body, was also an extended reflection of the cosmic pattern.[21] Thus, affliction in the king's body, as an intersection of these symbolic layers, represented larger disharmonies. Likewise, a solar eclipse or an invasion of the state carried implications for the king's personal health. If we understand the Shang turtle as a proxy body for the king's and, at the same time, a tool for the diagnostician, we can see why it functioned as a legitimate instrument to test proposals for healing. Like a physician's hands it could diagnose and heal.

The bone inscriptions that mention affliction (*ji*) were produced by the diviners of King Wu Ding and his sons from around 1200 to 1175 BCE. Although by that time, turtle plastrons seemed to be of greater prestige than the more common medium, bovine scapula, it is still remarkable that every inscription involving "afflictions" of the king's personal physical body is found on a turtle plastron (or a shard most likely, but not unequivocally, from a plastron). Divination regarding the extended political body could be found on either type of bone. Generally, a single bone (or in some cases, a set of bones) included a range of concerns that had to be addressed during specific ritual calendar cycles.

The social construction of the royal human body reflected in the oracle-bone inscriptions consisted of separately named afflicted parts mostly determined from the outside: head and head areas (eyes, mouth, nose, ears, tongue, teeth, throat), chest (inner and outer, perhaps referred to as "heart," *xin* 心), limbs and areas of the limbs (elbow, knees, feet, toes).[22] Although it is obvious that the Shang diviners chose particular areas of the turtle plastrons to use at particular times, it is impossible to correlate at this time the site on the bone and the site on the royal body.[23] There is no question that diviners were sensitive to the different areas of the turtle plastron body, the front versus the back, the sides, edges, middle areas. In some, positive and negative alternative outcomes were presented on the left or right halves of one surface of the bone. In others, we find the related inscriptions opposite each other on the front and back surfaces of bones. Exactly what factors dictated how the diviners used a bone over a ritual cycle is unknown and difficult to quantify. Generally, we can see that the back was reserved for applying the hot pokers and the front for reading the cracks. The sense is that the turtle body represents a spiritually enhanced medium for healing the physical ailments of the king as well as anything suffered by the king's extended social body, his kingdom.

The concept of "affliction" (*ji*) involved the vulnerability of places in the state or human body to harmful influence by outside forces (the act of *sui*) and, as represented in later medical literature, most likely indicated by feelings of pain (*tong* 痛). The sign representing a site of affliction was the graph ▨ (consisting of a "foot" 止 on top of a "bug" 虫). The category of "bug" includes snakes and turtles.²⁴ The graph, which has no clear descendant, is read by Qiu Xigui 裘錫圭 as meaning "harm" (*hai*) due to *sui*.²⁵ Diviners "reported" (*gao*) the afflictions to sets of ancestral spirits.²⁶ Ancestral spirits, normally charged to protect their descendants, could also be the sources of harm, therefore the *yu*-exorcism might be directed at them instead of the gift of a sacrifice.²⁷ The graph of the verb "to be afflicted" depicted a sideview of a person 人 on a pallet 爿 surrounded with drops 冫 of a liquid ▨. Some graphs of the verb include other elements that indicate actions associated with affliction. The elements include hands wielding implements, suggesting a healing strategy ▨ ▨. It is possible that such healing techniques were associated by outsiders with Shang practices. The word *yin* 殷 (*ʔər), later adopted by the invading Zhou for the conquered Shang people, also seemed to originally refer to a medical procedure involving a hand pointing a sharp object like an arrow toward the body, possibly having to do with the fecund or pregnant body ▨ ▨.²⁸ Implements for healing documented in Han literature included, besides lancing stones and hammers, also sticks, reeds, and arrows.²⁹ Examples of Shang *yu*-exorcism performance possibly with implements can be found throughout the vast bone corpus, but the inscriptions on hundreds of whole plastrons from a cache belonging to Wu Ding's sons in the Huayuanzhuang dongdi 花園莊東地 (HD) burial ground will be the focus of this essay since they represent an archaeologically attested set.³⁰ First, we examine six HD examples and then we explore the vocabulary of healing.

Exorcism and Examples from the Huayuanzhuang Turtle Plastron Corpus

The lines of each of the following inscribed HD plastrons are discussed in temporal units. We assume that the date assigned each divination record was linked to the actual day of the ritual cycle that the divination was performed. It is not always clear which day the proposed sacrifice was performed, but there is some suggestion that sacrifices were made on the stem days assigned posthumously to ancestors. It is unclear whether Shang diviners were sensitive to odd and even differences in the numerical value of temporal signs, which by the end of the Warring States represented *yang*/male and *yin*/female modes of cosmic influence.

HD 181: Affliction of the "Heart" and Exorcism

The form of the graph *ji* depicting the hand holding an implement is found on plastron inscription number 181.[31] HD 181 is a plastron with a thirty-five-line inscription written on days 1, 6, 7, 8, and 9 of the ten-day cycle (the so-called stem days in the stem-and-branch sexagenary calendar system). The diviner himself, or perhaps just the diviner's client, was named Zi 子 and was likely a son or heir of King Wu Ding.[32] During this ten-day cycle, the diviner tested a variety of proposals on different days aimed at two of the primary ancestral spirits that appear in the HD bones: Ancestress Geng 庚 (day 7), possibly a grandmother or great-grandmother spirit, and Zi Gui 癸 (day 10), possibly an older brother or male cousin who died before his time. An elder active in many of the divination performances and rituals was named Ding 丁, which likely refers to the living king Wu Ding, a powerful Shang king known from earlier OBI discoveries.[33] Since his wife, Fu Hao 婦好, also known in other OBI is mentioned here, it is possible that Zi was their child. A summary of the contents of HD 181 OBI by day is as follows:

> *Day 1* (lines 1–5): Zi asked about the performance of gift-giving, hunting, and ale libation rituals. The oracle tells him (*yue* 曰) there will be an unforeseen curse incurred during hunting.[34]
>
> *Day 6* (lines 6–18): Zi tries to figure out which types of animals and how many should be sacrificed to Ancestress Geng. Ding foresaw no danger, so they proceed with a ritual performance depicted with the graph 斅 (line 14, transcribed as "learning" *xue* 學, but perhaps "imitation" *xiao* 效) involving dancing and feasting. As a travel protection, Zi performs the *yu*-exorcism to Ancestress Geng (line 8). One danger that could come from travel was "affliction" (the graph written with a hand holding an implement).[35]
>
> *Day 7* (line 19): The oracle predicted that Zi's heart/chest 心 "affliction" would not linger (this time the graph for affliction is written without the sign of the hand holding the implement).
>
> *Day 8* (lines 20–25): Zi continued with the ritual activities, pledging offerings and dancing following Ding's lead. He also made sure to perform *yu*-exorcism rituals to Ancestresses Ji and Ding for his own protection (辛卜其禦子而于妣己眔妣丁).
>
> *Day 9* (lines 26–35): The idea is proposed of Zi dancing "without words" 亡言 while Ding led, suggesting the ritual or, perhaps,

healing value of not emitting sound. What sacrificial offerings should be presented were also queried as part of Zi's proposed visit to the shrine of Zi Gui 子癸, possibly for the next day, day 10 (a *gui* day).

From this plastron inscription, we see that *yu*-exorcism was performed on a regular basis along with animal sacrifices to procure the aid of particular ancestral spirits, especially as protection for travel or movement, such as while hunting or performing choreographed rituals. Even so his "heart" (*xin*), probably referring to the chest, suffered an affliction. The word "affliction" appears twice, each time written slightly differently. In the first case, where it was referring generally to any affliction that might be incurred during travel, the more complex graph, including the sign with the hand holding the implement, was written. When referring to the specific affliction he did incur, the graph leaves out that sign. It is unclear at this time if this distinction is meaningful or accidental, or if the more complicated graph was read by the ancient scribes as also including a reference to a required act of exorcistic hammering or attacking.

In the next five HD plastrons, we examine a word meaning "healing" but that may have graphically represented an early form of the exorcistic "binding" of demonic influences documented in third-century BCE texts. We have no clue how the Shang word may have been read and must rely on interpreting by context. Visually it shows two hands knotting a cord and as such seems to relate *conceptually* to knot-making, as in *jie* 結, a cognate of *jie* 詰 (spellbinding).[36] From the contents of five HD plastrons with this graph (HD 3, 44, 241, 247, 267), we get a sense of the larger magico-religious environment in which this type of healing, possibly through acts of "binding," took place. Basically, we see that the word was used in opposition to being "afflicted," and, like later healing rites, involved reporting to the ancestors and performing *yu*-exorcisms. In each case, translating the mystery HD word as "having bound the harm caused by the affliction" works as well as the more general definition of "healing." We first review the contents of each OBI example then proceed to an analysis of the graph.

HD 3: BINDING AFFLICTIONS

Plastron HD 3, consisting of seventeen lines, records divination testing on days 3, 6, 7, 8, and 9. The lines 8–9 which mention the healing-through-binding are placed in the lower half of the plastron on either side of the centerline. It is worth noting that this inscription also has two ways of writing "affliction." In line 10, a specific affliction incurred during traveling is mentioned and the graph is the standard form 㐬 (the curving line to the left in the graph is a part of a border line drawn on the bone to visually separate sections of inscriptions, not an element of the graph). It is possible that the undeciphered graph before *ji* was an unusually named body site or type of affliction (interpreted as 玄 *[ɢ]ʷi[n] over 鳥 *tˤiw?) 鳥. Adam Schwartz notes that "Dark Bird" is cited in later times as a progenitor of the Shang people, but he chooses to take it as a place name in the HD context.³⁷ However, the syntax of the sentence is very similar to a line in HD 446, line 6 with a "mouth affliction" suggesting the possibility of the word referring to a place on the visual body. The second more general term for "affliction" occurs in line 17 in the context of to having no afflictions while residing in the northern chamber. This graph is written with a full body 身 (with a line marking the trunk) instead of 人 on the pallet. This version also includes three hands (or, perhaps, three herb or foliage signs) around it instead of water drops 㾈.³⁸ If we understand the three signs to indicate the type of exorcistic healing, then perhaps the drops of liquid in the standard graph discussed earlier also indicate a healing method. The question remains whether a graph can visually indicate more than the simple semantic function of a pronounced "word" in a sentence. In other words, the variant graphs for "affliction" and "heal" might preserve details of the ancient treatment methods.

It is interesting that Zi Er's state of being healed was predicted to take place in five days (lines 8–9). This would be a *jia* (S1) day, the first "stem" day of the ten-day cycle, if we count day 7 (*geng*), the day of the record. Could that day, which coincided with Ancestress Geng's day, also be the day of the healing binding ritual? If so, then we must understand that the ritual's efficacy is dependent upon the calendar and the influence of particular ancestors whose spirits were perhaps most active on their sun/stem sign days.³⁹ A summary of HD3 OBI contents by day follows:

> *Day 3* (lines 1–5): Tested proposals regarding which and how many offerings to provide Ancestress Geng and whether or not Ding had to predict a concern.
> *Day 6* (lines 6–7): Tested proposals regarding the sacrifices to Ancestress Geng (day 7 is a *geng* day).
> *Day 7* (lines 8–9): It was predicted that Zi Er would "heal/have his harm bound" in five days, thus making *yu*-exorcism unnecessary (庚卜五日子而㾈。庚卜弗禦子而㾈).

Day 8 (lines 10–11): It was confirmed that even though he was afflicted while traveling, he would not die, and there would be no complications (辛卜貞往玄鳥疾不死。辛卜子弗難).

Day 9 (lines 12–17): It was determined that Ding should rest until day 2, providing no predictions. Zi could go hunting but he needed to issue a command first. It was suggested that if he resided in the northern chamber, his body would be free of afflictions (其宅北室亡疾).

HD 44: Healing Hands

Plastron HD 44 is broken and has only two lines remaining. They record that Zi's affliction would "not linger" but be "healed/bound" (子不延又 (有) 肰). The inscription with the healing word is in the upper-right quadrant of the plastron. The HD graph this time has an extra hand in the upper right. This then begs the question whether in fact the word typically read as "to possess, have," *you* 又 (有), should in fact be read as a matching hand on the other side of the graph (see fig. 6.1). This in turn suggests two graphs, the first of two hands read as "to offer," *gong* 共 (恭), and the second "the binding healing method."

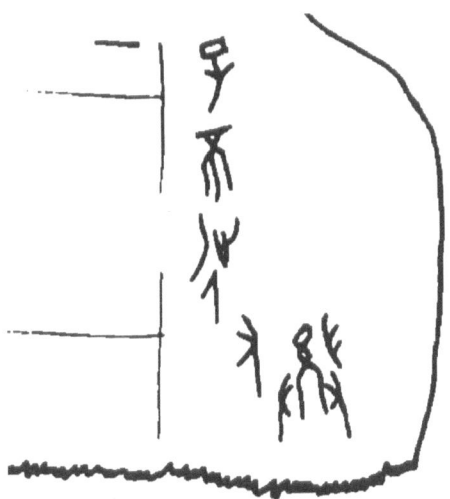

Figure 6.1. Detail of HD44: Healing Hands. *Source:* Author's graphic adapted from Huang Tianshu 黃天樹 comp., *Jiaguwen moben daxi* 甲骨文摹本大系, Vol. 26 (Beijing: Beijing daxue, 2022), no. 63657.

HD 241: Bound Slave

Plastron HD 241, consisting of thirteen lines, does not focus on the ten-day cycle but on particular days in the sexagenary cycle (consisting of days marked with both stem and branch signs): days 39, 42, 44, 48, and 50. Except for the first day *renyin* (day 39, stem 9 branch 3 [S9 B3]), all other days are even numbers. The graphs for the specific afflictions refer to Zi's abdomen as the site in line 8 and to the body of a *qiang* slave[40] in line 10. The graphic forms are standard (showing liquid drops rather than implements). The section of line 10, including the phrase with the HD healing term, stretches around in a half-circle from the centerline to the edge and back to the centerline of the plastron in the upper half, suggesting a need to inscribe a larger or specific section of the shell. The depiction of a knotted cord around the word for *qiang* slave is similar to the cord depicted in the graph for healing (see fig. 6.2). The shared element strongly suggests the ideas of knotting and binding. These ideas are further explored in the next section.

Day 39 (S9 B3, lines 1–4): Zi was hunting birds and animals.
Day 42 (S6 B6, line 5): (Four days later) sacrifices were performed for Ancestor Yi (a Stem Six ancestor).

Figure 6.2. Detail of HD241: Bound Slave. *Source:* Author's graphic adapted from Huang Tianshu 黃天樹 comp., *Jiaguwen moben daxi* 甲骨文摹本大系, Vol. 26 (Beijing: Beijing daxue, 2022), no. 63658.

Day 44 (S4 B8, lines 6–9): (Two days later) "Zi was afflicted in the abdomen by it (the travel)" (隹之疾子腹).

Day 48 (S8 B12, lines 10–12): (Four days later) a valued slave was afflicted and diviners tested whether it would be fatal or if he would heal that day. Sacrifices were made to Ancestress Geng, even though her official day was a S7 not S8.

Day 50 (S10 B2, line 13): Sacrifices were made to Gui Zi (on a S10 day, a Gui day).

It is possible that the valued slave mentioned in the OBI for day 48 had a name, Jade-Qiang, as indicated by the additional "jade" sign to the graph. Concern expressed over a slave's illness implies that this *qiang* was valuable, perhaps one with skills versus one among the hundreds sacrificed to the ancestors. Or that perhaps any slave's body no matter what function it served in Shang society was more valuable when not contaminated with an ill supernatural influence. Sacrifices in this OBI were offered to Ancestress Geng and Gui Zi. The OBI for day 48 is as follows: "Crack-making on Xinhai day, test the proposal that Jade-Qiang's affliction is not fatal. Zi prognosticated and said: 'The *qiang* may die today or possibly be healed through binding today'" (辛亥卜貞 玉[41]羌又 (有) 疾不死. 子占曰羌其死隹今其⺊亦隹今).

HD 247: THE HEALING REPORT

Plastron HD 247, consisting of sixteen lines, also focuses on the sexagenary calendar, specifying days 45, 46, 50, 51, 57, 60, 2, 14, 24, 26, and 27 (in this order if we read from the bottom of the bone upward). Only day 2 inscriptions included more than one line of text. Zi suffered from an affliction in or around the mouth. Instead of performing *yu*-exorcism, an announcement of "healing through binding" was sent to Ancestress Geng on the last day of the sexagenary calendar. This follows up the proposal that Ancestress Geng be denied sacrifices (which would include a human) because of Zi's mouth affliction. In the last line, Ancestress Geng is rewarded with sacrifices upon evidence that Zi did not experience anything negative, including affliction, while he was traveling. This set of inscriptions seems to serve more than one Zi.

The line about healing was inscribed in the lower left region of the plastron, beginning next to the centerline of the bone and going around in a circle until it meets the centerline again (see fig. 6.3).

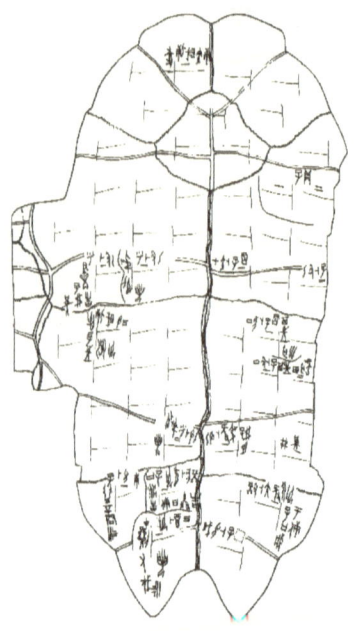

Figure 6.3. HD 246: The Healing Report. *Source:* Author's graphic adapted from Huang Tianshu 黃天樹 comp., *Jiaguwen moben daxi* 甲骨文摹本大系, Vol. 26 (Beijing: Beijing daxue, 2022), no. 63687.

Figure 6.4. Detail of HD 247 (lower left of centerline): Day 60. *Source:* Author's graphic adapted from Huang Tianshu 黃天樹 comp., *Jiaguwen moben daxi* 甲骨文摹本大系, Vol. 26 (Beijing: Beijing daxue, 2022), no. 63687.

	D27		
D2 D46	D51	D24 D14	D2
D57	D2 D60 D46	D2 D45	D50

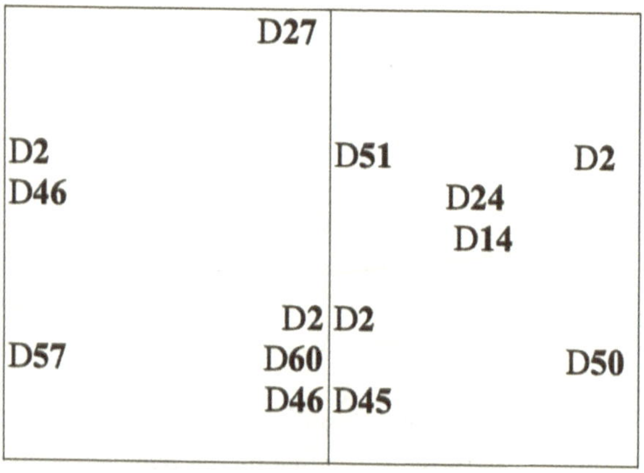

Figure 6.5. The Positioning and Numbering of Day Signs on the Plastron. *Source:* Created by the author.

The pattern of dates is distributed around the bone with days 45 and 46 near the bottom and day 27 at the top, suggesting that the rituals started in the middle of the sixty-day cycle. The four inscriptions recording divinations on the earliest day of the cycle, day 2, were in two pairs, one on the left and right edges of the middle section, and the other on the lower left and right of the centerline. Day 46 has two different sites of inscription, the lower left and the middle left regions of the bone. It is clear that placement of the proposals on the bone are purposeful as if sections of the body represented by the bone convey different power on different days.

> *Day 45* (S5 B9, line 1): Concern about Zi but the topic is obscured.
> *Day 46* (S6 B10, line 2): Tests whether the performance of *yu*-exorcism should include human sacrifice.
> *Day 50* (S10 B2, line 3): Tests not performing the *yu*-exorcism and proposed that Zi's mouth affliction might in fact be due to Ancestress Geng (presumably the spirit who would have received the sacrifices proposed in line 2).
> *Day 51* (S1 B3, line 4): For Zi Jin.
> *Day 57* (S7 B9, line 5): For Zi Yi performing the Shang sacrifice.
> *Day 60* (S10 B12, line 6): Again proposes no *yu*-exorcism for Zi's mouth affliction. Instead "announces" (*gao*) it to Ancestress Geng and says, "Healing/binding report" (癸亥卜弜禦子口疾告妣庚曰󰀀告).
> *Day 2* (S2 B2, lines 7–12): Shu 弔 (叔) called to assist, concern that Zi X might have difficulties.
> *Day 14* (S4 B2, line 13): Would there be "harm" if Zi goes hunting.
> *Day 24* (S4 B12, line 14): No calamity if Zi Jin travels.
> *Day 26* (S6 B2, line 15): Sacrifices to Ancestress Geng are proposed on day 26 because Zi was traveling to the Wan River 灣 to perform a *yu*-exorcism.
> *Day 27* (S7 B3, line 16): A Geng day, the sacrifices to Ancestress Geng were performed.

HD 467: Healing Bones

The inscriptions on plastron HD 467, consisting of eleven lines, also record specific days of the sexagenary calendar: days 35, 36, 37, and 45 (reading from the bottom up). Most of the lines concern religious activities by

132 | Constance A. Cook

different people at various sites, during archery practice and the capture of particular animals for sacrifices. Sacrifices and a Shang ritual were performed on day 37, a Geng day. The line, which we might read as "Zi's bones will perhaps heal just before the sun rises" (子骨未 (昧) 其㣇),⁴² is one of four inscribed lines placed in a square and separated by lines in the lower left quadrant of the shell. All eleven lines of the inscription are distributed among four quadrants of the shell (see figs. 6.6 and 6.7).

The choice of where to locate a particular inscription on a plastron is obviously intentional, even if the rationale is not obvious to us. It does seem to be associated with time. Although the line with the healing ritual

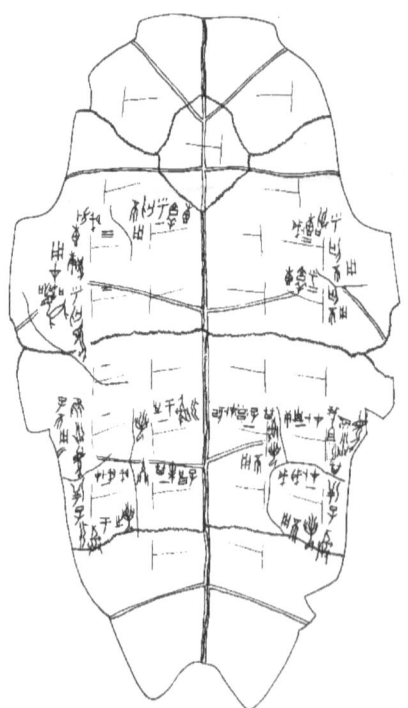

Figure 6.6. HD 467: Healing Bones. Source: Author's graphic adapted from Huang Tianshu 黃天樹 comp., *Jiaguwen moben daxi* 甲骨文摹本大系, Vol. 26 (Beijing: Beijing daxue, 2022), no. 63736.

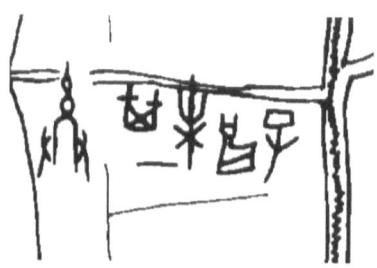

Figure 6.7. Detail of HD 467 (lower left of centerline). Source: Author's graphic adapted from Huang Tianshu 黃天樹 comp., *Jiaguwen moben daxi* 甲骨文摹本大系, Vol. 26 (Beijing: Beijing daxue, 2022), no. 63736.

is not dated, its location in the lower left quadrant suggests it took place around day 35, the only date that appears among the inscriptions in the lower left quadrant. On the other hand, as we saw in HD 247, the line recording the healing ritual is located in the same sector but has a different day than the other inscriptions in that quadrant. The diviners grouped the HD 467 records more or less by day. The inscriptions on the lower right quadrant are made on day 35 (S5 B5), day 36 (S6 B12), and day 37 (S7 B1). The upper left quadrant of inscriptions mentions a day 45 (S5 B9) and those of the upper right quadrant simply a Wu (S6) day, probably day 45 also. It is possible the healing ritual was divined about on a stem 5 (Wu) day, either day 35 or day 45.

The healing of bones in the *Heji* collection of oracle-bone inscriptions is expressed differently than we see here in HD.[43] For example, bone *Heji* 709 has nineteen proposals inscribed on the front with only one day, a Geng day (day 47, S7 B11), mentioned.[44] First, the diviner proposes that the afflicted body is evidence of a toxic state (貞有疾身佳有毒), but later the king claims there is no affliction, perhaps suggesting a successful healing ritual. There are two words that may have been used for the healing of bones used in the following lines. One is read as a shortened version of "to rise up" (*xing* 興 ▨ *qʰrəŋ, also written with up to two sets of hands),[45] and the other as "to get better" (*ying* 嬴 ▨ *ɢeŋ, read as *long* 龍 *mə-roŋ > *chong* 龍 *ɾoŋ?).[46] The first term seems to be particular to bone affliction and the second a general term of getting better, but perhaps we might consider them as different derivations of the same root word representing different contexts. The first term depicts a raised plank—in other more complex versions of the graph two to four hand signs might be added, possibly representing healing as a function of "lifting up" ▨. But the second graph depicts a curled dragon, likely significant only as a phonetic loan. Notably the inscriptions about the affliction and healing are recorded on either side of the centerline of the plastron in the lower half, written in somewhat of a T-shape. The remaining inscriptions on the upper half and two side wings of the plastron all concerned sacrifice contingencies, reaffirming the importance of sacrifice and ancestral spirits in the healing process, but also revealing that they were ritual stages separate in time.

The HD Graph for Healing

The variety of terms for healing and the use of graphs with different visual information for the same words suggest that the HD graph may also have harbored layered complexities. While used for a state of healing, it depicts the act of binding or knotting a cord and was applied in the larger context of *yu*-exorcism rituals.⁴⁷ Because the graph does not seem to connect graphically to a known descendant word, scholars interpret it from context and suggest *cuo* 搓 (*tsʰˤaj) "to polish, rub" > *chai* 瘥 (*tsʰˤraj) "to heal." There are no oracle-bone inscriptions or early Zhou examples of words written with the basic graph of 差, so, although the meaning fits, there is no way to prove that the word existed then. Other scholars note that the HD corpus has a similarly written graph with two hands and tied cords, found in the title Suo yin 索尹 "the Technician of Suo" (HD 125). The root meaning of the word *suo* 索 (*sˤak) can mean "tie, twist up with rope." The problem with this is that *suo* is found only as a place name in other inscriptions, and also the graph of two hands holding the knotted cord differs in two respects. In the *suo* graph, the top of the knot is split open showing two ends of the cord, and the two hands do not separately grasp the bottom ends of the cords. Similar problems accompany other attempts to interrupt the HD graph as a knotted cord depicted in the graphs *xi* 糸 or *su* 束.⁴⁸ Some suggest that the mystery graph should be read as 交 (*kˤraw) meaning "to cross," written . This graph is found in names in the *Heji* corpus and depicts a person with crossed legs rather than a cord being knotted with two hands.⁴⁹ Although none of these are optimal transcriptions for the HD graph, many assume a correlation between "healing" and "twisting, binding, knotting."

The concept of binding or tying up is confirmed in a slightly similar graph with two hands on either side of a knot in the sense of "to tie up" an ox (*niu*) found in *Heji* 387 (verso), 8945, and 1763, written as and as , although this "knot" in other contexts as we saw earlier with Dark Bird can be read as *xuan* 玄. As a knot or twist, the element is found on its own often simplified to a single cord with two bumps (knots) and read as *wu* 午 "go crosswise, resist."⁵⁰ Although the first version of this graph is not exactly the same as our mystery graph in terms of the placement of the hands, the phonetic *wu* (*m-qʰˤaʔ) links it to the graph from *yu*-exorcism (*m-qʰraʔ) originally written as a kneeling person holding a knotted cord , and simplified to , as on HD 181. It was a combination of 午, most likely the phonetic, and the kneeling-human semantic element (later simplified to 卩). The graph was also read as "drive a chariot, drive away" 御 (*ŋra-s), an act that would have involved two hands holding reins.

Kenichi Takashima notes that the phonetic *wu* might be active in another mystery graph , a verb applied only in the negative to mark certain bone cracks. The graph, deciphered as 午 over 口 and having no clear descendant graph, has been read visually as a "drill." This interpretation is no doubt influenced by the fact that it is used as a common crack notation and the fact that if the *wu* 午 was replaced with *bu* 卜 it would be *zhan* 占 (to prognosticate by crack-making). The upper twisted cord element, which looks like an Arabic numeral eight (as seen earlier) is often read pictographically as *xuan* (dark)[51] and the lower part imagined as a drill head, suggesting an unknown word "to carve, pierce, poke" and that the whole phrase could be read in the sense of "don't carve this crack (or poke the bone) here."[52] We find a version of the graph with two hands holding either a pole or the knotted cords over a triangular-shaped "mouth, cavity" element, but it seems likely to be a name or an activity associated with divination and sacrifice.[53]

The crack notion ▨▨▨ is read by Takashima as *bu wu zhu* 不吾 (悟) 黽 (*pə-ŋˤa-tro). He reads "the drill" phonetically as the word "going against" 吾 (*ŋˤa) > 悟 (*ŋˤak-s). More likely the graphic element he takes as *wu* 五 (five, usually written as a cross with two open ends) was *wu* 午 (*m-qʰˤaʔ, resist, crosswise).[54] Important to Takashima's reading is the idea that the object of the mystery verb, "spider" *zhu* ▨ (*tro), might refer to a spirit or numen of the bone, as it appears in statements associated with (and possibly even causing) supernatural harm.[55] The idea that the Shang believed the plastron had a spirit is suggested by the rare divination concerning "encountering Ghost Day" (*gou gui ri* 遘鬼日), in which the graph for "ghost, demon" (*gui* 鬼) included the semantic sign for "shell (cowry or turtle)" (*bei* 貝).[56] On the other hand, in HD 288 (line 9) we find the graph *zhu* (spider) read as a full verb. It is interpreted to be a phonetic loan for the verb *shu* 殊 (to cut, kill) in the phrase "capture but do not cut [deer]" (*huo bu zhu* 獲不黽 (殊)).[57] If we claim the noun that Takashima reads as "spider" was in fact a verb ("cut"), then together with the mystery word, we would have two verbs possibly representing carving or cutting. Alternatively, since a double verb would be unusual, is the object read as "spider" really something else?

What do spiders have to do with turtles? Since many graphs are identified by modern scholars simply from visual inspection, we cannot even be sure that the Shang read this graph as "spider."[58] Yao Xiaosui simply transcribes it as *min* 黽 (a kind of turtle, also found in a Warring States name for a turtle divination method).[59] Graphs representing turtles did vary, so perhaps "spiders," or whatever was represented by that graph, were considered visually similar in some sense or of similar mantic potential.[60] Turtle (*gui* 龜 *kʷə) graphs include ▨ ▨ ▨ (note the two hands added to the last example).[61] There is also a mystery graph with a turtle that indicates the result of an "affliction" due to a "loss" or death caused by ghosts fifty-one days earlier. It depicts a turtle over a pit with a supine human form in it 🝔.⁶² One noticeable difference between the graphs for spiders or turtles is the representation of the head (spider graphs tend to feature no head).

In sum, the graph read "spider" could possibly indicate an object used in divination that should not be pierced with a drill-like implement or had some ritual associated with "resistance" applied to it. If the word for "spider" was in fact a second verb, we still end up with the idea that the turtle should not be cut in this place at that time. If we understand the knot to indicate resistance to perverse supernatural influences, then perhaps the cutting of the turtle bone also symbolized a warding-off ritual, maybe even requiring a knotted cord attached to the knife or drill. By extension then, we can understand that successful resistance to bad influences could lead to healing.

Variant examples of the HD graph further suggest the value of the knotted cord but also reveal complexities in interpretation. For example, on HD 286, we find on lines 18–19 seemingly two versions of the healing/binding graph. One has three hands—the two holding the ends of the strings of the knot and another hand near the top of the knot. The other graph used in a related sentence shows a knot with no strings and only one hand alongside. Because the graphs described colors of jade, it is possible to imagine the graphs were loans with *you* 幽.⁶³ On the other hand, the addition of the specification "without side strings" in the second sentence matches the use of the graph with no dangling strings.⁶⁴ It seems to be a verb that modifies the jade tablet, which is perhaps bound with strings for presentation to Ding. In other words, we see examples of graphs containing more information than the general definition of the word.

> "Crack-making on a *bing* day (S3): [we] shall present to Ding a bound auspicious/dark jade tablet; Crack-making on a *bing* day, [we] shall present to Ding a jade tablet without side strings."
>
> 丙卜惠 🝔 吉圭再丁；丙卜惠 🝔 圭再丁亡緅.

This suggests that the knotting ritual involved in healing included the purposeful use of side strings.

Hands and Implements

Interestingly, the graph with an abbreviated version of the knot, clearly depicted as *wu*, is found with two hands but no side strings 🝔 on HD

458 as either a verb meaning "to pummel" or part of the name of a people who will be attacked. A similar graph but with the "mouth, cavity" element below and only one "knot" marked on the upright cord or pole 忠 is found in the *Heji* corpus in an unclear context, perhaps as part of a title. Scholars intrepreted this graph to represent "beat, pound," as either *wu* 杵 or *chong* 舂 (*s-toŋ).⁶⁵ The question then is whether the graph meaning to heal/bind could also imply the metaphorical or actual beating of the "toxin" in the afflicted area.

Another consideration is whether the lower half of the HD graph for healing/binding, the two hands holding two side strings, should actually be read as a separate graphic element. For example, the graph depicting two hands is routinely transcribed as *gong* 共, in the sense of "to offer up (with two hands)" (*kroŋʔ).⁶⁶ A rare variant of the graph with two hands holding an object 𢀖 depicts two hands holding a stone mallet or pestle: *gong* 工 (*kˤoŋ), written 𠙶 工. Scholars understand that this graph first depicted a stone mallet used to pound earth.⁶⁷ The word could have been a name in some cases, but in others, it seems to have been a procedure used to combat harmful supernatural influences (*sui*).⁶⁸ An exorcistic function is suggestive as, in fourth-century BCE Chu bamboo texts, healing afflictions involved an exorcistic process called *gong* 攻 (*kˤoŋ, attack), written with the phonetic 工 (tool) > (artisan, officer) and a single "hand" element 攵. This word is not found in the inscriptions of earlier eras. David Keightley discusses the possible link between the oracle bone graph of the *gong* "tool" and some sort of implement used to measure space; Han scholars felt it formed the basis of the graph for *wu* 巫 (shaman). Allan showed that the early graph for shaman that looked like two 工 in a cross shape was a depiction of the four quadrate cosmos.⁶⁹ Could we understand then that the act of "crossing" two implements symbolizing measurements of the cosmos had exorcistic power? Keightley sees the basic graph *gong* as operating in a "tool-work-accomplishment nexus" of meaning (incorporating the cognate "merit" *gong* 功) and thus could also extend to warfare, as in "to attack with success."⁷⁰ On Warring States sword inscriptions, we find the names of two officers with the two types of *gong*: one is an "artisan master" (*gongshi* 工師), chief officer in charge of works or ritual objects, and the other is a "grand attack technician" (*dagong yin* 大攻尹).⁷¹ Attacking enemies may have been conceptually similar to warding off pathogens in ancient China.

Two hands holding implements of various shapes appear in a number of undeciphered oracle bone graphs.⁷² Perhaps most interesting for our purposes are the rare graphs of two hands, each holding what looks like the ends of cords only or short pole-like implements, something that might be transcribed as two 支 or 攵 (or even two "father" elements, *fu* 父). *Heji* 14795, a plastron inscribed on both sides, shows two hands as one word and the knot *wu* following ▨ on the verso side. The meaning is uncertain. In *Heji* 13845, a fragment, hands with implements facing outward ▨, represent a word that is/seems to be connected to an affliction (*ji*).[73] These rare examples suggest the possibility that the HD graph was a combination of this graph with the knot *wu* element instead of simply the semantic idea of two hands holding side strings.

Another graph composed of a hand holding a long pole-like implement is that for "technician" *yin* 尹 (*m-qur?), a Shang ranking officer written as ▨▨ (this was probably the phonetic in the word *yin* 殷, the Zhou name for the Shang, mentioned previously). Yi Yin 伊尹 is a legendary Shang officer with magical healing powers.[74] The addition of a "mouth, cavity" element below the pole makes the graph represent the word *jun* 君 (*C.qur), which after the Shang era took on the meaning of "ruler."[75] In OBI, the two forms just seem to be graphic variations of the same word. Another variant might be a graph that appears to include *yin* with "thread, cord" elements (*xi* 糸 or *su*) instead of the "mouth, cavity" element.[76]

The idea of the HD graph being associated with holding an implement as key to healing finds support in the Warring States exorcist healing rituals that, like the Qin binding rituals, seemed to involve oral imprecations. The Chu ritual of "command and attack" (*ming gong* 命攻) most likely included vocalizing an invocation while applying an ancient stone "needle" to the affected area.[77] The Qin method of binding also involved imprecations and bodily motions:[78]

> To bind the afflicted harm (spiritual blame). . . . Announcing it is like binding it (with an accusation and spell); command . . . what ghosts detest are those who sit in a crouch, like a winnowing basket, move in interlinked fashion, or stand at a lean.
>
> 詰咎. . . . 告如詰之；道令 . . . 鬼之所惡彼窋 (屈) 臥箕坐，連行奇 (踦) 立.[79]

In the Qin example, the binding was through bodily motions rather than holding an object to the afflicted area to "poke" or "attack" as suggested by the Warring States Chu example, although this too involved "command" and "intent." Although over a thousand years separated the Shang from the Qin, evidence suggests that *yu*-exorcisms may have involved twisting or other movements that warded off ghosts and bound the site against their influence.

Conclusion

This essay examines the vocabulary of a healing in a set of inscribed turtle plastrons dating from the twelfth to thirteenth centuries BCE. To unlock the meaning of words without obvious descendants in later texts, the original graphs, words, and inscriptions are decoded within the religious context of the plastron as an instrument of healing. Later manuscripts describing exorcism and sacrifice practices reinforce the clues that the Shang treatments involved "binding" and protecting. Their inscribed sites on the bone was purposeful, suggesting the use of the turtle plastron as a symbolic body, which may or may not be pierced in certain places at particular times of the ritual calendar. The inscribed turtle plastrons record diviners' efforts to treat the sites of supernatural infection or "toxin" on the bodies of King Wu Ding and his family members. As instruments, the turtle shells mediated the exorcistic healing but also functioned as sacrifices. The turtle shells, after use, were stored, some polished like jade with the cracks filled with black or cinnabar pastes. All shells were eventually buried in pits.[80] Perhaps, like once animated human bodies, the used turtle shells had to be sealed in the earth to protect the living. On the other hand, these dismembered, pierced, and burnt shells, buried en masse, seem closer in status to sacrificed human captives than kings—whose bodies, once healed, remain above ground with access to the divine power of the Sky.

Notes

1. See Stephan N. Kory, "Cracking to Divine: Pyro-plastromancy as an Archetypal and Common Mantic and Religious Practice in Han and Medieval China," PhD diss., Indiana University, 2012. Use of the upper shells in Shang was rare.

2. Sarah Allan, *The Shape of the Turtle: Myth, Art, and Cosmos in Early China* (Albany: State University of New York Press, 1991). A revised edition appeared in Chinese in 2010: Ai Lan 艾蘭, *Gui zhi mi—Shangdai shenhua, jisi, yishu he yuzhouguan yanjiu* 龜之謎—商代神話、祭祀、藝術和宇宙觀研究 (Beijing: Shangwu, 2010).

3. Donald Harper, "A Chinese Demonography of the Third Century B.C.," *Harvard Journal of Asiatic Studies* 45, no. 2 (1985): 481–82.

4. Catherine Despeux, "Âmes et animation du corps: La notion de *shen* dans la médecine chinoise antique," *Extrême-Orient, Extrême-Occident* 29 (2007): 71–94. See Donald Harper's comments on the *renshen* 人神 system in "Dunhuang Iatromantic Manuscripts: P. 2856 R° and P. 2675 V°," in *Medieval Chinese Medicine: The Dunhuang Medical Manuscripts*, ed. Vivienne Lo and Christopher Cullen (London: RoutledgeCurzon, 2005), 136–37, 139, 149–54. Vivienne Lo also comments on

these taboos, in "Quick and Easy Chinese Medicine: The Dunhuang Moxibustion Charts," in Lo and Cullen, *Medieval Chinese Medicine*, 233–35. Recent discoveries of Qin medical texts in Wuwei 武威, Gansu, confirm the much earlier existence of a mobile human spirit (*shenhun* 神魂) within the body. See Harper, "Dunhuang Iatromantic Manuscripts," 151–53.

5. Vivienne Lo, "The Influence of Nurturing Life Culture on the Development of Western Han Acumoxa Therapy," in *Innovation in Chinese Medicine*, ed. Elisabeth Hsu (Cambridge: Cambridge University, 2001), 39.

6. Paul U. Unschuld, *Medicine in China: Historical Artifacts and Images* (Munich: Prestel, 2000), 30–31; Donald Harper, *Early Chinese Medical Literature: The Mawangdui Medical Manuscripts* (London: Kegan Paul International, 1998), 5, 81, 96.

7. Allan, *Shape of the Turtle*, 101, 106–07, 111–13, 121.

8. Hu Houxuan, "Lun Yin ren zhiliao jibing zhi fangfa" 論殷人治療疾病之方法, *Zhongyuan wenwu* 1984.4: 27–30.

9. Jao Tsung-I 饒宗頤 looks at the symbolism of spirit turtles from Neolithic to Han China as well as from India in "Lun gui wei shuimu ji youguan wenti" 論龜為水母及有關問題, *Wenwu* 1999.10: 35–37.

10. Following the *Shuowen*; Harper, *Early Chinese Medical Literature*, 96.

11. Harper, *Early Chinese Medical Literature*, 60–69, 78–82, 89–90. The recently discovered bamboo text *Tang zai chimen* 湯在啻門, currently in the Tsinghua University collection, reveals an early awareness of the influence of natural forces on the formation of the body, and of dialogue between a sage emperor and a minister-magical specialist, a format followed in the *Huangdi neijing* for knowledge transfer. See Li Xueqin 李學勤, ed., *Qinghua daxue cang Zhanguo zhujian* 清華大學藏戰國竹簡, vol. 5 (Shanghai: Zhongxi, 2015), 141–48.

12. For a discussion of Qiu Xigui's 裘錫圭 reading of *tuo* as *hai*, see Ken-ichi Takashima, *Studies of Fascicle Three of Inscriptions from the Yin Ruins*, 2 vols. (Taipei: Academia Sinica, 2010), vol. 2, 150–53n5, 262n1. For Qiu's original argument and the writing of 蚩 with one extra stroke, see Qiu Xigui, *Qiu Xigui xueshu wenji* 裘錫圭學術文集, 6 vols. (Shanghai: Fudan daxue, 2012), vol. 1, 206–11. A similar graph in which the 止 is replaced with 丰 was read in the *Yupian* 玉篇 as *du*, toxin (*[d]ˁuk). I suspect this would be a better reading than *hai*, harm: "蚩 *dowk (Middle Chinese), the old form of *du*: harm, evil, resentful" 蚩徒酷切古文毒字害也惡也恚也; see *Yupian* (*Siku quanshu* 四庫全書 ed.), 25.7a.

13. See Paul U. Unschuld on "evil *qi*" in *Huang Di nei jing su wen: Nature, Knowledge, Imagery in an Ancient Chinese Medical Text* (Berkeley: University of California Press, 2003), 89, 192–96, 220–22. See also Donald Harper, "Iatromancy, Diagnosis, and Prognosis in Early Chinese Medicine," in Hsu, *Innovation in Chinese Medicine*, 99–120; "Dunhuang Iatromantic Manuscripts," 134–64; and "Demonography," 459–98. See also Constance A. Cook, *Death in Ancient China: The Tale of One Man's Journey* (Leiden: Brill, 2006), 99–101 passim.

14. Archaic phonetic reconstructions follow the Baxter-Sagart Old Chinese reconstruction (version 1.1), January 10, 2016, accessed February 5, 2019, http://ocbaxtersagart.lsait.lsa.umich.edu. For the definition of *yu*, see David N. Keightley, *Working for His Majesty: Research Notes on Labor Mobilization in Late Shang China (ca. 1200–1045 B.C.), as Seen in the Oracle-Bone Inscriptions, with Particular Attention to Handicraft Industries, Agriculture, Warfare, Hunting, Construction, and the Shang's Legacies* (Berkeley: Institute of East Asian Studies, University of California, Berkeley, 2012), 356.

15. Harper, *Early Chinese Medical Literature*, 69.

16. C. A. Cook, *Death in Ancient China*, 84–85. See the extensive study by Vivienne Lo, "Spirit of Stone: Technical Considerations in the Treatment of the Jade Body," *Bulletin of the School of Oriental and African Studies* 65, no. 1 (2002): 99–128. See also Harper, *Early Chinese Medical Literature*, 92–93. Harper translates *jie* as "elimination ritual."

17. "Wushier bingfang," no. 126 in Ma Jixing 馬繼興, *Mawangdui gu yishu kaoshi* 馬王堆古醫書考釋 (Changsha: Hunan kexue jishu, 1992), 477; Harper, *Early Chinese Medical Literature*, 148, 261. Note that an oracle bone graph visually similar to an archaic Han graph for exorcistic hammering was composed of "bug" 虫 and a "hand holding something" and read as *shi* 它 + 攴 "to dismember" (as in a human sacrificial victim). See Chen Guangyu 陳光宇, Song Zhenhao 宋鎮豪, Liu Yuan 劉源, and An Maxiu 安馬修 (Matt Anderson), eds., *Shangdai jiagu Zhong-Ying duben* 商代甲骨中英讀本 / *Reading of Shāng Inscriptions* (Shanghai: Renmin, 2017), 189–90.

18. Harper, "Demonography," 475–76.

19. Marta Hanson, "The Hand Book: The Body-as-Technology in Chinese Medicine" and "Ritual Healing: The Body-as-Technology in Mid-Seventh-Century Tang China," unpublished manuscripts, February 26, 2018. For the technology of the hand, see her "Hand Mnemonics in Classical Chinese Medicine: Texts, Earliest Images, and Arts of Memory," in "Star Gazing, Firephasing, and Healing in China: Essays in Honor of Nathan Sivin," special issue, *Asia Major*, 3rd ser., 21, no. 1 (2008): 325–47.

20. Nathan Sivin, "State, Cosmos, and Body in the Last Three Centuries B.C.," *Harvard Journal of Asiatic Studies* 55, no. 1 (1995): 5–37.

21. For Warring States and Han analogies of the human body with the turtle's, see Mark Edward Lewis, *The Construction of Space in Early China* (Albany: State University of New York Press, 2006), 56, 72.

22. Body part graphs are identified by modern scholars visually, thus there is some debate. See Hu Houxuan, "Yin ren jibing kao" 殷人疾病考, *Jiagu xue Shang shi luncong* 甲骨學商史論叢 (Chengdu: Qi Lu daxue guxue yanjiusuo, 1942); Yan Yiping 嚴一萍, *Yin qi zheng yi* 殷契徵醫 (1951) collected in *Yan Yiping quanji* 嚴一萍全集 (Taipei: Yiwen, 1991); Du Zhengsheng 杜正勝, *Cong meishou dao changsheng: yiliao wenhua yu Zhongguo gudai shengming guan* 從眉壽到長生：醫療文化與中國古

代生命觀 (Taipei: Sanmin, 2005), 83. Later additions were added by Chen Shihui 陳世輝, "Yin ren jibing bu kao" 殷人疾病補考, *Zhonghua wenshi luncong* 中華文史論叢 4 (1963): 138. Fan Yuzhou 范毓周 corrected some of Chen's readings in his "'Yin ren jibing bukao' bianzheng" "殷人疾病補考" 辯正, *Dongnan wenhua* 東南文化 1998.3: 98–99. For a classic case of guesswork for a large array of body parts, see Zhang Wei 張煒, "Jiaguwen zhong de renti ji shengli renshi" 甲骨文中的人體及生理認識, *Zhongyi wenxian shizhi* 中醫文獻史志 1998.1: 12. For a more constrained identification, see Huang Tianshu 黃天樹, *Guwenzi lunji* 古文字論集 (Beijing: Xueyuan, 2006), 151.

23. This would involve analysis of data on thousands of bones, most of which are unfortunately simply shards.

24. Donald Harper notes the importance of "bug" imagery in illness categories and in the exorcistic performance of the Pace of Yu; *Early Chinese Medical Literature*, 74–75. See also Donald Harper and Marc Kalinowski, eds., *Books of Fate and Popular Culture in Early China: The Daybook Manuscripts of the Warring States, Qin, and Han* (Leiden: Brill, 2017), 129–33. "Bugs" and wind were both feared; Unschuld, *Huang di nei jing su wen*, 180–89. See also Sivin, "State, Cosmos, and Body"; Harper, "The Conception of Illness in Early Chinese Medicine, as Documented in Newly Discovered 3rd and 2nd Century B.C. Manuscripts (Part I)," *Sudhoffs Archiv* 74, no. 2 (1990): 210–35, and "Demonography."

25. See note 14 in this chapter.

26. Hu Houxuan, *Jiaguxue*, 322–24. The graph is from *Heji* 3273 recto.

27. David Keightley, *Sources of Shang History: The Oracle-Bone Inscriptions of Bronze Age China* (Berkeley: University of California Press, 1978), 104n44. Michael Puett describes ancestral spirits like other spirits as "controlling aspects of the natural world" and often arbitrary in their choice to harm or protect, see *The Ambivalence of Creation: Debates concerning Innovation and Artifice in Early China* (Stanford, CA: Stanford University Press, 2001), 25–27.

28. See discussion in Constance A. Cook and Xinhui Luo, *Birth in Ancient China: A Study of Metaphor and Cultural Identity in Pre-Imperial China* (Albany: State University of New York Press, 2017), 95–96.

29. Harper, *Early Chinese Medical Literature*, 161, 169.

30. For an excellent introduction to the site in English, see Adam Smith, "Writing at Anyang: The Role of the Divination Record in the Emergence of Chinese Literacy," PhD diss., UCLA, 2008.

31. Adam Schwartz has translated all the HD plastrons in "Huayuanzhuang East I: A Study and Annotated Translation of the Oracle Bone Inscriptions," PhD diss., University of Chicago, 2013. My translations are somewhat different in places than those of Schwartz.

32. Adam Smith, "Writing at Anyang," chap. 3. There were several Zi, but it is clear that Wu Ding was still living and that Zi was a blood relation; see Chang Yaohua 常耀華, *Yinxu jiagu feiwang buci yanjiu* 殷墟甲骨非王卜辭研究 (Beijing: Xianzhuang, 2006), 268–86.

33. This is also the assertion of Yao Xuan 姚萱, *Yinxu Huayuanzhuang dongdi jiagu buci de chubu yanjiu* 殷墟花園莊東地甲骨卜辭的初步研究 (Beijing: Xianzhuang, 2006), 24–39.

34. Line 3: "On a *jia* day div., Zi may go hunting: (the oracle) says: 'There will be a curse that is not foreseen'" (甲卜子其往田曰有祟非虞). The meaning of the word *yu* 虞, written 𓏍 (*[ŋ]ʷ(r)a, graph composed of a kneeling person with a large eye and "wood"—stalks?—semantics), which I translated as "foresee," is not clear. Some understand it as a loan for *you* 憂 (*ʔ(r)u), a common term in later divination texts to indicate a lingering concern over supernatural harm. The graph emphasizes the image of an "eye" above a "female" with "wood" elements added. As a noun, the word later refers to a woodsman or warden.

35. "On *ji* day div., have the many servitors direct an exorcism to Ancestress Geng with regard to (Zi's) travel" (己卜惠多臣禦往于妣庚). For line 14, Schwartz ("Huayuanzhuang," 384) reads the unusual graphic form for *ji* (discussed later) with the hand holding an implement as *yi* 疫 "fatigued" (in later texts, *yi* is a contagious illness). But since there are no other examples, this is unlikely. For somewhat similar variants of *ji*, see Yao Xiaosui 姚孝遂, ed., *Yinxu jiagu keci leizuan* 殷墟甲骨刻辭類纂, 3 vols. (Beijing: Zhonghua, 1989), vol. 3, 1184–85.

36. Harper, "Demonography," 471–75. I am not proposing a phonetic link between the ancient graph and the later word *jie* (*kˁi[t]).

37. Schwartz, "Huayuanzhuang," 201.

38. Schwartz prefers to read the graph as "cold" (*han* 寒), but given the many variants of *ji* (some with wood signs) and spotty evidence for *han*, I stick with the more common *ji*. See Schwartz, "Huayuanzhuang," 203.

39. Allan, *Shape of the Turtle*, 19–56; David Keightley, *The Ancestral Landscape: Time, Space, and Community in Late Shang China (ca. 1200–1045 B.C.)* (Berkeley: Institute of East Asian Studies, 2000), 37–53; Adam D. Smith, "The Chinese Sexagenary Cycle and the Ritual Foundations of the Calendar," in *Calendars and Years II: Astronomy and Time in the Ancient and Medieval World*, ed. John M. Steele (Oxford: Oxbow Books, 2011), 1–37.

40. For the determination that *qiang* indicates a class of subhuman (that was captured, enslaved, and sacrificed like an animal), see Campbell, *Violence, Kinship and the Early Chinese State: The Shang and Their World* (Cambridge: Cambridge University Press, 2018), 206–08.

41. Schwartz interprets the jade graph as *shu* 琡 "jadesmith"; see Schwartz, "Huayuanzhuang," 448.

42. Some read this last graph as "shoulder" 肩. On the debate, see Takashima, *Studies*, vol. 2, 143–45, 363, 469.

43. Guo Moruo 郭沫若, chief ed., and Hu Houxuan, ed., *Jiaguwen heji* 甲骨文合集, 13 vols. (Beijing: Zhonghua, 1978–1982).

44. See Takashima, *Studies*, vol. 1, 548–55.

45. For the full debate on this graph, see Takashima, *Studies*, vol. 2, 363n3, and Qiu Xigui, *Qiu Xigui xueshu wenji*, vol. 1, 473–84.

46. Takashima reads *ying* as *chong* 寵 "to be favored." See *Studies*, vol. 2, 107n12, for bones, vol. 2, 255–56n9.

47. Examples include HD 3, 44, 241, 147, 286, 458, 467, and *Heji* 22049. There may be other abbreviated *Heji* examples, but the inscriptions are fragmented.

48. See Yao Xiaosui, *Leizuan*, vol. 3, 1232–34.

49. For different interpretations of the HD graph, see Li Aimin 李愛民, "Jiagu wenzi kaoshi huizuan (2000–2010)" 甲骨文字考釋匯纂 (2000–2010), MA thesis, Jilin University, 2015, 571–81. For opinions regarding graphs with knotted cords open with dangling strings at both ends, some with hands, see 582–89.

50. Yao Xiaosui, *Leizuan*, vol. 1, 376.

51. For two examples reading it as *xuan*, see Yao Xiaosui, *Leizuan*, vol. 3, 1222. In one example, it is likely a color word, describing a bovine (*niu*). As a color word, I suspect it was an abbreviation for *you* 幽 (*ʔriw), the color of a bovine; see Yao Xiaosui, *Leizuan*, vol. 3, 1228. Note also the appearance of two of the knotted signs together read commonly as *zi* 兹 (*[ts]ə) for "this" or "here." The signs were clearly multivalent in terms of the words they could represent.

52. See Li Aimin, "Jiagu wenzi," 582, citing Dang Xiangkui's 黨相魁 (2000) opinion that the graph was an early form of "dangle" *xian* 縣 depicting a bronze weight dangling from a cord (a level used in construction). How it relates to the turtle crack is unknown. I know of no study that compares every example of this phrase with nearby cracks to see if the crack is left uncarved in connection to other cracks on the same or related bones. This would involve personal examination of each bone example. The idea that the spirit of the bone might reside in certain places of the bone and should be protected is enticing in light of the late Han and medieval practice of avoiding certain acupuncture points on days when the soul occupied that section of the body. See Despeux, "Âmes et animation du corps."

53. Ten examples are found in *Heji*. Note that a version of the graph with the full figure-eight version of 午 without the "mouth, cavity" or possibly "drill" element but with two grain 禾 elements is transcribed as Qin 秦 (*dzin). See Yao Xiaosui, *Leizuan*, vol. 1, 376.

54. Yao Xiaosui reads it as 午 over 口. It was clearly a verb since it could follow negatives *bu* and *wu*. See Yao Xiaosui, *Leizuan*, vol. 3, 1230–31.

55. *Heji* 15396 (recto). See Takashima, *Studies*, vol. 1, 716–17; vol. 2, 43.

56. Yao Xiaosui, *Leizuan*, vol. 2, 709. In late Warring States and Qin hemerology manuscripts, there are diagrams determining which days recently deceased ghosts would appear in particular places; see Harper and Kalinowski, *Books of Fate and Popular Culture*, 216–20.

57. In the same inscription, animals are "carved" 舌 (刮) in sacrifice. See Schwartz, "Huayuanzhuang," 501–02.

58. See Fan Yuzhou's criticism of the identification of graphs for parts of the body or illness, "'Yin ren jibing bukao' bianzheng," 99.

59. Yao Xiaosui, *Leizuan*, vol. 3, 1230–31. For the Warring States method of *xunmin* 訓黽, see Cook, *Death in Ancient China*, 101.

60. See *Heji* 809 (recto), 30853, and *Huai* 475 where it seems a turtle might be meant. The inscriptions refer to an "auspicious" spider, one that could heal, and something that could be imported (the import of turtles was noted routinely in OBI). See Yao Xiaosui, *Leizuan*, vol. 2, 693.

61. *Heji* 8996 (recto), 6480, 27653.

62. *Heji* 13751 (lower front right) and 13752 (upper front center).

63. Some read them as versions of the same word, which they interpret as *cuo* 瑳 (lustrous) or *xuan* 玄 (dark). Note HD 357 with 白圭 (white jade tablet) and HD 480 with 斋圭 (patterned jade tablet with nine dangling strings). A pattern could be achieved through incision or woven threads.

64. Note the similar sentence in *Heji* 32721: "On a *dingmao* day (day 4, S4 B4) test the proposal that the king may present a jade with strings" 丁卯貞王其再 珏絠. Yao Xiaosui reads the graph 絠 as *lian* 聯 (*Leizuan*, vol. 1, 236).

65. Zhongguo shehui kexueyuan kaogu yanjiusuo 中國社會科學院考古研究所, ed., *Xiaotun nandi jiagu* 小屯南地甲骨, 2 vols. (Beijing: Zhonghua, 1980–1983), no. 880.

66. See Keightley, *Working for His Majesty*, 299.

67. Liu Xinmin 李新民, "'Gong' zi ziyuan xinkao" "工"字字源新考, *Zhongguo wenzi yanjiu* 中國文字研究 2 (2007): 137–39.

68. See *Heji* 2795 (recto). Cf. *Heji* 2796, 13962, 14065 (recto); Li Xueqin 李學勤, Qi Wenxin 齊文心, and Sarah Allan 艾蘭, eds., *Yingguo suocang jiagu ji* 英國所藏甲骨集 (Beijing: Zhonghua, 1985), no. 809 (recto).

69. Keightley, *Working for His Majesty*, 300; Allan, *Shape of the Turtle*, 77–111.

70. Keightley, *Working for His Majesty*, 301–2.

71. Many examples of *gongshi* are found in the bronze inscription corpus. The title *dagong yin* is rare. See Zhongguo shehui kexueyuan kaogu yanjiusuo 中國社會科學院考古研究所, ed., *Yin-Zhou jinwen jicheng* 殷周金文集成, rev. ed., 8 vols. (Beijing: Zhonghua, 2007), no. 11670.2.

72. Yao Xiaosui, *Leizuan*, vol. 1, 376–80.

73. See Yao Xiaosui, *Leizuan*, vol. 1, 378. For the graph composed of a single hand holding up an implement, see vol. 1, 360–61.

74. See Sarah Allan, "'When Red Pigeons Gathered on Tang's House': A Warring States Period Tale of Shamanic Possession and Building Construction Set at the Turn of the Xia and Shang Dynasties," *Journal of the Royal Asiatic Society* 25, no. 3 (2015): 419–38.

75. Yao Xiaosui, *Leizuan*, vol. 1, 353–54.

76. Yao Xiaosui, *Leizuan*, vol. 3, 1232–33.

77. See the sources in note 17 in this chapter.

78. See Harper, "Demonography," 480–86.

79. *Rishu jiazhong* 日書甲種, in *Shuihudi Qin mu zhujian* 睡虎地秦墓竹簡, ed. Shuihudi Qin mu zhujian zhengli xiaozu 睡虎地秦墓竹簡整理小組 (Beijing: Wenwu, 1990), 212 (slips 24–26, verso, register 1).

80. Keightley, *Sources*, 10–15, 152–53; Roderick Campbell, "Animal, Human, God: Pathways of Shang Animality and Divinity," in *Animals and Inequality in the Ancient World*, ed. Benjamin S. Arbuckle and Sue Ann McCarty (Boulder: University Press of Colorado, 2014), 267.

7

Transcription Notes on the "Mind as Ruler" Section in the Tsinghua Bamboo Manuscript *The Heart Is Called the Center* (*Xin shi wei zhong* 心是謂中)

CHEN WEI

TRANSLATED BY CONSTANCE A. COOK

Filling Some Gaps in Explanations of *The Heart Is Called the Center*

The Tsinghua manuscript *The Heart Is Called the Center* (*Xin shi wei zhong* 心是謂中) is not long, but it is extremely important. It essentially connects the relationship between the "body" and "heart" (*shen xin* 身心) to the relationship between "heaven" and "man" (*tian ren* 天人), the fundamental philosophy behind Chinese political ideology. The first section (slips 1–3, up to *yi jun minren* 以君民人) is tentatively called "Mind as Ruler." This essay fills in a few gaps left by the editors' ample annotations. First, I transcribe the text into modern characters and then provide a commentary. Whenever I mention "editors," "the original transcription," and the "original commentary," it refers to the Tsinghua team and their treatment of *The Heart Is Called the Center* in the initial publication of the manuscript.[1] Square brackets will be used to mark off the slips and the numbered comments that follow.

Slips 1–3 of the Translated and Transcribed Text

[Slip 1:] Heart is the center. Located in the center of the body it is the ruler of it [1] and the eyes, ears, mouth, and X (limbs) are the four assistants [2]. The heart is therefore called the center [3]. The goodness enacted by the heart's (intentions) submits to the commands just like a shadow [4]. The size of (the response to the commands) emitted (as intended) by the heart [5] follows the commands like an echo [6]. [Slip 2:] If the heart wants to see something, then the eyes will visualize it; if the heart wants to hear something, the ears will listen to it; if the heart wants to talk about something [7], then the mouth will say it; if the heart wishes to reach somewhere [8], then the limbs will rise up. When the heart is quiet, nothing will be reached [9] and the entire body [Slip 3:] and four assistants will be completely still. It is up to the ruler to reflect upon this in order to rule the people.

【Slip 1】 心, 中. 尻 (處) 身之中以君之,【1】目, 耳, 口, ▇ 四者爲相.【2】心是胃 (謂) 中.【3】心所爲㳷 (美) 亞 (惡), 復何 (號) 若倞 (景).【4】心所出少 (小) 大,【5】因名 (命) 若颯 (響).【6】【Slip 2】心欲見之, 目古 (故) 視之; 心欲聞之, 耳古 (故) 聖 (聽) 之; 心欲道之,【7】口古 (故) 言之; 心欲甬 (通) 之,【8】▇古 (故) 與 (舉) 之. 心情 (靜) 母 (毋) 又 (有) 所至 (致),【9】百體,【Slip 3】四相莫不▇淩.【10】爲君者其監於此,【11】以君民人.

Commentary

[1] The punctuation here is that of the Tsinghua editors, but I am afraid it is not absolute. There are other possibilities. For example, the line could be read as "the heart, from the central place of the body, rules it" (心, 中尻 (處) 身之中以君之) instead of with a stop after *zhong* 中 (center).

[2] According to the Tsinghua editors, the graph ▇ (X) after the word *kou* 口 (mouth) may be transcribed as 纏 and read as *zhi* 肢 (limbs). They explain that it was composed of the element 糸 and the phonetic *shi* 適 and probably read as *zhi*. The graph read *shi* is classified in the *duan* initial and *xi* final group (*duan mu xi bu* 端母錫部), whereas the graph read *zhi*

is classified in the *zhang* initial and *zhi* final group (*zhang mu zhi bu* 章母支部). Both finals *zhi* and *xi* are cases of *yinru duizhuan* 陰入對轉 (turning of a *yin* or *ru* final into a *yang* final) and both initials *duan* 端 and *zhang* 章 ([*-ig] and [*-ik] respectively) are exact alliterative correspondents (*zhun shuangsheng* 準雙聲): [*t-] and [*tj-] respectively. The "four" refer to the eyes, ears, mouth, and limbs. *Mengzi* 孟子 7B.24 has: "The way the mouth is disposed toward tastes, the eye toward colors, the ear toward sounds, the nose toward smells, and the four limbs toward ease is human nature" (口之於味也，目之於色也，耳之於聲也，鼻之於臭也，四肢之於安佚也，性也).[2] Anciently, the "four assistants" were known as the "four limbs." Slip 45 of the Guodian 郭店 manuscript *Wuxing* 五行 has: "Ears, eyes, nose, mouth, hands, and feet, the six of them" (耳目鼻口手足六者).[3] Now this Tsinghua text takes the heart as ruler with the eyes, ears, mouth, and limbs as the *xiang* 相 (assistants). The *Guoyu* 國語 has the phrase "for the eyes to assist the heart" (以相心目), to which Wei Zhao 韋昭 (204–273 CE) commented: "*xiang* is to help" (相助也).[4]

Shan Yuchen 單育辰 (also known by the alias "ee" online) takes graph X as *can* 簪, read as *zu* 足 (foot), as he believes the orthography is not from the graph *di* 帝, and, therefore, is not from the *shi* 適 phonetic.[5] A similar graph is found in the Guodian and Shanghai Museum versions of *Ziyi* 緇衣, where it is used as *cong* 從 in the sense of "leisurely" (*congrong* 從容). He notes that *cong* was classified as *qing niu dong bu* 清紐東部 (a *tsʰeŋ class initial and a *tʕoŋ class final) and *zu* (foot) was *jing niu wu bu* 精紐屋部 (a *tseŋ class initial and a *qʕok class final), so they were close in sound.[6] Slip 2 goes on to say, "If the heart wishes to make use of something, the feet raise up" (心欲甬 (用) 之足故與 (舉) 之), which accords with this meaning.[7]

Wang Ning 王寧 agrees with Shan Yuchen's analysis and suggests that X was possibly a variant of *zong* 縱, read in bamboo manuscripts as *zhong* 踵 (heel), synecdoche for the foot.[8]

Strictly speaking, only the *cong* on slip 16 of the Guodian *Ziyi* matches up with the right half of the graph, as it appears twice in the Tsinghua text referring to the human body and organs. The graph *zhong* (heel) is classified as *zhang niu dong bu* 章紐東部 (a *taŋ class initial and a *tʕoŋ class final),[9] close to that of *cong* (leisurely). "Heel" can be explained as "foot." Examples of "heel" representing the "foot" include: (1) "feel with the two heels down" (以二垂踵感) in *Zhuangzi* 莊子 "Tiandi" 天地, as explained by Cheng Xuanying 成玄英; (2) "stretch the neck and lift the heel" (延頸舉踵) in the "Yu Ba-Shu xi" 喻巴蜀檄 by Sima Xiangru 司馬相如 (ca. 179–118 BCE), as explained by Li Zhouhan 李周翰 in the *Wenxuan* 文選; and (3) "pheasants rein in and turn on their heels" (雉胅肩而旋踵) in "She zhi fu" 射雉賦 by Shen Yue 潘岳 (247–300 CE), as explained by Liu Lang 劉良, also in the *Wenxuan*.[10] Thus, there is a good possibility that ▨ is *zhong* (heel).

The word *xiang* (assistant) is in opposition to the ruler (the heart) and the people (the body). It refers to the officials who help the ruler govern the people. The *Xunzi* 荀子 states:

> The prime minister should evaluate the men who lead the Hundred Bureaus, promulgate the essential principles for the adjudication of the Hundred Tasks, thereby to elaborate the official responsibilities to be assigned to each member of the court from ministers down to the most minor officials, to measure their achievement and effort, to assess their appropriate commendation and reward so that at the end of the year he can memorialize their accomplishments and bring them to the attention of the lord.[11]

> 相者, 論列百官之長, 要百事之聽, 以飾朝廷臣下百事之分, 度其功勞, 論其慶賞, 歲終奉其成功以效于君.

[3] Wang Li 王力 (1900–1986) explained that in archaic Chinese, the term *shi wei* 是謂 (is called) is formulaic (凝固形式).[12] The *Han shu* biography of Jia Yi contains the lines "Ritual propriety, righteousness, integrity, and having a sense of shame: *these are called* the four weft threads" (禮義廉恥, 是謂四維).[13] The *Ma Shi wentong* 馬氏文通 by Ma Jianzhong 馬建忠 (1845–1900) points out that "*shi* refers generally to the four [types of] nouns" (是字總指四名).[14] Li Maoxi 黎錦熙 (1890–1978) notes that *ci* 此 and *shi* 是 are both reflexive pronouns that are then followed by more details of the general objects to which they refer.[15]

Wang Guanjun 王冠軍 explains that the *shi* in *shi wei* is a pronoun like *ci* that refers back to the subject, purposely highlighting it. This is a common grammatical function in classical Chinese. Typically, the subject is placed outside of the sentence, setting up the topic, marked with *shi* to establish the basic structure.[16]

The Tsinghua manuscript phrase *xin shi wei zhong* 心是謂中 is at odds with examples found in pre-Qin literature and with scholarly understandings. As a general expression, the use of "heart" in such a way is unlikely. On the other hand, perhaps *shi* was used as a conjunction. The *Gushu xuzi jishi* 古書虛字集釋 notes that "*shi* is like *gu* 故, a word that connects topics" (是

猶故也, 申事之詞也).[17] In the *Xunzi* there is the line in which *shi* is used as *gu*: "Shun would not press his people to their limits, and Zaofu would not wear out his horses. *For this reason*, Shun never lost control over the people, and Zaofu never had his horses bolt out of control" (舜不窮其民, 造父不窮其馬. 是舜無失民, 造父無失馬也).[18] The word *shi* translated as "for this reason" can be understood as *shiyi* 是以. We find similar statements about Shun in the *Xinxu* 新序 and *Han shi waizhuan* 韓詩外傳 but with *shiyi* in place of *gu*, as in "*thus* Shun never lost the people" (是以舜無失民).[19] The *Jingci yanshi* 經詞衍釋 by Wu Changying 吳昌瑩 (Qing) notes that *shi* can stand for *shiyi*, meaning *shigu* 是故.[20] A speech by Guanzi 管子 in the *Zuo zhuan* has the phrases 寡人是徵 and 寡人是問, which the corresponding section of the "Qi Taigong shijia" 齊太公世家 chapter of the *Shiji* writes as 是以來責 and 是以來問.[21] The *Liji* uses *shigu* in a statement (是故仁人之事親也如事天) repeated only with a *shi* in the *Da Dai liji* (and no *gu*).[22] If the Tsinghua manuscript's use of *shi* is along these lines, then the editors' punctuation is possible.

[4] The Tsinghua commentary to *fu* 復 notes that the *Lunyu* "Yong ye" 雍也 chapter has "if someone comes back to me" (如有復我者), which the Huang Kan 皇侃 (Liang) commentary explains as "again" (又也).[23] I suspect the Tsinghua graph should be read *fu* 服 (serve). The *fu* meaning "again" is classified as *bing niu jue bu* 並紐覺部 (a *[b]ˤeŋʔ class initial and a *kˤruk class final) and the *fu* meaning "serve" as *bing niu zhi bu* 並紐職部 (a *[b]ˤeŋʔ class initial and a *tək class final), making them close in sound.[24] In the *Shangshu* "Shao gao" 召誥 there is the line "come to serve in the middle of the land" (自服于土中), in which *fu* (serve) is written in a later citation by Li Shan 李善 (630–689) as *fu* (again) (see *Wenxuan* "Xizheng fu" 西征賦).[25] Similarly, Zheng Xuan 鄭玄 (127–200) notes that one *fu* can be read for another ("the *fu* 復 [meaning 'again'] is sometimes given as *fu* 服 [meaning 'serve']" 或爲服) in the *Liji* line "when the ruler comes to mourn, then put the coffin clothes back on" (君吊則復殯服).[26] The word *fu* (serve) has the meaning of to practice or implement something. The Kong 孔 commentary explains the use of *fu* in the *Shangshu* 尚書 "Yue ming zhong" 說命中 line "Excellent! Yue, your words will be put into practice" (旨哉說乃言惟服) as putting something into practice through the act of praise ("He extols that which [Yue] said, permitting it all to be put into action" 美其所言皆可服行).[27] Wang Su 王肅 (ca. 195–256) explained this *fu* as *xing* 行 (to implement) similarly in the *Kongzi jiayu* 孔子家語 "Ru guan" 入官 line "The gentleman cultivates himself and returns to the Way, observing his inner words, he implements them" (君子修身反道察裏言而服之).[28]

I suspect that the word *he* 何 (what) should be read *hao* 號 (call) as they sounded similar in Old Chinese: *he* was *xia niu ge bu* 匣紐歌部 (a *[g]ˤr[a]p class initial and a *[k]ˤaj class final) and *hao* was *xia niu xiao bu* 匣紐宵部 (a *[g]ˤr[a]p class initial and a *[s]ew class final).²⁹ Some scholars suggest that the element *kao* 丂 was the phonetic.³⁰ The word *hao* can mean "to command." The Kong commentary to the *Shangshu* "Jiong ming" 冏命 line "issuing commands and effecting orders, there was no one who was not good. The people were thus at peace and the myriad nations all grateful" (發號施令罔有不臧；下民祇若萬邦咸休) explains it as "issuing commands and effecting orders, no one was not good. The people respectfully followed his mandates and the myriad states all praised his changes" (發號施令無有不善；下民敬順其命萬國皆美其化).³¹ Zheng Xuan explains the use of *hao* in the *Liji* "Yue ji" 樂記 line "called to order with bells" (鏗以立號) as "*hao* is to order, as in what was used to alert the masses" (號號令所以警衆也).³²

The Tsinghua editors explain *ruo* 若 as *yi* 以, citing the *Zhouyi* quote preserved in the *Liji* "Jingjie" 經解: "Even a slight error can wind up having vast consequences" (差若毫厘謬以千里). Alternatively, I suggest that the *ruo* that appears in this line and in the next line of the Tsinghua text should be read as *ru* 如 (to be like), and that the two lines are parallel.

The Tsinghua editors read *jing/liang* 倞 as *liang* 諒, in the sense given by the *Shuowen* of "to be trustworthy" (信也). They provide two examples of its use as "sincere" or "trustworthy" from the *Liji*. The "Yue ji" 樂記 has: "The gentleman said: '(The practice of) ritual music cannot even for one instant separate from one's person. If one regulates the heart through the perfection of music, then a heart easy and forthright, tender and faithful is naturally produced. Once the heart is easy and forthright, tender and faithful, then it is joyful. With joy comes calm; with calm comes long endurance; with long endurance comes celestial-abilities; and with celestial-abilities comes divinity (君子曰：禮樂不可斯須去身；致樂以治心則易直子諒之心，油然生矣，易直子諒之心生則樂，樂則安，安則久，久則天，天則神).³³ In the chapter "Ziyi" 緇衣 it has: "Thus the gentleman says little, only enacting [his intentions] in order to complete his trustworthy character, so people will not exaggerate their praise or suppress their disgust" (故君子寡言而行以成其信則民不得大其美而小其惡).³⁴

I note that the phonetic *jing* 京 found in *jing* 景 by the editors is also found in *ying* 影 (shadow). This reading is likely as the following text has the word *xiang* 響 (echo) in the line "follow the commands like an echo" (因名若響). The words for "shadow" (written as either *ying* 影 or *jing* 景) and "echo" were often paired in ancient texts. For instance, in the *Xunzi*

荀子 "Chen dao" 臣道 there are the lines: "They are able to honor their lord above and love the people below. Their governmental ordinances and edicts and their instructions for transformation are imitated by the people just as a shadow follows its object. They respond immediately whenever they encounter changed circumstances with the quickness and speed of an echo" (上則能尊君下則能愛民; 政令教化刑下如影; 應卒遇變齊給如響).³⁵ In the *Guanzi* 管子 "Mingfa jie" 明法解, it states: "The obedience of those below to their superiors would be like the response of an echoing sound; the way of ministers behaving toward their rulers would be like shadow following form" (下之從上也如響之應聲; 臣之法主也如景之隨形).³⁶ The *Huainanzi* 淮南子 "Zhushu" 主術 likewise states: "The world follows them as an echo responds to a sound or a shadow imitates the form (that casts it)" (天下從之如響之應聲影之像形).³⁷

[5] The editors explain the word *chu* 出 (go out) as *xing* 行 (to go, enact), as in the line of the *Da Dai liji* 大戴禮記 "Zhu yan" 主言: "Will I not die if my ruler's words are not put into action?" (吾主言其不出而死乎).³⁸ I suggest that *chu* is parallel to the word *wei* 爲 in the previous line, and that it refers to the commands that come from the heart as ruler.

[6] The word *yin* 因 can mean "pursue, comply, compliable." Wei Zhao explains *yin* as *jiu* 就 in the *Guoyu* line: "Their people suffer repeated acts of greed and cannot be relied on (其民沓貪而忍不可因也).³⁹ Yin Zhizhang 尹知章 (660–718 CE) explains that *yin* could mean "to abandon the self and follow things, thus it is called *yin*—to comply" (舍己而隨物故曰因), as in the *Guanzi* line: "Those who comply with it are the ones who abandon the self and take things as their model" (因也者舍己而以物爲法者也).⁴⁰

The editors took the word *ming* 名 to refer to the actual name of something based on the *Shiming* 釋名 gloss: "*ming* 'name' is *ming* 'clarify' 明. Naming reality makes differences clear" (名明也; 名實使分明也).⁴¹ They cite usages in the *Mengzi* 6B.6 line: "Chunyu Kun said: 'The first to give names to reality was man. Later the naming of reality continued of its own accord'" (淳于髡曰: "先名實者爲人也; 後名實者自爲也"); and in the *Guanzi* "Jiu shou" 九守 statement: "Revise names while observing reality and examine reality while fixing names, so that names and reality produce each other, turning to mutually produce emotions. When names and reality are appropriate, then there will be proper governance; when they are not appropriate, then there will be chaos" (修名而督實按實而定名, 名實相生反相爲情, 名實當則治不當則亂).⁴²

I suggest that *ming*, in this instance, has the verbal meaning of "to command" instead. The Wei Zhao commentary to the *Guoyu* "Zhouyu xia"

周語下 line "One speaks by believing in names and clarifies by means of the movement of time; name in order to effect government and movement in order to reproduce" (言以信名明以時動; 名以成政動以殖生) claims that "*ming* is to command. . . . Commands are made to effect government (名號令也. . . . 號令所以成政也).⁴³ In another example, *ming* (name) was substituted for *ming* 命 (to command) in the "Gong Zhongpeng wei Han guo zhang" 公仲倗謂韓國章 section of the Mawangdui text *Zhanguo zonghengjia shu* 戰國縱橫家書: "Commanding the war chariots to fill the roads" (名 (命) 戰車滿道路).⁴⁴ The same phrase is originally found with the graph *ming* 命 in the *Shiji*.⁴⁵ We find a similar substitution in reverse between the transmitted and Mawangdui B manuscript versions of the transmitted *Laozi* phrase "If we don't hear a name while listening, we call it inaudible" (聽之不聞名曰希).⁴⁶

The editors suggest that the graph 䖵 is *xiang*, written 蚼 or 蠁 and read as *xiang* 響, glossed by the *Shuowen* as "sound" (*sheng* 聲).⁴⁷ The commentary by Du Yu 杜預 (222–284 CE) on the *Zuo zhuan* Zhao 12.11 line "Presently his words with the king seem like noise" (今與王言如響) explains that "the word *xiang* 響 was also written *xiang* 綱; they sounded the same" (響本又作綱音同).⁴⁸ The Kong commentary explains that the *Yijing* "Xici shang" 繫辭上 line "Thus if the gentleman wants to do something or go somewhere, he will ask about it and through words receive a command that is like a sound [of response]" (是以君子將有爲也將有行也問焉而以言其受命也如響) in fact "refers to how the stalks receive a person's command then report on the auspiciousness to the person like an echo" (謂蓍受人命報人吉凶如響之應聲也).⁴⁹ In the Tsinghua text, the words *xiang* 相, *liang* 諒, and *xiang* 響 all rhyme.

I note that the Du commentary to the *Zuo zhuan* passage mentioned earlier actually means that the line is making fun of obeying the king's intention, being like an echo. From the *Yijing* and *Zuo zhuan* usages and commentaries, we can understand that the basic meaning of *xiang* is "to echo," and that thus in the Tsinghua text, it is reflective of the word "shadow" (*jing* as *ying*) discussed earlier.

[7] The editors suggest that *dao* 道 (way) refers to a person's experience and understanding of reality, such as in the *Xunzi* "Jiebi" 解蔽 line, "What do men use to know the Way? I say that it is the mind. How does the mind know? I say by its emptiness, unity, and stillness" (人何以知道? 曰心. 心何以知? 曰虛壹而靜).⁵⁰

I believe that *dao* is parallel to *shi* 視 (visualize), *ting* 聽 (hear), and *ju* 舉 (raise up) and is connected to *yan* 言 (words), but in the ordinary sense of "to say." In his collection of Han dynasty commentaries on the *Book of Songs*, Wang Xianqian 王先謙 (1842–1918) cites a Lu 魯 explanation that "*dao* is to speak or tell" (*dao shuo ye* 道說也) for the *Shijing* 詩經 "Qiang you ci" 墻有茨 line, "What is said within the fence cannot be disclosed" (中冓之言不可道也).[51] Tang period commentator Yang Liang 楊倞 argues that "*dao* means speech" (*dao yan ye* 道言也) in his exegesis of the *Xunzi* "Tian lun" 天論 phrase "superior men speak only of their [i.e., Heaven and Earth's] constants" (君子道其常).[52]

[8] The Tsinghua editorial team reads *yong* 甬 as *yong* 用, but as Shui Zhigan 水之甘 has noted, this interpretation is not appropriate if we take the graph in the subsequent line as *zu* 足 (foot) or *zhong* 踵 (heel). Rather, Shui believes the *yong* 甬 should be read as *tong* 通, which the *Shuowen* explains as "to reach" (*da* 達). This fits with Wei Zhao's explanation of *tong* as "to reach or arrive" (*zhi* 至) in the *Guoyu* "Jin yu, er" 晉語二 phrase: "Since the way is far, it is hard to reach" (*dao yuan nan tong* 道遠難通).[53] I am in complete agreement on this point.

[9] For the Tsinghua text phrase *xin qing wu you suo zhi* (心情母(毋)又(有)所至), the editors explain *qing* 情 (emotion) as *yu* 欲 (desires). In the *Xunzi* "Zheng ming" 正名 chapter, it states that "emotions are the substance of nature" (情者性之質也), while the "Ru xiao" 儒效 chapter claims "as teachers and models are grasped by way of the emotions" (而師法者所得乎情), to which Yang Liang comments that *qing* is "happiness, anger, love, and hate, all responses to outside phenomena" (情謂喜怒愛惡, 外物所感者也).[54] Slips 35–36 of the Shanghai Museum bamboo-slip manuscript *Xingqing lun* 性情論 has the line "Mourning and joy represent the greatest apogee of emotion" (用情之至【者, 哀】樂爲甚).[55]

Considering the larger meaning of the Tsinghua text, we should read "heart" together with the line that follows, taking *qing* (emotion) as *jing* 靜 (quiet) instead. Earlier the text had four sentences concerning how the physical senses respond to the plans of the heart, for instance: "If the heart wants to see something, then the eyes will visualize it." The sentence with "If the heart is quiet" (*xin jing* 心靜) begins the obverse circumstance, that is the state of having no desires when the heart is quiet.

Slips 4–5 of the Tsinghua *Guan Zhong* 管仲 manuscript have: "If the heart is not quiet the hands will be agitated. If the heart is without plans, then the eyes and ears can relax (心不情(靜)則手燥心亡(無)圖則目耳豫). According to the editors, *yu* 豫 can be read as *ye* 野, as the Kong commentary to the *Liji* "Tangong" 檀弓 phrase "So crude!" (若是野哉) explains and means "not ritually appropriate" (*bu da li ye* 不達禮也).

They also note that *yu* and *ye* both contain the phonetic element *yu* 予.⁵⁶ In fact, *yu* 豫 itself can mean "lazy." Cai Shen's 蔡沈 (1167–1230) collected commentary explains *yu* as *dai* 怠 in the *Shangshu* "Hongfan" 洪範 line "An attribute of laziness is to be constantly warm" (曰豫恆燠若).⁵⁷ Xiang Zonglu's 向宗魯 (1895–1941) commentary cites a Mr. Guan 關氏 similarly for the *Shuoyuan* 說苑 line "The elderly lord is in front and ought not be passed; the minor lord is in back and ought not lag" (老君在前而不踰; 少君在後而不豫).⁵⁸ The Tsinghua *Guan Zhong* usage is thus along these lines.

[10] The lower half of the graph following the word *bu* 不 is not clear. The Tsinghua editorial team believes the component is *tian* 田. They argue that the character form consists of an abbreviation for *ma* 馬 (horse) on top with *tian* (field) on the bottom, writing a word that could mean "escape" (*yi* 逸). I suggest that the lower part is *nie* 囡 (net) instead, which the *Shuowen* explains as "To take in something and store it. From *kou* and *you*. Read as *nie*" (下取物縮藏之. 从囗从又. 讀若聶).⁵⁹ Slip 23 of the Shanghai Museum *Ziyi* manuscript writes *nie* as ▨ in the line "The friends that helped you, helped with perfect manners" (朋友卣 (攸) 聶 (攝), 聶 (攝) 以威義).⁶⁰ Allowing that my conjecture about *nie* is correct, then the Tsinghua graph can be explained as "a swift horse" (*nie* 騙) or "to quiet" (*nie* 攝), in the sense of "to settle down, pacify" (*anding* 安定). Yan Shigu 顏師古 (581–645) cites Meng Kang 孟康 (fl. 220–250) explaining *nie* as *an* 安 in the *Han shu* "Yan Zhu zhuan" 嚴助傳 line "the world was settled" (天下攝然).⁶¹ Li Shan 李善 cites the *Han shu yinyi* 漢書音義 to explain *nie* in the *Wenxuan* "Quanjin biao" 勸進表 line "one who resists an enlightened demeanor will not be skillful in pacifying" (抗明威以攝不類).⁶² *Nie* is *ni niu ye bu* 泥紐葉部 (a *C.nˤ[ə]* class initial and a *lap class final) and *zhe* 耴 (drooping) is *duan niu ye bu* 端紐葉部 (a *tˤor class initial and a *lap class final) [*t-ap]. They sounded similar and were loaned for each other. Wang Niansun 王念孫 (1744–1832), in the entry for *dan'er* 耽耳 (drooping ears) in *Dushu zazhi* 讀書雜志, records "Father Kua's ears drooped northward" (夸父耽耳在其北方) from the *Huainanzi*. To this, Gao You 高誘 (fl. 205–210 CE) explains that "the drooping ears refer to the ears hanging down to the shoulders. *Dan* can be read as *zhe*, as in pleated skirts, or as *nie*, as in using two hands to work the ears" (耽耳耳垂在肩上耽讀褶, 衣之褶, 或作攝以兩手攝耳). Wang notes however that the words *zhe* and *nie* had very different pronunciations than *dan*, meaning that *dan* could not have been read as either *zhe* or *nie*. The *dan* 耽 here was a later interpolation for *zhe* 耴. The *Shuowen* explains *zhe* 耴 as "ears drooping, a *xiangxing* (pictograph) of ears drooping downward. In the *Chunqiu zhuan* it has: 'The name *zhe* in

Qin Gongzi Zhe was given to him due to his drooping ears'" (耳垂也, 从耳下垂象形; 春秋傳曰: 秦公子耴, 耴者其耳下垂, 故以爲名). In the *Yupian* 玉篇, the word *zhe* is given the *fanqie* spelling of *zhu she qie* 豬涉切 (Old Chinese [*tr-ap]) and defined as drooping ears. Thus, the Gao commentary notes, "*Zhe'er* refers to ears that hang down to the shoulders" (耴耳耳垂在肩上). The *Guangyun* 廣韻 also notes that "*zhe'er* was the name of a state" (耴耳國名). In this case, *zhe* can be written as *nie* 聶. The *Shanhaijing* 山海經 "Haiwai bei jing" 海外北經 statement: "The state of Nie'er is east of Wuchang, the people there use their two hands to work their ears, they hang down and rest in the ocean's waters" (聶耳之國在無腸國東爲人兩手聶其耳縣居海水中).[63] This is why the Gao commentary gives as an example that people "used two hands to work the ears, resting in the ocean" (以兩手攝耳居海中) cited before. The reason the "Haiwai bei jing" wrote *nie* instead of *zhe* is because they sounded similar. The *Jiyun* 集韻 explains, "*Nie* 馹 is defined in the *Shuowen* as 'horse galloping' and also written as *nie* 驜" (馹說文馬步疾也或作驜).[64] In the Tsinghua text the *nie* 馹 could be read as *zhe* 軏. In the *Zhuangzi* "Da sheng" 達生, we find the usage *zhe'ran* in the sense of "unmoving":

> As an underling undertaking the construction of a bell-stand, I dare not ever squander my energy, so I fast in order to quiet my heart. After fasting for three days, I dare not harbor ideas of congratulation, award, rank, or payment; after fasting for five days, I dare not harbor ideas of criticism or praise of my skill or lack thereof; after fasting for seven days, I—unmoving (*zhe'ran*)—forget my body and its four limbs.
>
> 臣將爲鐻未嘗敢以耗氣也, 必齊以靜心. 齊三日而不敢懷慶賞爵祿, 齊五日不敢懷非譽巧拙, 齊七日輒然忘吾有四枝形體也.[65]

The *Jingdian shiwen* explains *zhe'ran* as "the image of not moving" (*budong mao* 不動貌), to which Cheng Xuanying 成玄英 (fl. 631 CE) adds "*zhe'ran* is the image of not daring to move" (輒然不敢動貌也).[66] The idea of a quieted heart and four limbs not moving fits nicely with the literary mood of the Tsinghua text as well.[67]

The editors suspect that the graph 洰 is a complex form of 沵, which is read as *chen* 湛 (沉) (deep, sink).[68] It is understood in the context of this manuscript to be *yichen* 逸沉, or "self-indulgent sinking into depravity." Now I note that *chen* was written *shen* 沈 in ancient texts, which can refer to stagnation, being stuck, or coming to a stop.⁶⁹ The *Guangya* 廣雅 ("Shigu, san" 釋詁三) defines *shen* as "to stop" (*zhi* 止).⁷⁰ Wei Zhao defines *shen* as "stagnant or stuck" (*zhi* 滯) in his commentary to the *Guoyu* line "in order to raise up those who are stuck and crouched over" (*yi yang shenfu* 以揚沈伏).⁷¹ This is close to the idea of being settled, as with the reading of *nie* 聶 as *nie* 攝 or *zhe* 輒.

[11] The word *jian* 監 means "to draw lessons from, to reference." Ancient texts also write *jian* 鑑 (mirror, reflect), for which the *Guangyun* gives the gloss "to warn or admonish, also written as *jian*" (誡也昭也亦作監).⁷² In the *Shangshu* "Shao gao" there is the line: "I cannot but admonish those of Xia and those of Yin" (我不可不監于有夏亦不可不監于有殷).⁷³

Notes

1. Li Xueqin 李學勤, ed., *Qinghua daxue cang Zhanguo zhujian* 清華大學藏戰國竹簡, vol. 8 (Beijing: Zhongxi, 2018), 14–15 (original-size photos), 87–90 (enlarged photos), 138–52 (transcription).

2. *Mengzi zhushu* 孟子注疏, in *Shisanjing zhushu* 十三經注疏, ed. Ruan Yuan 阮元 (1815; rpt. Beijing: Zhonghua, 1980), 2775 ("Jinxin xia" 盡心下). Translation after *Mencius: A Bilingual Edition*, trans. D. C. Lau, rev. ed. (Hong Kong: Chinese University Press, 2003), 319.

3. Jingmenshi bowuguan 荊門市博物館, ed., *Guodian Chu mu zhujian* 郭店楚墓竹簡 (Beijing: Wenwu, 1998), 34, 151.

4. Xu Yuangao 徐元誥, *Guoyu jijie* 國語集解, rev. ed. (Beijing: Zhonghua, 2002), 263 ("Jinyu, yi" 晉語一, no. 7).

5. Shan Yuchen 單育辰, *Chu di Zhanguo jianbo yu chuanshi wenxian duidu zhi yanjiu* 楚地戰國簡帛與傳世文獻對讀之研究 (Beijing: Zhonghua, 2014), 121–24.

6. For the transcription of traditional *fanqie* readings and Li Fang-Kuei reconstructions, the editors consulted with David P. Branner in January 2019. He places a hyphen between initial and final so as to avoid committing to the medials and tones of the full Li Fang-Kuei reconstruction. The editors also consulted the *Baxter-Sagart Old Chinese Reconstruction, Version 1.1 (20 September 2014)* by William H. Baxter (白一平) and Laurent Sagart (沙加爾), https://ocbaxtersagart.lsait.lsa.umich.edu/BaxterSagartOCbyMandarinMC2014-09-20.pdf.

7. See [Shan Yuchen], post no. 2 to "Qinghuajian ba *Xin shi wei zhong chu du*" 清華簡八《心是謂中》初讀, *Jianbo wang jianbo luntan* 簡帛網簡帛論壇, November 18, 2018, http://www.bsm.org.cn/forum/forum.php?mod=viewthread&tid=4373.

8. Wang Ning 王寧, post no. 9 to "Qinghua jian ba *Xin shi wei zhong chu du*," November 19, 2018, http://www.bsm.org.cn/forum/forum.php?mod=viewthread&tid=4373.

9. Tang Zuofan 唐作藩, *Shangguyin shouce* 上古音手冊, rev. ed. (Beijing: Zhonghua, 2013), 209.

10. For the Tang commentators to the Liang period *Wenxuan* by Xiao Tong 蕭統 (501–531), see *Liuchen zhu Wenxuan* 六臣注文選 (Beijing: Zhonghua, 1987), 820 (44.2a) and 180 (9.16b). The phrase *zhui zhong* 垂鍾 in *Zhuangzi* was written as *fou zhong* 缶鍾 in the unified edition (通行本); see Lu Deming 陸德明, *Jingdian shiwen* 經典釋文 (Beijing: Zhonghua, 1983), 379 ("Zhuangzi yinyi zhong" 莊子音義中, 27.13a).

11. *Xunzi jijie* 荀子集解, comp. Wang Xianqian 王先謙, 2nd ed. (Beijing: Zhonghua, 2013), 265 ("Wangba" 王霸). Translation after John Knoblock, *Xunzi: A Translation and Study of the Complete Works*, 3 vols. (Stanford, CA: Stanford University Press, 1998–1994), vol. 2, 166.

12. Wang Li 王力, *Hanyu shigao* 漢語史稿, rev. ed. (Beijing: Zhonghua, 1980), 357.

13. *Han shu* 漢書 (Beijing: Zhonghua, 1964), 48.2246 ("Jia Yi zhuan" 賈誼傳).

14. Ma Jianzhong 馬建忠, *Ma Shi wentong jiaozhu* 馬氏文通校注, comm. Zhang Xishen 章錫深 (Beijing: Zhonghua, 1954), 135.

15. Li Jinxi 黎錦熙, *Bijiao wenfa* 比較文法, rev. ed. (Beijing: Zhonghua, 1986), 179.

16. Wang Guanjun 王冠軍, "Gu Hanyu 'shi wei' jiegou bianzheng" 古漢語"是謂"結構辯證, *Xuzhou shifan xueyuan xuebao* 徐州師範學院學報 1984.1: 127–30.

17. Pei Xuehai 裴學海, *Gushu xuzi jishi* 古書虛字集釋 (Beijing: Zhonghua, 1984), 813.

18. *Xunzi jijie*, 645 ("Ai Gong" 哀公). Translation after Knoblock, *Xunzi*, vol. 3, 264 (emphasis added).

19. *Xinxu jiaoshi* 新序校釋, annot. Shi Guangying 石光瑛, 2nd ed. (Beijing: Zhonghua, 2009), 711 (5 "Zashi" 雜事, no. 12); *Han shi waizhuan jianshu* 韓詩外傳箋疏 (Chengdu: Bashu, 1996), 164 (2.12).

20. Wu Changying 吳昌瑩, *Jingci yanshi* 經詞衍釋 (Beijing: Zhonghua, 1956), 177–78.

21. *Chunqiu Zuo zhuan zhengyi* 春秋左傳正義, in *Shisanjing zhushu*, 1792 (Xi 4.1); *Shiji* 史記 (Beijing: Zhonghua, 1959), 32.1489.

22. *Liji zhengyi* 禮記正義, in *Shisan jing zhushu*, 1612 ("Ai Gong wen" 哀公問); *Da Dai liji huijiao jizhu* 大戴禮記彙校集注, ed. Huang Huaixin 黃懷信, 2 vols. (Xian: San Qin, 2004), 95 ("Ai Gong wen yu Kongzi" 哀公問於孔子).

23. *Lunyu jijie yishu* 論語集解義疏, comm. He Yan 何宴 and Huang Kan 皇侃 (*Siku quanshu* 四庫全書 ed.), 3.27b.

24. Tang Zuofan, *Shangguyin shouce*, 45, 47.

25. *Shangshu zhengyi* 尚書正義, in *Shisan jing zhushu*, 212; *Liuchen zhu Wenxuan*, 190 (10.6b).

26. *Liji zhengyi*, 1582 ("Sang da ji" 喪大記).

27. *Shangshu zhengyi*, 175.

28. *Kongzi jiayu* 孔子家語, comm. Wang Su 王肅 (*Sibu congkan* 四部叢刊 ed.), 5.17a.

29. Tang Zuofan, *Shangguyin shouce*, 56, 57.
30. Zhang Ru 張儒 and Liu Yuqing 劉毓慶, *Hanzi tongyong shengsu yanjiu* 漢字通用聲素研究 (Taiyuan: Shanxi guji, 2002), 161–62.
31. *Shangshu zhengyi*, 246.
32. *Liji zhengyi*, 1541.
33. *Liji zhengyi*, 1543.
34. *Liji zhengyi*, 1651.
35. *Xunzi jijie*, 292. Translation modified from Knoblock, *Xunzi*, vol. 2, 198.
36. *Guanzi jiaozhu* 管子校注, comp. Li Xiangfeng 黎翔鳳 (Beijing: Zhonghua, 2004), 1221.
37. *Huainanzi jiaoshi* 淮南子校釋, comp. Zhang Shuangdi 張雙棣 (Beijing: Beijing daxue, 1997), 898. Translation after John Major et al., *The Huainanzi: A Guide to the Theory and Practice of Government in Early Han China* (New York: Columbia University Press, 2010), 299.
38. *Da Dai liji*, 3 ("Zhu yan" 主言).
39. *Guoyu jijie*, 469 ("Zhengyu" 鄭語).
40. *Guanzi jiaozhu*, 776 ("Xin shu shang" 心術上).
41. *Shiming* 釋名 (*Sibu congkan* ed.), 4.26b ("Shi yanyu" 釋言語).
42. *Mengzi zhushu*, in *Shisan jing zhushu*, 2737 ("Gaozi xia" 告子下); *Guanzi jiaozhu*, 1046.
43. *Guoyu jijie*, 109–10 ("Zhou yu xia," no. 6).
44. Mawangdui Han mu boshu zhengli xiaozu 馬王堆漢墓帛書整理小組, ed., *Mawangdui Han mu* boshu 馬王堆漢墓帛書, vol. 3 (Beijing: Wenwu, 1983), 75 (col. 260).
45. *Shiji*, 45.1870 ("Han shijia" 韓世家).
46. *Laozi Daodejing zhujiaoshi* 老子道德經注校釋, annot. Lou Yulie 樓宇烈 (Beijing: Zhonghua, 2008) 31 (*zhang* 14); Guojia wenwuju guwenxian yanjiushi 國家文物局古文獻研究室, ed., *Mawangdui Han mu boshu*, vol. 1 (Beijing: Wenwu, 1980), 96 (col. 228 下–229 上).
47. Xu Shen 許慎, *Shuowen jiezi: fu jianzi* 說文解字: 附檢字 (Beijing: Zhonghua, 1963), 3A.58.
48. See Lu Deming, *Jingdian shiwen*, 281 ("Chunqiu Zuo zhuan yinyi zhi wu" 春秋左傳音義之五, 19.13a).
49. *Zhouyi zhengyi* 周易正義, in *Shisanjing zhushu*, 81.
50. *Xunzi jijie*, 467. Translation after Knoblock, *Xunzi*, vol. 3, 104.
51. Wang Xianqian 王先謙, *Shi sanjia yi jishu* 詩三家義集疏 (Beijing: Zhonghua, 1987), 220. Translation after Arthur Waley, *The Book of Songs: The Ancient Chinese Classic of Poetry* (New York: Grove, 1996), 39.
52. *Xunzi jijie*, 368.
53. Shui Zhigan 水之甘, post no. 19 to "Qinghua jian ba *Xin shi wei zhong chu du*," December 5, 2018, http://www.bsm.org.cn/forum/forum.php?mod=viewthread&tid=4373&extra=&page=2.

54. *Xunzi jijie*, 506 ("Zheng ming") and 170 ("Ru xiao"). Translation of the line in "Zheng ming" after Knoblock, *Xunzi*, vol. 3, 136.

55. Ma Chengyuan 馬承源, ed., *Shanghai bowuguan cang Zhanguo Chu zhushu* 上海博物館藏戰國楚竹書, vol. 1 (Shanghai: Shanghai guji, 2001), 270–71.

56. Li Xueqin, ed., *Qinghua daxue cang Zhanguo zhujian*, vol. 6 (Shanghai: Zhongxi, 2016), 111, 114. This point was brought to my attention by Li Tianhong 李天虹.

57. Cai Shen 蔡沈, *Shujing jizhuan* 書經集傳 (*Siku quanshu* ed.), 4.26b.

58. Xiang Zonglu 向宗魯, *Shuoyuan jiaozheng* 説苑校證 (Beijing: Zhonghua, 1987), 361 ("Zhi gong" 至公).

59. *Shuowen*, 6B.129.

60. Ma Chengyuan, *Shanghai bowuguan cang Zhanguo Chu zhushu*, vol. 1, 67. Translation of the *Shijing* ode quoted here (Mao no. 247 "Jizui" 既醉) is after Waley, *Book of Songs*, 248.

61. *Han shu*, 64A.2777.

62. *Liuchen zhu Wenxuan*, 701 (37.36b).

63. Wang Niansun 王念孫, *Dushu zazhi* 讀書雜志 (Shanghai: Shanghai guji, 2014), 2077 ("Huainan neipian di si, di xing" 淮南內篇第四, 地形).

64. *Jiyun* 集韵, comp. Ding Du 丁度 (*Siku quanshu* ed.), 10.55b ("Ye yun" 葉韻).

65. *Zhuangzi jishi* 莊子集釋, comp. Guo Qingfan 郭慶藩, 2nd ed. (Beijing: Zhonghua, 2004), 658–59.

66. *Zhuangzi jishi*, 659n4.

67. Wang Niansun 王念孫, *Guangya shuzheng* 廣雅疏證 (Shanghai: Shanghai guji, 2016), 660 (*juan* 4, *xia* 下, entry for "*nie* is quiet 㘝靜也") states: "*Nie* is like *tie* 怗, with light or heavy pronunciations. In the *Yupian* (it has the *fanqie* spelling of) *nai qie* 乃箧, with a gloss of *mo* 莫 "nothing, still like night." The *Han shu* 'Yan Zhu zhuan' has 'when the world is under control, people can live in peace' to which Meng Kang comments: '*nie* is *an*, with a *fanqie* pronunciation of *nu xie fan* 奴協反 [*n-ap].' *Zhuangzi* 'Tianzi fang pian' has 'motionless as if not a person at all' to which Guo Xiang comments: 'the peak of being anchored in silence.' The *Jingdian shiwen* likewise records that *zhi* 慹 has a *fanqie* spelling of *nai ye fan* 乃牒反 [*n-ap]. The sound and meaning of *nie* 㘝, *nie* 㩒 and *zhi* 慹 were all the same. *Zhuangzi* "Da sheng pian' has 'so still that one forgets that one has a body with four limbs,' to which the *Jingdian shiwen* records that '*zhe* 輒 has a *fanqie* pronunciation of *ding xie fan* 丁協反 [*t-ap]. *Zhe ran* is like not moving.' The words *zhe* and *nie* 㘝 are the same in sound and meaning" (㘝猶怗也語有輕重耳; 玉篇: 乃箧切云㘝莫也; 漢書嚴助傳: 天下㩒然人安其生, 孟康注云: 㩒安也, 音奴協反; 莊子田子方篇: 慹然似非人, 郭象注云: 寂泊之至也. 釋文慹乃牒反, 㘝㩒慹聲義並同. 莊子達生篇: 輒然忘吾有四枝形體也. 釋文: 輒丁協反, 輒然不動貌, 輒與㘝亦聲近義同). Following Wang's explanation, we know that when used in the sense of "being at peace," *nie* 㩒 and *zhe* 輒 were interchangeable.

68. Huang Dekuan 黃德寬, "Shi xinchu Zhanguo Chu jian zhong de 'chen' zi" 釋新出戰國楚簡中的 "湛" 字, *Zhongshan daxue xuebao (shehui kexue ban)* 中山大學學報 (社會科學版) 2018.1: 49–52.

69. *Yupian* (*Sibu congkan* ed.), 19.4b ("Shui bu" 水部) takes *chen* 沉 as a common form of *shen* 沈. The *Kangxi zidian* 康熙字典 cites the *Zihui* 字彙, which claims that *chen* 沉 is the same as *shen* 沈; see Hanyu dacidian bianzuanchu 漢語大詞典編纂處, ed., *Kangxi zidian (biaodian zhengli ben)* 康熙字典: 標點整理本 (Shanghai: Hanyu dacidian, 2002), 557–58.

70. *Guangya shuzheng* 廣雅疏證, comm. Wang Niansun 王念孫 (Beijing: Zhonghua, 1983), 93 (3B.3a).

71. *Guoyu jijie*, 118 ("Zhouyu xia" 周語下, no. 7).

72. *Guangyun* (*Sibu congkan* ed.), 4.66a ("Jian yun" 鑑韻).

73. *Shangshu zhengyi*, 213.

8

Texts, Historicity, and Metaphors in Early China
Reading *Tang Resides Near the Mound of Tang*
(*Tang chuyu Tangqiu* 湯處於湯丘) in the
Tsinghua Collection of Warring States Bamboo Manuscripts

SHIRLEY CHAN

Many pre-Qin texts offer compelling evidence of identifiable formulations of the language of persuasive discourse.[1] These texts used various rhetorical devices to convey the (semi-)hidden or complex meanings of philosophical or political messages. This chapter focuses on the text *Tang Resides Near the Mound of Tang* (*Tang chuyu Tangqiu* 湯處於湯丘) in the Tsinghua collection of Warring States (475–221 BCE) bamboo manuscripts as an example of the use of historicity and metaphors in pre-Qin writings. The recovered text uses historical personages of the legendary Shang King Tang and his minister to present political ideas with cooking and bodily metaphors. Through establishing the connection between culinary skills and statecraft, past and present, the discussion of the *Tang chuyu Tangqiu* manuscript reveals how authors of the early texts imagined and constructed a rhetorical discourse that presents a holistic approach to understanding the world, temporally and spatially—the human realm is seen as part of the cosmic order and how,

---

I would like to heartily thank Constance Cook and Sue Wiles for proofreading and formatting. I am also grateful to the reviewers for their very helpful comments.

across time and space, humans live by the same universal principle(s). This study will also include other early texts such as the *Tang zai Chimen* 湯在啻門 in the same Tsinghua collection.

Introduction

The origins of Greek rhetoric are marked by the emergence of the word *rhetorike* and it is conventionally believed that rhetoric was first developed and studied in ancient Greece in the fifth century BCE.[2] Commonly perceived as an art of persuasion for the purpose of changing thought and action at social, political, and individual levels, rhetoric played a significant role in different cultures through representation of the power and impact of language.[3] Recently, it has become generally accepted that rhetorical practices have been universally shared, albeit with culturally specific experiences and conceptualization.[4] Recovering these different rhetorical traditions will allow us to promote understanding and appreciation of diverse communication patterns, cultural values, and human experiences. As an artistic use of oral and written expression, Chinese rhetorical discourse offers a rich body of knowledge and practice.

Studying the rhetoric in ancient Chinese philosophical manuscripts will help us further comprehend the thinking patterns, and even the development of ancient Chinese worldviews, whereas on the other hand being able to read these philosophical texts through the lens of their worldviews can help us grasp the deeper and broader meaning behind these philosophical messages. For example, metaphor is not only a literary rhetorical device but also a phenomenon involving reasoning to obtain the maximum possible cognitive effect. The general conceptual system in which we live and think is metaphorical in nature.[5] Most scholarly work on ancient Chinese metaphorical rhetoric has focused on Daoist texts.[6] One such is Sarah Allan's *The Way of Water and Sprouts of Virtue*, in which the characteristics of water have been drawn out to illustrate the meanings of Dao.[7] Others have analyzed the weighing of body parts as a metaphor for action, in the *Mozi* (a book compiled under the name of Mozi, ca. 470–391 BCE) and the *Lü shi Chunqiu* (Master Lü's Spring and Autumn Annals, compiled around 239 BCE).[8]

Research into Chinese rhetoric in many other major ancient Chinese texts is lacking. This is particularly the case for the hitherto lost ancient manuscripts recently recovered, for example, the bamboo-slip manuscripts acquired by Tsinghua University in 2008. This cache of Warring States (475–221 BCE) bamboo-slip manuscripts is a valuable collection dated to before the purported burning of the books by the First Emperor of Qin in 213 BCE that destroyed many ancient books. The manuscripts have attracted scholarly attention as original texts providing a new understanding of the evolution of the Chinese philosophical tradition. Due to the relatively recent discovery of the corpus, an important and yet underexplored area of study is the philosophy of writing and rhetorical discourse in these manuscripts. In this case we will focus on historicity and metaphor in early Chinese texts that concern ancient Chinese philosophy and history. Based on the recent recovered texts from the Tsinghua Bamboo Slip corpus, the current study will focus on two aspects of rhetoric: (1) how historical narratives and metaphors were employed in the ancient texts, which were largely concerned with statecraft and ideal rulership during the golden age of Chinese philosophy in the Warring States period, and (2) what the newly recovered texts tell us about rhetoric in Chinese political philosophy.[9]

First, historical narratives were an embodiment of knowledge with foregrounded values and truths drawn from the past. Historicity was frequently used to empower the message(s) in the texts concerned. I use the term "historicity" referring to past events presented through varied forms such as history, myth, or popular memory with the purpose of presenting philosophical and political agendas rather than accurately representing factual events.[10] Engaging with the historical materials in the Tsinghua slips, this chapter explores how the past was mobilized as powerful ideological capital in diverse political debates and ethical dialogues before the rise of the First Emperor of Qin (Qin Shi Huangdi, 259–210 BCE). Appeals to the past in early China could have been deliberate ways of articulating political thought and challenging ethical debates during periods of crisis.[11] I will draw on examples of historicity to showcase how, in philosophical discourse, history was not merely an account of past events. On the contrary, it could be a high-stakes enterprise involving contested notions of heritage, origin, and authority that reflected concerns and interests in the present. The ancient wisdom in historical anecdotes was justified as evidence of valid knowledge and timeless truths that continued to inspire current and future generations.

Second, the study will show how the principle of nature and everyday activities (e.g., culinary preparation as a way of achieving bodily pleasure and nourishment) were considered an integral part of statecraft and rulership. This is based on the hypothesis that the same principle that was shared between nature and human was also common to daily life and sociopolitical functionaries. This assumption is where metaphor and the meanings of metaphors come into play. By giving the "nameless" names and the undescribed description, metaphor imparts fresh knowledge to the symbolic creations that can help us understand how ancient Chinese philosophers engaged in this world and derived meaning from their surroundings. Given the importance of metaphor to our understanding not only of ancient Chinese philosophy but also of Chinese cultural values, the current study of rhetoric in the newly recovered bamboo manuscripts will advance our understanding of the Chinese worldview on which conceptual metaphor is based. That is, taking life and philosophy in its totality rather than in its parts, humans are considered as beings evolving in a multidimensional cosmos (past-and-present, human-and-nature). Within the multidimensions of sociopolitical concerns in the early texts, the human realm is seen as part of the natural world and the present and future as a continuum of the past; humans share the same universal principle across time and space, especially if we can perceive universality in a nondimensional point and eternity in one timeless moment. The conceptual historical narratives and metaphorical discourse present a holistic approach to understanding the world, temporally and spatially. As part of human experience, this knowledge and its related activities were born and developed in their own social, political, and cultural contexts, surviving through orality and literacy.

Art, Myth, and Ritual before Zhou

Art and writing were an integral part of knowledge and the effort to understand and make sense of the universe and the cosmic order in ancient China. This quest for knowledge and creativity, in the forms of divination, mythology, numerological arrangements or almanacs, emerged from the immediate concerns of an agricultural society to help the ruling class conceptualize and adjust to making important decisions and conducting administrative business, ritual ceremonies, and the deployment of the military.[12] Before the Zhou, the Chinese believed in the existence of a number of powerful deities. Shangdi 上帝, or God on High in anthropomorphic terms, possessed supreme powers over humans and nature. Art and writing were mythical and religious in nature. Cultural and social discourse was utilized or facilitated by poets, performers, and religious leaders for creating relationships between the worlds of God/Heaven, ancestors/spirits, and humans. As part of their religious expression, myth, art, and ritual in Shang, as in other early cultures, could be considered a form of metaphor. They went beyond depicting the "real" world to allude to a meaningful and sacred representation of the religious dimension through various motifs and decorative art.[13] The motifs were continually transformed, crossing the boundary between the living and the dead when, for example, used to decorate vessels for food offerings or for ritual washing, or to mark shamans to allow them to communicate with the spirit world.[14] Ritual and mythical art were patterns designed with sacred meanings intended to communicate with another world. They were therefore characterized with effective features of "distortion, disjunction," and "conjoining of different animals."[15] From the Xia to the Shang dynasties, the rhetorical experience was mostly characterized by mythological and ritualist communications, including oral transmission, divination accounts, and musical and ceremonial performances. Metaphors and symbolism were largely presented in the form of images, signs, symbols, and odes, in which the ancients constructed meaning with their perceptions of the world across space and time.

Developed from knowledge derived in the quest for understanding Heaven and Earth through divination and ritual practice, art and writing have had important sociopolitical significance since the very beginning. They were a manifestation of wealth and political authority facilitated by several interrelated factors: kinship hierarchy, moral authority of the ruler, military power, exclusive access to gods and to ancestors (through rituals, art, and the use of writing), and access to wealth itself. This ancient Chinese characteristic "has been woven into the overall pattern of ancient art, myth and politics."[16] The three dynasties of Xia (ca. 2070–1600 BCE), Shang (ca. 1600–1046 BCE), and Zhou (ca. 1046–256 BCE) are believed to have been founded by different clans, each of which was characterized by a mythological ancestor and a name and totem used by the entire clan. The clans competed for rulership through qualifications in the mythological sense, lineage rules codified in rituals, but also through deeds deserving the support of the ruled.[17] This legitimacy of deservedness based on merit was later referred to as "Heaven's Mandate" (*tianming* 天命) in the Zhou, as revealed in early literary texts such as the *Documents* (*Shu* 書) and the *Odes* (*Shi* 詩), which described the virtue of the Western Zhou elites as a means of connecting Heaven, the spiritual world, and humans. Kings and lineage ancestors accomplished meritorious deeds, which were sometimes magical or supernatural. Myths and rituals, as expressed through tangible objects such as temples, tablets, treasures and associated records, inscriptions and writings, provided the sanction, the reminder, and the symbol for the solidarity of lineages and the pathway to political power.[18]

Texts, Historicity, and Metaphor

Together with the development of writing and literary texts, mythological traditions and legends evolved and were transmitted by literate men from the beginning of Zhou with different elements, such as systematized historical anecdotes, the use of correlative thinking, and the praising of deeds and achievements of high ancestors or dynastic founders or ancient kings in historical narratives.[19] As the creative age of China's great classical and philosophical literature, the Zhou offers us a huge amount of texts containing knowledge associated with the human experiences and codes of conduct linked to the ancestors and ancient kings.[20] These codes enabled the living to communicate with Heaven and the spirits as well as to predict the future from historical patterns, which in turn were modeled on earlier kings' exemplary behavior. Mantic knowledge and the accounts of divination were subverted in philosophical writings and textual construction, as political rhetoric became increasingly important to interpreting the triad relationship of Heaven, Earth, and Man. In philosophical texts, the focus on systematizing moral principles and philosophical concepts in connection with the cosmic order became distinct from technical knowledge. In the Zhou period, the Mandate of Heaven, awarded by means of ancestral merit and virtue, reinforced the idea that an individual's moral power was key to justifying the success and achievement of a state or a ruler. The fall of a state, on the other hand, was largely due to immoral tyranny and the subsequent loss of the mandate.

Philosophical writings and texts had the purpose of preserving elements of "truth" in the form of lengthy speeches, historical narratives, policy recommendations, and predictions. In this context, "historicity" meant focusing on the claims of the value of knowledge about the past (denoting historical experience of a truth rather than making an accurate representation of the event itself). While it is impossible to verify the historical actuality and authenticity of the persons and events, reference to them as part of history signifies their meaning and authority.[21] Historicity and accounts of past events in the texts provided political and intellectual authority. Narratives and speeches in a historical setting could be adapted and made subject to constructions of meanings based on implicit value commitments. As such, historical and current examples became used for a powerful means of persuasion in many early texts, such as the *Book of Odes*, the *Book of Documents*, the *Zuo zhuan*, and the *Guoyu*.[22] These texts based on the accounts of the past were consciously presented as "another type of truth, allegorical or metaphysical rather than literal."[23]

As representations of the wisdom of the early kings, ministers, and historically significant personages, writing and inscribed artifacts were of special import and symbolized key cultural values.[24] By the end of the Warring States, text production based on lineage narratives (probably originally memorized and adapted from mythology, historical events, legends, songs, and tales) was made possible by the literati, who were educated and trained for political positions or as successors of the ruling class. These texts focused on the retention of cultural patterns and how to preserve the knowledge and wisdom of the sage kings and cultural heroes, who had created success stories through meritorious behavior and good deeds that enabled them to connect with Heaven and the spirits, bringing peace to All Under Heaven.[25] The magical importance of Heaven's regulation of daily life on earth was no longer primarily perceived through divination, but by means of human (re)interpretation and philosophical determination of truth. Literati employed accounts of the past and narratives attributed to earlier rulers to articulate political theories and philosophical ideas.[26] One notable intellectual group, the Ruists, held that the tradition of preserving, producing, and transmitting these historical stories and moral examples of sage kings was a duty and a source of political inspiration.[27] Furthermore, it was believed that cosmological principles informed human behavior; metaphors and imagery employed in art and writing reflected the relationship of the abstract and concrete principles intrinsic to the natural and human worlds. Correlative thinking such as *yin yang* 陰陽 and *wuxing* 五行 (the five phases) were increasingly incorporated into art, philosophy, literature, and politics.[28]

Political crisis and chaos that marked the Warring States period in pre-Qin China led to a flourishing of different schools of thought, all responding to the need for solutions to sociopolitical issues. Strategists, thinkers, itinerant scholars, and masters of different schools all came into contact with exponents of rival systems of thought and felt compelled to promote their own ideas. They not only had to face competition between the different schools, but they also had to convince state rulers to embrace the political ideals they espoused. Therefore, their methods for presenting new ideas had to be engaging and convincing. The speakers/authors presented their views by drawing upon relevant stories, allegories, anecdotes, and tales. In the process, they employed irony, satire, similes, metaphors, and hyperbole.[29]

One such example is the manuscript *Tang chuyu Tangqiu*.

Tang Resides Near the Mound of Tang

The following section will discuss textual rhetoric in early texts based on the manuscript *Tang chuyu Tangqiu* 湯處於湯丘 in the Tsinghua University collection of the Warring States Bamboo Slip corpus (TBS or *Qinghua jian* 清華簡), acquired in 2008. The corpus was written in Chu script and dated to the mid- to late Warring States period (480–221 BCE).[30] The textual contents are mostly historical and philosophical in nature; they evince a literary style that seems to be similar to the "Counsels" (*Mo* 謨 chapters in the *Book of Documents*) that feature a discussion between the king and his minister. The *Tang chuyu Tangqiu* manuscript records the conversation of Tang and Yi Yin on state affairs and the ideal ruler. The manuscript consists of nineteen bamboo slips, each with a length of about 44.5 cm and a width of about 0.6 cm.

The text is significant in exemplifying the implication of historical narratives in philosophy and the use of metaphor to draw political lessons. First, the use of historicity occurs in the context of a dialogue between Tang 湯 and Yi Yin 伊尹, the founding figures of the Shang 商 dynasty (ca. 1600–1046 BCE), the earliest ruling dynasty of China to be established in recorded history. Set against the historical background of how Tang succeeded in overthrowing Jie 桀, the last king of Xia 夏, the text articulates political philosophy in which true kingship is revealed through an account of the past based on Tang's story. The historical narrative lends textual authority and exemplifies the role of history in philosophical texts, that is, the practice of retelling and remarking on historical events and personages; the texts are making retrospective judgments and compelling arguments for future behavior, a rhetorical pattern found in many historiographical speeches.[31]

In addition to historical narratives, the text offers us an opportunity to explore metaphors of the human body and human life used to promote a particular ideology for governing a state. This feature of metaphors employed categorical correlations between different objects; "substitutions" or "references" were drawn where parts of these objects were assumed to share the same natural characteristics. These correlations integrated the references, providing deeper meanings than possible without the metaphor.[32] In the *Tang chuyu Tangqiu*, references to the state and the operative parts of the political entity were made and compared to the human body and other aspects of human life. Readers were expected to participate in the layered dialogue through the context of providing references from common knowledge about cooking and nourishment, governing and prosperity. These metaphors correlated the human body with the political body, suggesting political philosophy was embedded in the philosophy of life or nature and inseparable from the understanding of basic needs of human life, such as sensual pleasure, body nourishment, and social consensus.

In the *Tang chuyu Tangqiu*, the legendary ruler, Tang 湯 of Shang 商, and his minor minister (*xiaochen* 小臣), Yi Yin, discussed how to win a state. This text and another from the same corpus, the *Tang zai Chimen* 湯在啻門, both recorded deliberations regarding the establishment of the Shang dynasty and, as such, were historical in nature.[33] The speeches discussed the ideal qualities in a ruler and their political implications. The dialogue between ruler and minister thus fit into a long tradition of using speeches and anecdotes to express essential cultural and historical values. The bamboo manuscripts have been dated to the fourth century BCE, whereas the historical context of the story belongs to the end of the Xia period, when Cheng Tang, the founder of Shang, was being advised by Yi Yin on the principles of being a good ruler and how to conquer Jie 桀, the ruler of Xia, who had lost the people's faith. The text is an example of flourishing historical discourses linking historical accounts with early philosophical writing for the purpose of revealing a meaningful truth. The narrative and conversation between Tang and his advisor could be an adapted fictive pre-Zhou story reflecting the evolving concerns of the Warring States–period authors: the Mandate of Heaven and the justification to rule, the ideal rulership, the roles of ruler and minister and the relationship between the two. It was an accepted idea that the successes of legendary figures would inspire the current and future ruling class.[34]

The story began with introducing the talented chef Yi Yin, who accompanied Princess Xin as a servant and part of her dowry when she married Tang. Yi Yin's culinary talent was acknowledged by the effect it had on Lady Xin:[35]

> The minor minister was good at cooking by applying a technique of harmonization (blending the ingredients). There was this Lady Xin who, having tasted his cooking, stopped taking all other delicious and aromatic food, with the result that her body recovered from illness with increased strength, improved visual and auditory acuity, her heart-mind properly guided, and with a feeling of complete ease and lack of restraint.

(小臣) 善為飤 (食) 言 (烹) 之和，又 (有) 莘之女飤 (食) 之，絕
飤 (芳) [1] 旨以䭇(餕)，身體倦 (痊) 劦 (平)，九㝢 (竅) 發明，以
道 (導) 心䜣 (噫)，惜快以恒。

This passage displays the aesthetics of bodily pleasure, that is, the gastronomic delight that Lady Xin experienced through her senses, her heart-mind, and her body as a whole. Stories of Yi Yin, originally a cook and later employed as a minister, appear in other texts, such as the *Lunyu* 論語, the *Mozi* 墨子, the *Han Feizi* 韓非子, the *Shuoyuan* 說苑, and the *Chu ci* 楚辭.[36] However, none of these texts contain such a detailed description of the bodily pleasure brought on by Yi Yin's exceptional culinary skill of "harmonization" (*shan wei shi peng zhi he* 善為飤烹之和). The scenario in the Tsinghua bamboo manuscript of the historical scene elaborated with the body and politics schema could be a surviving example of Warring States textuality reworked into a set of coded judgments and philosophical schema responding to the sociopolitical environment. The key metaphorical framework is provided by the word "harmonization" (*he* 和), which connotes pleasure through soothing, healing, nourishing, improving, and thus bringing the person to an optimal state of well-being, both mentally and physically. It is said that after tasting this delicious food, Tang asked if the technique of harmonization in cooking could be applied to bringing harmony to the people (此可以和民乎).[37] Tang's question leads us to expect that a larger emotional, sensuous, and moral dimension of "harmonization" (*he*) would arise (beyond that of the royal body) if a similar technique could be applied in governing. While the earlier passage illustrated the bodily pleasure a person gained from the well-blended ingredients in food, the conversation went on to show that "harmonization" applied equally to the well-being of the individual and the prosperity of the people. Yi Yin further confirmed that this strategy could be used to unify the people and conquer the Xia. But what is the meaning of harmonization in state affairs? It is through Tang's praise of Yi Yin that we get the first glimpse that this concept was the guiding principle for the state:

> Now the minister was able to display prominently the many qualities of appropriate actions, so as to harmonize the people, restore the regulation of the four seasons, attend Offices of the Nine Affairs, and perform services at the altars of the spirits of the land and grain for a long time . . .

今少 (小) 臣能廬 (閭) 章 (彰) 百義，以和利萬民，以攸 (修) 四
時之正 (政)，以執 (設) 九事之人，以長奉社稷 . . .

So far, we can see a rhetorical discourse common to other early texts: Yi Yin's symbolic humble beginning as a chef and ultimate promotion to political advisor to Tang and a comparison of culinary techniques to governing skills.[38] The existence of these other accounts implies that, while the production of these histories is not clear, they were pervaded by similar moral and cultural values and persuasive devices.[39] The text, which could have been varied and adapted with past or existing tales, was not intended to explain historical events but to evaluate tested knowledge of and the philosophy behind statecraft. The metaphorical association of cooking with statecraft revealed that both shared the same principles.

Just as in culinary skills, it was necessary to understand the successful blending of ingredients, so was it necessary in governing to grasp and satisfy the people's needs and unite them in harmony. Great care and attention were essential in both cases.[40] In the preceding passage, Tang used the evidence of Yi Yin's culinary knowledge as the qualification for being a good minister. This description by Tang served as an illocutionary force inviting readers to make the same assumption. The metaphor of cooking and statecraft included the idea that good government, like good cooking, was fundamental to the physical and mental nourishment of the people, to their very survival, in fact.

The analogy between food preparation and statecraft has a near parallel in the *Guoyu* 國語 (Discourses of the States). Shi Bo 史伯 of Western Zhou used the metaphor of a body to praise the sage kings for harmonizing the five flavors to suit the taste of food and the six sounds to suit hearing:

> Therefore, the early kings mixed Earth with Metal, Wood, Water, and Fire, and produced a variety of things; they thereby harmonized the five flavors in order to temper tastes, strengthened the four limbs in order to guard the body, harmonized the six measures of sounds to improve the hearing, aligned the seven parts of the body to maintain the heart/mind, balanced the eight body parts to complete the whole person, established the nine records to set up pure virtues, and put together the ten rules to regulate the multitude. . . . Therefore, the kings set up residence in the fields of the nine peripheries, and harvests were regularly collected to support multitudes of people. The Zhou learned the lessons and applied them and taught the people adequately and harmonized (*he*) them as one whole. In this way, it (achieved) harmony at the highest level.

> 故先王以土與金木水火雜，以成百物。是以和五味以調口，更四支
> 以衛體，和六律以聰耳，正七體以役心，平八索以成人，建九紀以
> 立純德，合十數以訓百體。. . . . 故王者居九畡之田，收經入以食兆
> 民，周訓而能用之，和樂如一。夫如是，和之至也。[41]

The epitome of "harmony" (*he*) was its application to state affairs, as it enabled diverse elements to work together. In the preceding passage from the *Guoyu*, different components of government affairs were compared to body parts (mouth, ears, heart/mind, etc.). Working together, the state would be, like the body, ultimately "in harmony and joy as one" (*hele ru yi* 和樂如一). The term *hele ru yi* suggests that joy was closely connected with harmony, functioning to enable humans to recognize their full being as a whole, as lived experience.[42]

The bodily metaphor for polity in *Tang chuyu Tangqiu* became evident when Yi Yin referred to the ruler of Xia, Jie, as an "illness" (*ji* 疾):

> Tang also asked the minor minister, "What if I conquer Xia?" The minor minister replied, "You have shown reverence to the fearsome decree of Heaven; you have reverentially performed sacrifices and acted with virtue and benevolence to our people, as if they were a part of your body. As for the illness of Jie, your majesty should be able to take over Xia!"
>
> 湯或 (又) 昏 (問) 於少 (小) 臣：「吾戔 (翦) 夏女 (如) 台？」少 (小)
> 臣含 (答)：「句(后) 古 (固) [13] 共 (恭) 天畏 (威)，敬祀，弔 (淑)
> 慈我民，若自事朕身也。傑 (桀) 之疾，句 (后) 將君又 (有) 夏
> 才 (哉)!」

"The illness of Jie" (*jie zhi ji*) referred to Jie's moral corruption and the illness it caused in the ideal political body. Yi Yin suggested that Tang would succeed in winning over the people because he would serve them as if they were part of his own body (*ruo zishi zhenshen* 若自事朕身); the metaphor revealed a close relationship between ruler and ruled. The *ji* of Jie referred to his having not taken good care of his people and having inflicted mayhem on the state. Thus, Yi Yin explained the moral nature (*de* 德) of Xia, saying:[43]

> As to the moral nature of the Xia (government), it was devoted to goods and commodities and thus caused confusion; it changed the rules every season; people were perplexed and in doubt

and fled in large numbers due to severe penalties in the state. Hence the Xia king was not able to achieve his goal (of ruling his state properly).

又 (有) 夏之悥 (德), 事貨以惑, 旹 (春) 秋改則, 民人諏 (趣) 貣 (忒), 型 (刑) [12] 亡 (無) 卣 (攸) 恋 (赦), 民人皆悐 (務) 禺 (偶) 離, 夏王不得亓 (其) 圖.

In stark contrast to the Xia king, who was politically corrupt, according to Yi Yin the ancient sages were able to show love and care for their people (just as if they were part of their own bodies):

Tang again asked the minor minister: "How is it said that the ancient sages had self-regard?"

湯或 (又) 睧 (問) 於少 (小) 臣: "古 [14] 先= (之先) 聖人, 可 (何) 以自悥 (愛)?"

The minor minister replied: "The ancient sages could be said to have self-regard because they never caused confusion, never adopted those doubtful (policies) or chose delicacies to eat; they used all the five flavors with no particular preference; they did not have overly adorned clothing; their equipment was not carved or decorated; they did not impose cruelty and killing but shared benefits with their people. Hence this could be called having self-regard."

少 (小) 臣酓 (答): "古先= (之先) 聖人所以自悥 (愛), 不事睧 (昏), 不處 (居) 矣 (疑); 飤 (食) 時不旨 (嗜) 珍, 五味 [15] 皆哉, 不又 (有) 所僚; 不備 (服) 華文, 器不斵 (雕) 鏤; 不瘧 (虐) 殺, 與民分利, 此以自悥 (愛) 也."

Tang again asked the minor minister: "How can one be a (good) ruler? How can one be a (good) minister?"
　　The minor minister replied: "To be a ruler is to love the people, to be a minister is to serve with reverence."
　　Tang further asked: "How does one love the people?"
　　The minor minister replied: "Those who had traveled afar were allowed to end the journey; those who were called to toil were allowed to rest; those who were hungry were given food.

When people from afar flocked to (the king), even deep water and high mountains could not stop them, was this not (his) loving the people?"

湯或 (又) 聆 (問) 於少 (小) 臣: "為君奚 [16] 若? 為臣奚若?"
少 (小) 臣會 (答): "為君惡 (愛) 民, 為臣共 (恭) 命."
湯或 (又) 聆 (問) 於少 (小) 臣: "惡 (愛) 民女 (如) 台?"
少 (小) 臣會 (答) 曰: "遠又 (有) [17] 所亟 (極), 勞又 (有) 所思 (息), 飢又 (有) 所飤 (食), 罙 (深) 開 (淵) 是淒 (濟), 高山是逾, 遠民皆亟 (極), 是非惡 (愛) 民虎 (乎)?"

The metaphors of "body nourishment" and "cooking" appear in the Tsinghua manuscript *Tang chuyu Tangqiu*, where they likewise conceptualized correlative relationships within the human realm.

Nourishment of one nourishes the other. Cooking and statecraft both require *de* and *he* for success. The manuscript provides conceptualization of the significance of life and the undertaking of such significance in relation to other aspects of the human realm. Life and the attributes and constituents of life such as *de* 德 (moral quality) and *he* 和 (harmonization) were elaborated in the text illustrating how these constituents of life played an effective part in shaping and affecting not only individuals but the people and the state as a whole. The symbolic function of "culinary skills" and "cooking" in statecraft lies in the idea of how the way of ruling and the relationship between ruler and ruled can affect human survival and the prosperity of society in the same way as cooking and food affect a human body. The text demonstrates that a good ruler could manage political and cosmological order with the same principle of cooking and nourishment. Through cooking as a way of providing bodily nourishment, readers were urged to relate these life discourses with statecraft, and the associated conceptualization of *de* and *he* as an essential part of people's lives both as individuals and as part of the sociopolitical entity. In essence, *de* was demonstrated through a ruler's love for his people, that is, to benefit the people through harmonization of differences. Within this context, *Tang chuyu Tangqiu* drew on the interrelated political ideas of "harmonizing the people" (*hemin* 和民, strip 3), "benefiting the people by harmonization" (*yi he li min* 以和利民, strip 8), and "loving the people" (*ai min* 愛民, strip 17).[44] When the last passage is concluded with a statement that a ruler's loving people was demonstrated when "those who were called to toil were allowed to rest; those who were hungry were given food," the author of the text reiterates the connection between food and well-being, and the ruler's care and the good of a larger world.

More on *de* 德 and *ji* 疾

The discussion so far has shown how the metaphor of the body was politicized in the *Tang chuyu Tangqiu*. The story's not-so-subtle moral was that the state, like the body, could only function well when all the parts were in harmony: the ruler and his ministers must work together for the good of the people. This concept of the state emphasized fitness and well-being over illness, the latter occurring when the ruler and his government failed to perform their roles. Harmonization in a state meant that government officials must act modestly, not spending extravagantly, and ensure that the state operated properly so that everyone could benefit. The people should be well looked after by the ruler as if they were his own body. This is the concept of moral integrity (*de*), which was the essential constituent of life and social prosperity. Conceptual metaphors not only shape our communication but also structure the way we think and act.[45] Metaphors are in turn shaped by cultural values. That is, metaphor is derived from cultural conceptions while its use in rhetoric, and as a cognitive force, plays a role in the formation of ideas.[46] Sources of metaphors in different cultures naturally vary. Early Chinese thinkers assumed that nature and human society shared common principles and that people could be understood by observing nature. Therefore, nature became the source of the metaphor used in a process of systematic abstraction, in which the moral quality of *de* can be seen as the abstraction of the idea of life and well-being.[47] As we can see in many early texts, the cultivation of *de* resulted in happiness, well-being, and prosperity for individuals and society at large. According to the *Laozi* 老子, "All things were produced by *dao* and nourished by *de*. . . . Therefore, all things without exception honor *dao*, and exalt *de*" (道生之，德畜之. . . . 以萬物莫不尊道而貴德). In the *Zhuangzi* 莊子, "Geng Sang Chu" 庚桑楚, "Life is what gives opportunity for the display of *de*. Nature is the substantive character of the life" (生者，德之光也; 性者，生之質也), and in "Tiandi" 天地, "What enables all things to live and/or to produce is *de*" (物得以生謂之德). Then in the *Guanzi* 管子, "Xinshu, one" 心術一, "What can be called *de* is the residence of *dao* and is what enables all things to live" (德者，道之舍，物得以生). The *Liji* 禮記 comments on how *de* and *qi* worked together to bring about nature and the qualities of all things: "All (of the musical activities) have the effort of exhibiting the brilliance of *de*, stirring up the harmonious action of the four *qi*, and displaying the natures and qualities of all things" (奮至德之光, 動四氣之和, 以著萬物之理).⁴⁸

The influence of *de* on the body and the mind is apparent in adages preserved in the *Analects* 論語: "The wise are free from perplexities; the benevolent from anxiety; and the courageous from fear" (知者不惑, 仁者不憂, 勇者不懼); "The wise find pleasure in water; the benevolent find pleasure in hills. The wise are active; the benevolent are tranquil. The wise are joyful; the benevolent are long-lived" (知者樂水, 仁者樂山; 知者動, 仁者靜; 知者樂, 仁者壽).⁴⁹ The *Guanzi*, "Zhong Kuang" 中匡, explicitly states that it is through the proper guiding of blood-*qi* that one grows his years and grows his heart-mind and *de* (道血氣以求長年長心長德).⁵⁰ It was a common assumption in early China that moral cultivation involved cultivating one's person as a whole and that the process of cultivation transformed the person both physically and mentally.⁵¹

De, variously rendered as inherent power, character, integrity, morality, virtue, or goodness has been regarded as a kind of quality of a person in relation to people and to the cosmos.⁵² To continue the idea of bodily metaphor we discussed earlier, one important aspect of *de* was how one's inherent quality was actualized and thereby to shape or influence people's lives and well-being. That is, *de* was not only an important element for the survival and growth of natural life, it was also an important test of sociopolitical stability and prosperity. Texts in the Warring States period reflected the idea that lacking good *de* represented a defect, like an illness (*ji*).⁵³ In the *Tang chuyu Tangqiu*, this state describes the failure to cultivate *de*. To avoid this state, Xunzi 荀子 emphasized the importance of the rules of propriety (*li* 禮) in both individuals' lives and the state's well-being:⁵⁴

> If one inclines to goodness only so as to regulate *qi* and nurture life, one is following Peng Zu; but if it is done in order to cultivate one's person and to display his name prominently, one is matching Yao and Yu. To be appropriate in different times (and circumstances), so to better deal with the destitute is what propriety is truly about. In general, when it comes to blood-*qi*, intent and will, knowledge and deliberation, if regulated by propriety, all will be freely flowing; if not regulated by ritual, all will be abrupt, confused, and remiss. Eating or drinking, clothes

and dress, at home or resting abroad, to move or to be still, all should be harmonized and regulated by propriety; by not following propriety, all will be ensnared and decline into illness. In countenance and manner, in advancing and receding, in haste and walking, propriety will bring elegance; without propriety all will be rude, obstinate, wayward, defying, mediocre, and thus wild. Therefore, without propriety, no one will be able to live, nothing can be accomplished, and no state will be at peace.

扁善之度, 以治氣養生, 則後彭祖; 以脩身自名, 則配堯禹. 宜於時通, 利以處窮, 禮信是也. 凡用血氣, 志意, 知慮, 由禮則治通, 不由禮則勃亂提僈; 食飲, 衣服, 居處, 動靜, 由禮則和節, 不由禮則觸陷生疾; 容貌, 態度, 進退, 趨行, 由禮則雅, 不由禮則夷固, 僻違, 庸眾而野. 故人無禮則不生, 事無禮則不成, 國家無禮則不寧.

Xunzi's detailed account makes us aware how the rules of propriety could regulate *qi* and nurture life by "harmonizing and regulating" all activities (由禮則和節). To put it briefly, cultivating *de* involved harmonizing *qi*, the vital force for all living things. In the *Tang zai Chimen*, a metaphor of human life was used to describe the attributes of *de* and *qi*. The text started with Tang's questions concerning whether any ancient wisdom explained how the universe was formed, how life was created, and what "completed" a state (古之先帝, 亦有良言請至於今乎? 少臣答曰: 有哉! 如無有良言請至於今, 則何以成人? 何以成邦? 何以成地? 何以成天?). The repetition of the word *cheng* 成 (to complete) as the focus of the conversation indicated more than the mere physical existence of these entities. It also included the flourishing achievements of humans and what constituted the highest good.[55]

In *Tang zai Chimen*, Yi Yin applied the image of the development of the fetus into a person as a metaphor for statecraft in multiple layers from the human to the cosmic: "completing a man," "completing a state," "completing earth," and "completing heaven." According to Yi Yin, the human body was an entity composed of five kinds of vital energy (*wuwei zhi qi* 五味之氣) and only with *de* could it prosper and reach its full development (*de yi guang zhi* 德以光之).[56] The key element for the development of each layer was *qi*. The state, as a political body, also embodied *qi*. Different kinds of *qi* would affect, shape, and change the physical and mental states of individuals and society as a whole. The intertwined relationship of the individual and the state, ruler and ruled, and bodily function and statecraft, all pivoted on *qi* and *de*:

> People develop according to (the proper) time. When their *qi* was rising, they grew and became healthy; when their *qi* was vigorous and abundant, they were strong. This is the order (of the development of human life). When their (different kinds of) *qi* was blended and was complete it was to form (vital) energy. When the *qi* was harried, people aged; when the *qi* slowed, they failed; when the *qi* was rebellious and confused, they would abandon themselves, which would cause illness and calamity. When the *qi* became crooked and came to an end, the people also showed the exhaustion of their will.

> 民乃時生. 其氣晉 (歇) 發 (治), 是其為長且好哉. 其氣眛 (奮) [8] 昌, 是其爲當(壯). 氣 (融) 交以備, 是其爲力. 氣戚 (促) 乃老, 氣 (徐) 乃歇, 氣逆亂以方 [9], 是其為疾殃. 氣屈乃終, 百志皆窮.

In this passage, the notion of body and life was presented in *qi*. This prominent position of *qi* is nowhere in the *Tang chuyu Tangqiu*. Here, the different phases of human life reflected the ebb and flow of *qi*. First, in the preceding paragraph, the use of the term *min* 民 (people) instead of *ren* 人 (man) suggests that the phenomenon could scale upward from the individual to the society. Second, there was *qi* and *de*. Yi Yin drew a distinction between good *de* (*meide* 美德) and bad *de* (*e'de* 惡德), pointing out that good *de* protected the state and the people, causing prosperity, whereas bad *de* led to suffering and the collapse of the state:[57]

> When *de* (moral quality) is profoundly bright and replete with righteousness, it is called excellent *de*; it can protect and complete (the state). When *de* is full of flaws causing the state to perish, it is called bad *de* (being morally corrupt). . . . When people are suffering for no reason this is called bad affairs. . . . When government affairs are in chaos and become irregular, bodies of the people will completely collapse, causing them to be on their own, and this is called bad government.

> 德濬明執信以義成, 此謂 [13] 美德, 可以保成; 德 (變) 丞執譌以亡成, 此謂惡德. . . . 病民無故, 此謂惡事. . . . 政 (禍) 亂以無常, 民 [16] 咸解體自卹 (恤), 此謂惡政.

This passage could be taken as an elaboration on the idea of "flourishing by means of *de*" (*de yi guang zhi* 德以光之), mentioned earlier. With good moral behavior and benevolent government, the state and the people are cared for; without *de*, the people suffer and collapse, just like the state. It is clear that *qi* and *de* were both essential constituents of life and well-being. Excellent *de* ensured the proper flow of *qi*, the vital energy of all things. In the *Tang chuyu Tangqiu* the harmonious operation (*he*) of all things also represented the blending of different kinds of *qi*, such as the *wuxing* (five elements): water, fire, metal, wood, and earth (*shui* 水, *huo* 火, *jin* 金, *mu* 木, *tu* 土).⁵⁸ "The five kinds of (*qi*) were imbued in all things, from music to grain" (以成五曲, 以植五穀). A close reading elucidates the metaphorical relationship, where music was symbolic of ritual and grains, recognized as an important food source; significantly, ritual and food were vital to satisfaction of the senses and well-being. Apart from being a natural process, the political consciousness of a state, like the human body, was realized through ritual and music. *Tang zai Chimen* ends with Tang's response: "These are simply great words from the ancient kings that one should not alter" (唯古之先帝之良言, 則可 (何) 以改之). The author of this text, through Tang's claim, asserted that what had been passed down from the ancient kings was timeless truth. It not only showed a historical commitment to this lesson but, more significantly, it provided justification for fourth-century BCE political ideology.

Conclusion

Art and writing served significant purposes of facilitating sociopolitical power in early China. The tradition of having power and authority manufactured through art, myth, and ritual since the Shang continued into the Zhou period. The focus of this chapter is a recovered text dated to the Warring States period when thinkers and strategists through writing and texts constructed and communicated their knowledge regarding the creation of power and authority in polity. Historicity and metaphors were effectively used in rhetorical discourse as powerful forms of persuasion in the early texts. This chapter shows how the newly discovered bamboo manuscript *Tang chuyu Tangqiu* employed these devices to advance political ideas. Persuasion took the form of success stories of ancient sage kings. The text started with an advisory discussion between Tang (as the ideal ruler) and Yi Yin (as the talented minister) representing the qualities of, respectively, good rulers and ministers. There were layers of historicity in the text: the conversation between Tang and Yi Yin created the historical framework within which political philosophies and guiding principles were established through ancient precedent(s) and legitimized by their success, providing unifying values and "truth" that transcended time and space. A careful reading of the text shows that harmony and harmonization (*he*) were the key concepts critical to statecraft. This was exemplified in the metaphor of cooking and harmoniously blending ingredients, resulting in not only delicious food but healing nourishment crucial to well-being. By analogy, a state could be well governed only by applying the principle of harmonization. Throughout the text, readers were guided by the sharp contrast between a good ruler (as exemplified by Tang and other sage kings) and a bad one (e.g., Jie). In traditional historical accounts, the latter was conquered by the former. The Mandate of Heaven could continue only by following ancient wisdom, which was aesthetically appealing and morally inspiring through the carefully crafted rhetorical device. In terms of the moral qualities required of a ruler, the *Tang chuyu Tangqiu* may not have offered anything particularly new when compared to many Warring States texts. This author nevertheless hopes that reading the recovered text(s) would help us add a small explanatory note to the ongoing discussion on philosophical discourse in early China: the conversation between historical ideal personalities of ancient king and minister served as an illocutionary voice to enforce truth and knowledge. The communication of such knowledge with the use of historicity and metaphor was itself a holistic approach to understanding the world.

Notes

1. Studies of Chinese philosophical texts have mainly focused on "what" was said, rather than "how" it was said and "why" it was said the way it was.

2. Eric Havelock, *The Literate Revolution in Greece and Its Cultural Consequences* (Princeton, NJ: Princeton University, 1982).

3. Veron Jensen, "Rhetorical Emphases of Taoism," *Rhetorica* 5 (1987): 219–29; Brian Vickers, *In Defence of Rhetoric* (Oxford: Clarendon, 1988).

4. Xing Lü, *Rhetoric in Ancient China, Fifth to Third Century BCE: A Comparison with Classical Greek Rhetoric* (Columbia: University of South Carolina Press, 1998).

5. George Lakoff and Mark Johnson, *Metaphors We Live By* (Chicago: University of Chicago Press, 1980).

6. Chad Hansen, *A Daoist Theory of Chinese Thought* (New York: Oxford University Press, 1992); Havelock, *The Literate Revolution*; Sarah Allan, *The Way of Water and Sprouts of Virtue* (Albany: State University of New York Press, 1997).

7. Allan, *Way of Water*.

8. Griet Vankeerberghen, "Choosing Balance: Weighing (*quan* 權) as a Metaphor for Action in Early Chinese Texts," *Early China* 30 (2005–2006): 47–89; Carine Defoort, "Heavy and Light Body Parts: the Weighing Metaphor in Early Chinese Dialogues," *Early China* 38 (2015): 55–77.

9. Accounts of past events and historical figures were represented, exercised, and manipulated in diverse and complex ways, with different agendas. Sarah Allan has analyzed the text *When Red Pigeons Gathered on Tang's House* (*Chijiu zhi ji Tang zhi wu* 赤鳩之集湯之屋) contained in the same Tsinghua collection. The text has the same historical personages of Yi Yin, Tang, and Tang's wife from the *Tang chuyu Tangqiu* 湯處於湯丘, but the stories are very different in nature. In the *Tang chuyu Tangqiu*, Yi Yin was a political advisor to Tang, whereas in *Red Pigeons*, he was a shamanistic healer. See Sarah Allan, "'When Red Pigeons Gathered on Tang's House': A Warring States Period Tale of Shamanic Possession and Building Construction Set at the Turn of the Xia and Shang Dynasties," *Journal of the Royal Asiatic Society* (2015): 1–20.

10. It is sometimes difficult to make a distinction between popular memory and history that is "routinely blurred in people's minds." See Paul Cohen, *History and Popular Memory: The Power of Story in Moments of Crisis* (New York: Columbia University Press, 2014), xii–xiv. This study will not delve into that discussion, although it is possible that the power of a compelling story from the past comes from its distortion or exaggeration by myth or political manipulation. For relevant discussion on myths and history of ancient China, see Bernhard Karlgren, "Legends and Cults in Ancient China," *Bulletin of the Museum of Far Eastern Antiquities*, no. 18 (1946): 199–365; and Sarah Allan, *The Shape of the Turtle: Myth, Art, and Cosmos in Early China* (Albany: State University of New York Press, 1991).

11. Accounts of events in early Chinese texts such as the *Shangshu*, the *Zuo zhuan*, and the *Guoyu* preserve elements of truth in most of their narrations; personalities and moral qualities of the key figures seem to be consistent. Also see David Schaberg, "Social Pleasures in Early Chinese Historiography and Philosophy," in *The Limits of Historiography: Genre and Narrative in Ancient Historical Texts*, ed. Christina S. Kraus (Leiden: Brill, 1999), 1–26. Martin Kern has argued that the *Shangshu* is not a collection of historical documents but "a work of political rhetoric and philosophy." See Martin Kern, "Early Chinese Divination and Its Rhetoric," in *Coping with the Future: Theories and Practices of Divination in East Asia*, ed. Michael Lackner (Leiden: Brill, 2018), 255–88.

12. Kern, "Early Chinese Divination," 266–67.

13. I benefit largely from K. C. Chang and Sarah Allan, who have provided detailed studies in these areas. See Kwang-chih Chang, *Art, Myth and Ritual: The Path to Political Authority in Ancient China* (Cambridge, MA: Harvard University, 1983); Allan, *Shape of the Turtle*.

14. Allan, *Shape of the Turtle*, 145–63.

15. Allan, *Shape of the Turtle*, 169. In the decoration of bronze vessels of the mythic art from perhaps 1600 to 950 BCE "animals are shown in full vigor, whom man treats with affection, reverence or awe." Some animals and birds could also carry the significance of omens. Michael Loewe, *Divination, Mythology and Monarchy in Han China*, University of Cambridge Oriental Publications 48 (Cambridge, UK: Cambridge University, 1994), 39–40. See also, Elizabeth Childs-Johnson, "The Metamorphic Image: A Predominant Theme in Shang Ritual Art," *Bulletin of the Museum of Far Eastern Antiquities* 70 (1998): 5–171.

16. Chang, *Art, Myth and Ritual*, 8.

17. Chang, *Art, Myth and Ritual*, 33.

18. Chang, *Art, Myth and Ritual*, 41.

19. Allan, *Shape of the Turtle*, 174–76.

20. This is not to suggest that the time before Zhou had no writing or knowledge in relation to human experiences and ancestral conduct. However, most of the texts available to us today were either dated to the Western Zhou (1100–771 BCE) or the Eastern Zhou (770–221 BCE). For example, scholars have generally agreed that even the earliest historical texts such as the *Shangshu* that mentioned *tianming* or the Mandate of Heaven would have been written in Zhou, although the idea or theory might have had its roots in Shang thought. See Sarah Allan, *The Heir and the Sage, Revised and Expanded Edition: Dynastic Legend in Early China*, SUNY series in Chinese Philosophy and Culture (Albany: State University of New York Press, 2017), 1–6.

21. Parallels to many of these historical accounts or legendary figures appeared in early texts such as the *Book of Odes*, the *Book of Documents*, the *Zuo zhuan*, and the *Guoyu*. References to history in pre-Qin philosophical texts can be seen in the *Lunyu*, the *Mozi*, the *Works of Mencius*, and the *Xunzi*. For a discussion of appeals to history in the *Xunzi*, see Paul R. Goldin, "Appeals to History in Early Chinese Philosophy," *Journal of Chinese Philosophy* (2008): 79–96. Goldin's article extends Antonio S. Cua's insight in "Ethical Uses of the Past in Early Confucianism: The Case of Hsün Tzu," *Philosophy East and West* 35, no. 2 (1985): 133–56.

22. For a discussion of how philosophical traditions in early China adapted accounts of the past to their purposes, see Mark Edward Lewis, *Writing and Authority in Early China* (Albany: State University of New York Press, 1999), 99–145.

23. Allan, *Shape of the Turtle*, 175. For a study of metaphor and mythology in Indo-European tradition, see Eve Sweetser, "Metaphor, Mythology and Everyday Language," *Journal of Pragmatics* (1995): 585–93.

24. Li Feng and David Prager Branner, *Writing and Literacy in Early China: Studies from the Columbia Early China Seminar* (Seattle: University of Washington Press, 2011), 301.

25. For example, pre-Shang "history" in the early texts can be understood as "a later transformation and systematization of Shang myth" (Allan, *Shape of the Turtle*, 175).

26. Lewis, *Writing and Authority*, 99–145.

27. The Ruists were not the only intellectual group who applied rhetoric in writings; Daoist texts are well known for their rich imagination and frequent use of metaphor. Complexity and ambiguity in references to other literary sources and traditions were common features of early Chinese discourse, both oral and written. The different ways of conceptualizing and applying metaphor could be as colorful and lively. Just like different geographical cultures, philosophical cultures use and understand metaphors differently. Sometimes an analogy is used to highlight the commonality of things that seem to be contradictory; at other times it is to compare and contrast the particularity or uniqueness of the objects in the same category. We need to be sensitive to the complexity and diversity of the rhetoric when reading these texts. For example, Ruists and Daoists applied different characteristics of water to metaphorize and argue for their different views of human acts and the cosmic order.

28. Allan, *Shape of the Turtle*, 176.

29. Shirley Chan, "Identifying Daoist Humour: Reading the *Liezi*," in *Humour in Chinese Life and Letters: Classical and Traditional Approaches*, ed. Jessica Milner Davis and Jocelyn Chey (Hong Kong: University of Hong Kong Press, 2011), 73–88.

30. The Tsinghua Bamboo Slips were donated to Tsinghua University in July 2008 by an alumnus of the university. The precise location and date of the illicit excavation that yielded the slips remains unknown although, according to the donor, the manuscripts were purchased at an auction outside China. The very large size of the collection, 2,400 slips, and their unique contents make it one of the most important discoveries of early Chinese texts to date. See Liu Guozhong, *Introduction to the Tsinghua University Bamboo-Strip Manuscripts*, trans. Christopher J. Foster and William N. French (Leiden: Brill, 2016). The transcribed text used in this study is based on Tsinghua daxue chutu wenxian yaniu yu baohu zhongxin 清華大學出土文獻研究與保護中心, *Qinghua daxue cang Zhanguo zhujian (wu)* 清華大學藏戰國竹簡 (伍) (Shanghai: Zhongxi, 2015), vol. 5, pt. 2: 134–36.

31. See Lewis, *Writing and Authority*, 99–145. Also see Schaberg, "Social Pleasures," 10–11.

32. See Stephen R. Bokenkamp, "Chinese Metaphor Again: Reading—and Understanding—Imagery in the Chinese Poetic Tradition," *Journal of the American Oriental Society* 109, no. 2 (1989): 211–21, www.jstor.org/stable/604426, accessed September 19, 2020. Also see, Pauline Yu, "Metaphor and Chinese Poetry," *Chinese Literature: Essays, Articles, Reviews (CLEAR)* 3, no. 2 (1981): 205–24. Since the most influential texts tended to be philosophical in nature, meaning can always be detected from the use of derogative or commendatory terms. Also, correspondences were drawn from various elements of the natural world to illustrate human values. For example, the *Huainanzi* draws numerological correspondences between time distinctions, the *wuxing*, and the constituents of the human body. The human body, as a microcosmos, corresponded to the external world, the macrocosmos.

33. Both texts share a similar writing style, script form, and historical content. The fundamentals of historiographical practice are also evident in the *Tang zai*

Chimen. The narrative begins with the date, *jihai* day of the first month (*zhengyue jihai* 正月己亥), and the place, Chimen 啻門, where readers assume the conversation took place. Cheng Tang asks Yi Yin: "Are there any good words from the ancestral kings that can apply to the present?" (古之先帝亦有良言情至於今乎?). This sets up the correlation between historical events or personages and the philosophical or political ideas of the present. Yi Yin replies: "Certainly there are. Without any good words passed down to the present, how could a human be complete? How could a state be complete? How could the earth be complete? And how could Heaven be complete? (小臣答 [1] 曰: 有哉. 如無有良言情至於今, 則何以成人? 何以成邦? 何以成地? 何以成 [2] 天?). Yi Yin's response confirms the essential cultural values of the ancient correlative wisdom.

34. See Gilles Boileau, *Politique et rituel dans la Chine ancienne* (Paris: Collège de France, Institut des hautes études chinoises, 2013).

35. The English translations of *Tang chuyu Tangqiu* are mine and are necessarily preliminary.

36. For example, see the *Lunyu* "Yanyuan" and the *Mozi* "Shangxian, er." The *Mozi* "Shangxian, er" also records Yi Yin as a chef later appointed a minister by Tang. For discussion on the associations between culinary art, human senses, and ritual culture, see Roel Sterckx's *Food, Sacrifice, and Sagehood in Early China* (New York: Cambridge University Press, 2011).

37. Li Chenyang, "The Ideal of Harmony in Ancient Chinese and Greek Philosophy," *Dao: A Journal of Comparative Philosophy* 7, no. 1 (2008): 81–98.

38. See note 31 in this chapter.

39. For example, the Mandate of Heaven had been transformed from its religious and mythical sense to a moral and philosophical concept: only those who demonstrated moral quality were legitimate rulers.

40. Readers would have been reminded of the saying attributed to Laozi in the *Daodejing*: "Governing a great state is like cooking small fish" (治大國若烹小鮮).

41. *Guoyu*, "Zheng yu" 鄭語. See Shanghai Normal University, *Guoyu quanyi* 國語全譯, Vol. 1 (Shanghai: Shanghai Guji, 1978), 507. Translation adapted and modified from Li Chenyang, "The Confucian Idea of Harmony," *Philosophy East and West* 56, no. 4 (2006): 585.

42. Early Confucian and Daoist texts shared a rich vocabulary for sensuous pleasure in food, drink, music, and ritual: joy (*le* 樂), pleasure (*yue* 悦), being at ease (*an* 安), good (*shan* 善), beauty (*mei* 美).

43. For *de* 德 as "moral quality" or "moral nature," see "Shenda" 慎大, *Lüshi Chunqiu* 呂氏春秋, which has a description of Jie's behavior and the subsequent fall of Xia at the hands of Tang, with Yi Yin's strategic aid.

44. An example of the "interrelated" harmonization is "to share the benefit with the people, this is what loving the people refers to" (與民分利, 此以自愛也).

45. Lakoff and Johnson, *Metaphors We Live By*.

46. Allan, *Way of Water*. Allan has argued that root metaphor is more than just rhetorical figurative language. Metaphor itself is grounded in a specific abstraction of ideas.

47. Allan, *Way of Water*. Allan used water and plants as examples to show how early Chinese philosophers assumed that natural laws could be applied to the human world. The movement of water and the growth of plants were root metaphors in Chinese philosophy.

48. *Daodejing*, see, Chen Guying 陳鼓應, *Laozi jinzhu jinyi* 老子今注今譯 (Beijing: Zhonghua shuju, 2020), 89; *Zhuangzi*, see, Guo Xiang 郭象, Lu Dewen 陸德文, Xuan Ying 玄英, and Guo Qingfan 郭慶藩, *Zhuangzi jishi* 莊子集釋 (Taibei: Taiwan Zhonghua shuju, 1970), 391–401; Zhao Shouzheng 趙守正, *Guanzi tongjie* 管子通解, vol. 2. (Beijing: Beijing jingji xueyuan, 1989), 7; *Liji*, "Yueji" 樂記, see Sun Xidan 孫希旦, *Liji jiejie* 禮記集解 61 *juan*, vols. 9–16 (Rui'an Sunshi 瑞安孫氏 1861). Digitalized in 2012.

49. *Lunyu*, "Zihan" 子罕. See Roger T. Ames and Henry Rosemont Jr., *The Analects of Confucius: A Philosophical Translation, a New Translation Based on the Dingzhou Fragments and Other Recent Archaeological Finds*, Classics of Ancient China (New York: Ballantine Books, 1998), 132. "Yongye" 雍也, Ames and Rosemont, *Analects of Confucius*, 108.

50. *Guanzi*, "Zhong Kuang," *Zhao Shouzheng* 1989, 15.

51. See discussion on Mencius and the Mawangdui *Wuxing* manuscript in Mark Csikszentmihalyi, *Material Virtue: Ethics and the Body in Early China* (Leiden: Brill, 2004).

52. Arthur Waley, *The Way and Its Power: A Study of the Tao Te Ching and Its Place in Chinese Thought* (London: Allen & Unwin, 1934; New York: Grove, 1958); Victor H. Maier, *Tao Te Ching: The Classic Book of Integrity and the Way, by Lao Tzu; An Entirely New Translation Based on the Recently Discovered Ma-wang-tui Manuscripts* (New York: Bantam Books, 1990).

53. The word *ji* 疾 has a number of overlapping connotations: (1) illness (*Han Feizi* 韓非子, "Yulao" 喻老: 君有疾在腠理, 不治將恐深; *Analects*, "Yongye" 雍也: 伯牛有疾, 子問之); (2) suffering and pain (*Shiji* 史記, "Huji leizhuan" 滑稽列傳: 問之民所疾苦); (3) fault or disadvantage (*Mengzi*, "Liang Hui Wang, II" 梁惠王下: 寡人有疾, 寡人好勇).

54. *Xunzi*, "Cultivation" 修身. Wang Xianqian 王先謙, *Xunzi jijie* 荀子集解, 2 vols., vol. 1, ed. Shen Xiaohuan 沈嘯寰 and Wang Xingxian 王星賢 (Beijing: Zhonghua, 1988), 4.

55. Possibly Tang and Yi Yin's conversation could be compared to the Greek exploration of *eudemonia*, commonly translated as happiness or welfare; it is traditionally accepted that *eudemonia* included virtue, health, wealth, and beauty. Note the lengthy discussion of *de* and "completion" in Constance A. Cook, *Ancestors, Kings, and the Dao* (Cambridge: Harvard Asia Center, 2016). Cook traces the tradition

from Western Zhou bronze inscriptions up through Eastern Zhou manuscripts. See also "Contextualizing 'Becoming a Complete Person' in the *Tang zai Chimen*," in "Qinghua daxue cang Zhanguo zhujian (wu) guoji xueshu yantaohui lunwenji," ed. Li Xueqin, Sarah Allan, and Michael Lüdke, *Qinghua jian yanjiu* 清華簡研究 3 (2019): 183–93.

56. Tsinghua daxue, *Qinghua daxue cang Zhanguo zhujian (wu)*, 142–43.

57. References to people as the body of the state are also found in *Guanzi* 管子, "Junchen, xia" 君臣下; *Zhao Shouzheng*, 458.

58. These were mentioned toward the end of the *Tang zai Chimen*.

9

Some Remarks on the Value and Inner Meaning of the Way of Archery

CHEUNG KWONG-YUE

TRANSLATED BY CONSTANCE A. COOK

The flush of newly discovered bamboo manuscripts provides new tools to understand pre-Qin culture and education. For example, the "Yijie" 猗嗟 section of the *Kongzi shilun* 孔子詩論 manuscript (slip 22), presently stored in the Shanghai Museum collection, has a line that must be compared with a line in the ode of the same name in the "Airs of Qi" (Qi feng 齊風) in the transmitted *Book of Odes* (*Shijing*). The *Kongzi shilun* has:

"Yijie" says: "Four arrows return to control chaos"—I delight in it.

於 (猗) 差 (嗟) 曰: 四矢殳 (反), 以御亂, 吾憙之.[1]

The corresponding transmitted *Shijing* passage says:

When he dances, never losing his place,
When he shoots, always piercing.
Swift his four arrows fly
To quell mischief on every side.

舞則選兮, 射則貫兮. 四矢反兮, 以禦亂兮.[2]

In the *Han Odes* 韓詩 version of these lines, the word written *fan* 反 is recorded as *bian* 變;[3] they were both *bang* initials and *yuan* finals 幫母元部 and hence loaned for each other. In Chu bamboo-slip manuscripts, the archaic graph 㢋 could be read as either *fan* or *bian*. This is a prime example of how a newly discovered text, unseen by earlier scholars, is a great boon to our understanding. This chapter examines the archery ritual to reveal its modern value to self-cultivation.

"Four arrows" (*sishi* 四矢), in the preceding ode, refers to the number of arrows used in the ancient archery ritual. They were also referred to as *sihou* 四鍭 (four arrows) or *shengshi* 乘矢 (a four-in-hand of arrows). For example, *sihou* in the Da Ya ode "Xing wei" 行葦:

> The painted bows are strong,
> The four arrows well balanced;
> They shoot, all with like success;
> The guests are arranged according to their merits.
> The painted bows are bent,
> The four arrows, one after another, are aimed.
> The four arrows are as though planted;
> The guests must be arranged according to their deportment.
>
> 敦弓既堅, 四鍭既鈞; 舍矢既均, 序賓以賢. 敦弓既句, 既挾四鍭; 四鍭如樹, 序賓以不侮.[4]

The term *shengshi* appears in the "Lilou, xia" 離婁下 chapter of the *Mengzi* 孟子 and the "Xiangsheli" 鄉射禮 and "Dasheli" 大射禮 chapters on the archery ritual in the *Yili* 儀禮.[5] *Sheng* 乘 clearly refers to a set of four from the expression "held on to three (arrows) and put another under his arm" (搢三而挾一個) found in the "Xiangsheli" and "Dasheli" chapters.[6] The word *sheng* in the chapter "Shengma" 乘馬 in *Guanzi* 管子 is defined as involving four horses: "a single *sheng* is with four horses" (一乘者, 四馬也).[7] A battle chariot equipped with four horses probably included a squad of three armed soldiers along with seventy-two foot soldiers and, if we count support infantry, a total of maybe a hundred personnel. An army of one thousand *sheng* would be ten thousand strong. The word *sheng* can also imply "four" in other contexts. For example, the *Zuo zhuan* 左傳 records that, when the Qin 秦 army reached Hua 滑, Zheng 鄭 merchant Xuan Gao 弦高 used a *sheng* as vanguard, including twelve cattle, to feast the army (以乘韋先牛十二犒師).⁸ And the "Shaoyi" 少儀 chapter of the *Liji* 禮記 mentions "a gift of a *sheng* of pots with wine, bundled dried meats, and one dog" (其以乘壺酒, 束脩, 一犬, 賜人). Zheng Xuan 鄭玄 (127–200) explains that "a *sheng* of pots is four pots" (乘壺, 四壺也). Kong Yingda 孔穎達 (574–648) explains how the word *sheng* first applied to horses could be applied to pots (四馬曰乘, 故知四壺酒, 亦曰乘壺酒).⁹

The fact that the four arrows were the standard of the archery ritual can be traced back to the late Shang. Presently stored in the National Museum in Beijing, the Zuoce Ban *yuan* 作冊般黿 (a bronze turtle) has a thirty-three-graph-long inscription with the line: "The king shot first one and then three arrows, not a single one wasted" (王一 (?) 射, 囗 (?) 射三, 率無廢矢).¹⁰ In total the king shot off four arrows and they all hit the target. We see that the bronze soft-shelled turtle, cast as proof of the king's feat, has been cast with four arrows sunk so deeply into the turtle's back that only a short section with feathers is sticking out for each. While it is difficult today to imagine fully what the ancient archery ritual was like, ancient texts, such as those previously mentioned, as well as bronze inscriptions, like those from the Yu *fangding* 馭方鼎, Ling *ding* 令鼎, and Yi *hegai* 義盉蓋, among others, reveal clues. We define a seven-step process: (1) "the supervisor of archery requests the archery (ritual)" (*sishe qing she* 司射請射), (2) "three pairs wait their turn to shoot" (*san'ou si she* 三耦俟射), (3) "the supervisor of archery guides the archery (ritual)" (*sishe you she* 司射誘射), (4) "making the losers drink" (*yin bushengzhe* 飲不勝者), (5) "presenting [rewards] to the score counter" (*xian huozhe* 獻獲者), (6) "regulating the archery (ritual) with music" (*yi yue jie she* 以樂節射), and (7) "seated at the feast toasting each other, bringing the ritual to a close" (*zuoyan lüchou, zhong li* 坐燕旅酬, 終禮).

The supervisor of archery formally opened the ceremony after the host and the guests had all toasted each other with wine. This is described in the *Yili* in two similar passages, first in the "Xiangsheli" and then in the "Dasheli," with the supervisor performing a set choreography in the ritual hall and taking up the bow and four arrows:

> The supervisor of archery moved to the west side of the hall, bared his left arm, bowing and yielding, he proceeded to take out the bow when he reached just west of the steps, along with a *sheng* of arrows that he clasped under his arm. He then ascended [the hall] from the western stairs.

司射適堂西, 袒決遂取弓于階西, 兼挾乘矢, 升自西階.¹¹

The supervisor of archery approached the side passage, bared his left arm, bowing and yielding, proceeded to grasp the bow, carrying a *sheng* of arrows under his arm, then he sited the arrow along the riser on the outside [edge] of the bow and hooked the string with his right thumb. From a position in front of the stairs, he said: "May the governing official request the archery [ritual]."

司射適次, 袒決遂執弓, 挾乘矢, 於弓外見鏃於枎, 右巨指鉤弦. 自阼階前曰: 為政請射.¹²

These two chapters continue to describe the second step in the archery ritual in which three pairs of shooters wait their turns:

The three pairs of shooters all bared their arms and proceeded. The supervisor grasped the risers of the bows from the left and the strings of the bows from the right, and then handed over the bows followed by the arrows [to the shooters]. The three pairs held on to three arrows [each] and put another under [each of] their arms. The supervisor of archery first arranged them in position to the southwest of where the target is set up, facing east. The three pairs all approached from the west side of the supervisor of archery and stood to his southwest facing east, with the uppermost to the north waiting his turn.

三耦皆袒決遂, 有司左執柎, 右執弦, 而授弓, 遂授矢. 三耦皆執弓, 搢三而挾一個. 司射先立于所設中之西南, 東面. 三耦皆進由司射之西, 立于其西南, 東面北上而俟.¹³

Then [the supervisor] announced: "Grandee and grandee, and gentleman driver to grandee." Then he proceeded to move to the front of the western stair, faced east, and looked to the right. He then commanded those in charge to bring in the archery equipment. When all the archery equipment had been brought in, the bow and arrows of the lord were moved to the eastern hall. Those of the guests were parked below the western hall along with the targets, tallies, and full feasting dishes. No one grasped their bow and arrows. All bows and arrows lay ready,

Some Remarks on the Value and Inner Meaning of the Way of Archery | 193

along with the wooden board [for making sure the arrow shafts were even], then [each] proceeded in turn.

遂告曰:"夫與大夫,士御於大夫." 遂適西階前, 東面右顧, 命有司納射器. 射器皆入, 君之弓矢, 適東堂; 賓之弓矢與中, 籌, 豐, 皆止于西堂下, 眾弓矢不挾. 總眾弓矢, 楅, 皆適次而俟.[14]

The concept of two people competing as a pair was called *ou'she* 耦射. We can see some of the people who shot together mentioned in Zhou bronze inscriptions. The Yu *fangding* praises Yu, owner of the bronze vessel, for serving as an opponent of the king in archery (馭方卿王射). The Ling *ding* 令鼎 notes that whenever the king performed archery, the supervisor and young clansmen joined the shoot (王射, 有司眔師氏小子會射). The Yi *hegai* refers to the Zhou king along with the top state officers performing the great archery (ritual) (*dashe*).[15]

The *Yili* chapters continue to step three when the supervisor of archery "guides the shots":

The supervisor of archery faced east to the north of the three pairs of shooters. Each holding three [arrows] with another under their arms, they were bowed in. . . . guiding the shooting, until a *sheng* of arrows [was shot by each].

司射東面立于三耦之北, 搢三而挾一個, 揖進. . . . 誘射, 將乘矢.[16]

The supervisor of archery enters the side chamber, holding three arrows and another under his arm. Coming out of the side chamber, he faces west, bows, and then faces north to the stairs and bows. Ascending the hall, he bows and then facing the target to the north, he bows. When he approaches the target, he bows, and retreats slightly back down from the target to guide the archery [shooting].

司射入于次, 搢三挾一個; 出于次, 西面揖, 當階北面揖, 及階揖, 升堂揖, 當物北面揖, 及物揖, 由下物少退, 誘射.[17]

After the shooting (stage one) were two more stages, the drinking and the counting up of the catch. The three stages (*sanfan* 三番) in the performance included: archery (*she* 射), drinking (*yin* 飲), and counting the score (*shu huo* 數獲). Each stage had different sets of specialists responsible. The fourth step of the ritual was drinking, where the loser was made to drink (*yin bushengzhe*). This involved a choreography of arranging the winners and the losers into two lines. The line of winners ascended the hall first. Then the losers ascended to toast the winners in a display of decorous behavior. After the toast came the ritual of presenting the game to the lord. The sum of the total numbers of game was then divided by the number of arrows that actually hit the target and then further divided by the number of guests. The supervisor of horses ranked the successful shooters and oversaw the setting up of sacrificial meat stands in honor of the ruling lord.

A key aspect of the archery ritual was the use of music to regulate the motion of events. It also inspired and entertained the guests. The "Xiangsheli" notes that the supervisor of horses faced east and ordered the music regulator to entertain the guests with music. In response, the music regulator faced east and ordered the grand master to play the song "Zouyu" 騶虞 with equal intervals (between each movement) (司馬 . . . 東面命樂正曰, 請以樂樂於賓. . . . 樂正東面命大師曰, 奏騶虞, 間若一).[18] This not only helped to control the timing of the performance but also added an air of refinement to it. It inspired the guests to move to the final stage of the archery ritual, when everyone sat down to a feast of full dishes and gave toasts to each other, thus bringing the ritual to an end.

The Archery Ritual as Art

The seven stages presented earlier are the general pattern followed for the performance of the archery ritual. It was one of the six arts (*liuyi* 六藝) that comprised male elite education as described in the "Baoshi" 保氏 chapter in the "Diguan" 地官 section of the *Zhouli* 周禮:

> Raise the sons of state by means of the Dao, instructing them in the Six Arts: the first is the five types of ritual, the second is the six types of music, the third is the five types of archery, the fourth is the five types of chariot driving, the fifth is the six types of writing, and the sixth is the nine types of calculation.
>
> 養國子以道, 乃教之六藝: 一曰五禮, 二曰六樂, 三曰五射, 四曰五馭, 五曰六書, 六曰九數.[19]

We know from the recent discovery of manuscripts, as well as from transmitted texts, that there was an integral connection between ritual and music. Hence, it is not surprising to see even an archery ritual regulated by music. The "Yueji" 樂記 chapter of the *Liji* 禮記 explains the relationship:

> Music comes out from inside [oneself] and ritual is created on the outside. Since music comes from inside it is quiet, and since ritual is created on the outside it is ornate.

樂由中出, 禮自外作. 樂由中出故靜, 禮自外作故文.[20]

The mutual coordination of ritual and music is also something that those who cultivate *de* must take into consideration. Self-cultivation through the performance of ritual music produces *de* 德, an inner power that results in virtuous behavior.[21] The "Yueji" notes that "being accomplished in both ritual and music is what is meant by possessing *de*" (禮樂皆得, 謂之有德). Slip 54 of the *Yucong, san* 語叢三 in the Guodian 郭店 collection of Chu bamboo-slip manuscripts notes, "Music is what those accomplished in *de* find pleasurable" (樂, 備德者之所樂也).[22] Slip 29 of *Zun de yi* 尊德義 in the Guodian corpus explains, "There is no greater expression of *de* than in [the performance of] ritual and music" (德者且莫大乎禮樂). Slip 26 of *Liu de* 六德 notes, "Humanness is internal, and propriety is external. [The performance of] ritual and music are the same as this" (仁, 內也; 義, 外也. 禮樂, 共也).[23] These Guodian texts reaffirm the relationship between ritual and music recorded in the "Yueji."

The discourse connecting acting humanely (*ren* 仁) with the performance of ritual (*li*) is attributed to the Ru 儒 cultural tradition. The intimate connection between the performance of ritual and behavior provided the foundation of morality. As a form of self-cultivation, a self-cultivated man would experience "luminous *de*" (*mingde*) and "respectful *de*" (*jingde*), two terms that appeared in Western Zhou bronze inscriptions. The performance of archery ritual as regulated by music also provided men with an opportunity to cultivate *de*.

The connection between the ancient archery ritual and Confucian propriety is evident in the *Analects* 3.7:

> The Master said, "The *junzi* (superior man) has nothing with which he contends, yet must this be so in the practice of archery?

Bowing and yielding to others, he ascends the hall, descends and drinks, and through this competition remains a *junzi*."

子曰: 君子無所爭, 必也射乎! 揖讓而升, 下而飲, 其爭也君子.²⁴

We know from the previous discussion that the practice of bowing, ascending, descending, and drinking are all part of the choreography of the archery ritual. The connection between archery and ritual is affirmed in the "Sheyi" 射義 chapter of the *Liji* 禮記: "The many lords and ministers devoted themselves to archery through the practice of ritual and music" (諸侯君臣, 盡志於射, 以習禮樂).²⁵ Thus, we know that both the practice of ritual and of music are required to become proficient in archery. Elsewhere the same chapter notes:

Thus, the archers, in advancing, retiring, and circling around, had to focus on proper ritual, inwardly making their intentions align, and outwardly making their bodies straight. This way, they held bows and arrows both judiciously and firmly and then could be said to hit the mark. This way one can observe their virtuous conduct.

故射者, 進退周還必中禮, 內志正, 外體直, 然後持弓矢審固; 持弓矢審固, 然後可以言中. 此可以觀德行矣.²⁶

The link between the development of virtuous behavior and the practice of archery is further noted in this chapter, where it says:

The archers expressed the way of humane behavior and sought through the practice of archery to correct themselves. So once in a properly aligned position, they shot. But if they missed the mark, no resentment was expressed toward the winner. Instead, they reflected upon the causes within themselves.

射者, 仁之道也. 射求正諸己, 己正然後發, 發而不中, 則不怨勝己者, 反求諸己而已.²⁷

In fact, the preceding statement was drawn from a similar line in *Mengzi* 孟子 2A.7:

> The humane person is like an archer who shoots only after making himself properly aligned. And if when he shoots, he misses the mark, he holds no resentment toward the winner but simply reflects on the cause within himself.
>
> 仁者如射，射者正己而後發，發而不中，不怨勝己者，反求諸己而已矣。²⁸

The phrase "reflects on the cause within himself" (*fanqiu zhu ji* 反求諸己) is found again in *Mengzi* 4A.4, where it states that "whoever is unsuccessful at what they do should reflect on the causes within themselves. Once they are properly aligned the whole world will turn to them" (行有不得者，皆反求諸己。其身正，而天下歸之).²⁹ The idea is found also in the Chu bamboo-strip manuscript from Guodian, *Qiongda yi shi* 窮達以時 (slip 15): "Thus the noble man is earnest about returning to himself" (君子惇於反己).³⁰ In antiquity, people had the sense of performing service to rectify themselves or have their proper self "stand up" (*xingshi lishen* 行事立身). In essence, this was the point of education in the Ru tradition. As expressed in the *Xunzi* 荀子 ("Xiu shen" 修身): "Ritual is enacted through properly aligning one's body" (禮者所以正身也).³¹ In essence, making oneself an upright moral person also involved physical choreography. The archery ritual was a complex series of stages including advancing and retreating, circling around, positioning oneself, holding the bow and preparing the shot, then shooting the arrows at the target, being ranked, preparing sacrificial foods, and celebration. The ceremony melded the cultivation of personal temperament with the prescription for self-reflection resulting in the nurturing of the humanity and virtue inherent in a *junzi*. Thus, the concepts expounded in the *Daxue* 大學 and popularized during the Song (960–1269) of "the investigation of things" (*ge wu* 格物), "advancing knowledge" (*zhi zhi* 致知), "intentions with integrity" (*chengyi* 誠意), "aligned heart/mind" (*zheng xin* 正心), and "self-cultivation" (*xiu shen* 修身) evolved as the Chinese method for moral education.

The long history of the archery ritual involves the essentialized blend of ritual, music, and virtue and not simply the art of archery. The deeper meanings found hidden in the bounty of traditional culture have the power to correct the human heart and create changes in ways that should not be ignored.

Notes

1. Ma Chengyuan 馬承源, ed., *Shanghai bowuguan cang Zhanguo Chu zhushu* 上海博物館藏戰國楚竹書, vol. 1 (Shanghai: Shanghai guji, 2001), 11.
2. *Mao Shi zhengyi* 毛詩正義, 5.2.15b–16a, in *Shisanjing zhushu* 十三經注疏, coll. Ruan Yuan 阮元 (1764–1849), 8 vols. (Taipei: Yiwen, 2007), vol. 2, 202. Translation modified from Arthur Waley and Joseph R. Allen, *The Book of Songs* (New York: Grove, 1996), 83.
3. Fan Jiaxiang 范家相, *Sanjia Shi shiyi* 三家詩拾遺 (*Siku quanshu* 四庫全書 ed.), 5.13b–14a.
4. *Mao Shi zhengyi*, 17.2.4a–6b, in *Shisanjing zhushu*, vol. 2, 601–02. Waley and Allen, *Book of Songs*, 247–48.
5. *Mengzi zhushu* 孟子注疏, 8B.2a, in *Shisanjing zhushu*, vol. 8, 151. For the term *sheng shi* in "Xiangsheli" and "Dasheli," see *Yili zhushu* 儀禮注疏, 11.17b and 17.14a, in *Shisanjing zhushu*, vol. 4, 117 and 202.
6. *Yili zhushu*, 12.1b and 17.13b–14a, in *Shisanjing zhushu*, vol. 4, 124 and 202.
7. Li Xiangfeng 黎翔鳳, *Guanzi jiaozhu* 管子校注, 3 vols. (2004; rpt., Beijing: Zhonghua, 2015), vol. 1, 90.
8. *Chunqiu Zuo zhuan zhushu* 春秋左傳注疏, 17.14a (Xi 僖 33.1), in *Shisanjing zhushu*, vol. 6, 289.
9. *Liji zhushu* 禮記注疏, 35.16a, in *Shisanjing zhushu*, vol. 5, 633.
10. The Zuoce Ban *yuan* is kept in the National Museum of China, Beijing.
11. "Xiangsheli," in *Yili zhushu*, 11.17b, in *Shisanjing zhushu*, vol. 4, 117.
12. "Dasheli," in *Yili zhushu*, 17.11, in *Shisanjing zhushu*, vol. 4, 201.
13. "Xiangsheli," in *Yili zhushu*, 12.1, in *Shisanjing zhushu*, vol. 4, 124.
14. "Dasheli," in *Yili zhushu*, 17.11b–12a, in *Shisanjing zhushu*, vol. 4, 201.
15. See inscriptions 2810, 2803, and 9453 in *Yin Zhou jinwen jicheng* 殷周金文集成, ed. Zhongguo shehui kexueyuan kaogu yanjiusuo 中國社會科學院考古研究所, rev. ed., 8 vols. (Beijing: Zhonghua, 2007).
16. "Xiangsheli," in *Yili zhushu*, 12.1b–3a, in *Shisanjing zhushu*, vol. 4, 124–25.
17. "Dasheli," in *Yili zhushu*, 17.13b–14a, in *Shisanjing zhushu*, vol. 4, 202.
18. "Xiangsheli," in *Yili zhushu*, 12.23–24a, in *Shisanjing zhushu*, vol. 4, 135.
19. *Zhou li zhushu* 周禮注疏, 14.6b, in *Shisanjing zhushu*, vol. 3, 212.
20. *Liji zhushu*, 37.12b–13a, in *Shisanjing zhushu*, vol. 5, 668.
21. See the discussion of this relationship in Constance. A. Cook, *Ancestors, Kings, and the Dao* (Cambridge, MA: Harvard University Asia Center, 2017).
22. *Liji zhushu*, 37.8a, in *Shisanjing zhushu*, vol. 5, 665.
23. For texts and translations, see Scott Bradley Cook, *The Bamboo Texts of Guodian: A Study & Complete Translation* (Ithaca, NY: East Asia Program, Cornell University, 2012), 883 (*Yucong, san*), 661–64 (*Zun de yi*), 786–92 (*Liude*).
24. *Lunyu zhushu* 論語注疏, 3.4a ("Bayi" 八佾), in *Shisanjing zhushu*, vol. 8, 26.

25. *Liji zhushu*, 62.4b, in *Shisanjing zhushu*, vol. 5, 1015.
26. *Liji zhushu*, 62.1b–2a, in *Shisanjing zhushu*, vol. 5, 1014.
27. *Liji zhushu*, 62.13a, in *Shisanjing zhushu*, vol. 5, 1020.
28. *Mengzi zhushu*, 3B.8b ("Gongsun Chou shang" 公孫丑上), in *Shisanjing zhushu*, 66.
29. *Mengzi zhushu*, 7A.8b ("Lilou, shang" 離婁上), in *Shisanjing zhushu*, 126.
30. S. Cook, *Bamboo Texts of Guodian*, 464.
31. Liang Qixiong 梁啟雄, *Xunzi jianshi* 荀子簡釋 (Beijing: Zhonghua shuju, 1983), 21.

10

The Meaning of the Graph and Word *ge* 革 in the Huayuanzhuang East Oracle Bone Corpus and Related Questions

Han Yujiao

Translated by Constance A. Cook

While reading oracle bones, the author has come upon two observations: the first concerns the proper interpretation of certain sacrificial terms, and the second regards the importance of symmetry in the divination pattern on the turtle plastron.

The Word and the Graph *ge* 革

In the Huayuanzhuang East (*Huayuanzhuang dongdi* 花園莊東地, hereafter *Huadong*) oracle bone corpus, *ge* appears as follows:[1]

(1a) *Huadong* 474.4: 己巳卜: 子祼告其柬革于匕 (妣) 庚. 一 二
Crack-making on *jisi* day, Zi presents *guan*-libation and announces perhaps X *ge* should go to Ancestress Geng. 1, 2.

(1b) *Huadong* 474.5: 率酻革. 不用. 一
The whole (process of the rituals contains) the *you*-libation and *ge*. Do not use (this divination). 1.

(2) *Huadong* 491: 庚午: 酒革匕 (妣) 庚二小宰, 鬯卣一, 才 (在) 狀, 來自獸 (狩). 一 二

On *gengwu* day, make the *you*-libation and *ge*-ritual to Ancestress Geng with two specially pen-raised lambs and offer one *chang*-vessel of fragrant millet wine, at Da, (when Zi) comes (back) from the hunt. 1, 2.

Examples 1 and 2 are found on two plastrons concerning the same topic. The graph *ge* is written respectively as ⿰, ⿰, and ⿰ meaning in each case the name of a sacrifice.[2] It appears in the formula "verb of sacrifice + *ge* + (to) object of sacrifice + sacrificial animal." The verbs of sacrifice are modified by the words X 束 and *you* 酒, so it is necessary that we understand them before we begin to unpack the meaning of *ge*. In the following examples, we see that X is used to describe the manner of animal sacrifice:

(3) *Huadong* 228.8: 丁亥卜: 吉 (佶) 牛束于宜.

Crack-making on *dinghai* day, strong bovine is X in the *yi*-ritual (ritual of presenting meat on a chopping board).

(4) *Huadong* 522: 賈馬其束. 二

Trader's horse, perhaps X it. 2.

The meaning of the verb of sacrifice *you* in oracle bones has been a source of debate. Some feel it is not a method of sacrifice at all but, in fact, a stage in the larger sacrificial process.[3] In examples 1a and 1b, we see by contrast that X involves animal sacrifice. In fact, X only appears as a verb of sacrifice in the *Huadong* corpus, whereas elsewhere it is the name of the western wind. Qiu Xigui 裘錫圭 notes that since the oracle bone graph 束 looks like something wound around wood that the basic meaning must be to wrap around.[4] Yao Xiaosui 姚孝遂 (1926–1996) also pointed out that the names of ancient sacrifices all derived from animal sacrifices and that the name implied the method.[5] So, it is possible that X in the *Huadong* corpus refers to some sort of "wrapping around" (*chanshu* 纏束) sacrificial action.

Hence, *ge* in example 2 must be an animal sacrifice method, specifically with regard to the two specially pen-raised lambs, and then something similar in example 1. The *Shuowen jiezi* 說文解字 ("Gebu" 革部) explains *ge* as: "Animal skin with the fur removed, *ge* is to change it" (獸皮治去其毛, 革更之). Ji Xusheng 季旭昇 notes how the oracle bone graph looks like animal skin spread for tanning.[6] The graph and word *ge* then represents both the animal sacrifice and the method of cutting open the animal skin and removing the fur.

The Word and the Graph *pi* 皮

Another sacrificial term in the *Huadong* corpus confirms that *ge* was a sacrificial term.

> (5) *Huadong* 149.4: 丁未卜: 其侑 (禦) 自且 (祖) 甲, 且 (祖) 乙至妣 庚, 晋 二牢, 麥 (來) 自皮鼎酉興. 用. 一 二 三
> Crack-making on *dingwei* day, perhaps perform the *yu*-exorcism ritual for ancestors from Ancestor Jia, Ancestor Yi, down to Ancestress Geng, record two specially pen-raised bovines, come from the *pi ding you xing*. Use (this divination). 1, 2, 3.
>
> (6) *Huadong* 550.1: . . . 麥 (來) 自皮鼎酉 . . .
> . . . come from *pi ding you* . . .

The use of *pi* 皮 in examples 5 and 6 is the same. The *Huadong* editors recognize *pi* as a place name.[7] Huang Tianshu 黃天樹 reads *pi* as *bi* 彼 and understands example 5 as asking if it is okay whether Zi 子, from that place where Ding Jiu 鼎酒 rituals are performed to (Zi) Xing, comes (to a temple) to perform a sacrifice to ancestors including from Zu Jia 祖甲 and Zu Yi 祖乙 down to Bi Geng 妣庚.[8] We believe however that the *pi* in this phrase should be understood as *ge* and read in the sense of a verb of sacrifice. In addition, the three words, *pi ding you*, in examples 5 and 6 should be understood as three verbs of sacrifice linked together, a phenomenon we see elsewhere such as with the phrase *you X fa* 酉彳伐 in *Heji* 32099: "Divined on a *gengyin* day, perform *you X fa* rituals to ancestors including from Shang Jia and the Six Shi, with three Qiang captives and three bovine, to the Six Shi with two Qiang captives and two bovine, up to the Xiao Shi, with one Qiang captive and one bovine" (庚寅貞: 酉彳伐 自上甲六示三羌三牛, 六示二羌二牛, 小示一羌一牛).[9]

The word *ding* 鼎 can also be a verb of sacrifice in the oracle-bone inscriptions, as we see on *Heji* 1826: "Prepare meat sacrifice for Ancestor Ding, perform offering ritual by burning small pig and split-open, specially pen-raised sheep, saying, 'Do not split open and *ding* (them).' 1, 2 announcements" (山 (侑) 于且 (祖) 丁, 尞 (燎) 豰卯宰, 曰勿卯鼎. 一 二

告). Qiu Xigui claims that *ding* means to fill a *ding*-vessel with something for sacrifice, such as with the heads of the enemy as seen in the *Yi Zhou shu* 逸周書 ("Shifu" 世俘): "King Wu then disposed of Zhou shooting a hundred evil ministers, punishing those Jia on the Right and the Heirs (by putting their heads) in a *ding*: when the Grand Master cut those forty men's heads, they were as a group of lords (put) in the *ding*" (武王乃廢於紂矢惡臣人百人，伐右厥甲，小子鼎；大師伐厥四十夫，家 (塚) 君鼎). *Heji* 30997 has "perhaps perform the *ding* sacrifice using thirty dogs" (其鼎，用卅犬) and *Heji* 19962 has "sacrifice a pig for Mu Geng, performing *ding*. Use it" (屮母庚豕，鼎。用).[10] In both cases, the word *ding* has the same function, that is, the idea of the sacrificial act of filling a *ding* with sacrificial victims. This was likely the meaning in examples 5 and 6.

The word *pi* 皮 is defined in the *Shuowen jiezi* ("Pibu" 皮部): "*Pi* refers to when the *ge* is peeled off an animal" (剝取獸革者謂之皮). Duan Yucai 段玉裁 (1735–1815) notes:

> *Bo* 剝 (to peel) is to *lie* 裂 (split apart), as in to split apart the *ge* from the meat. What is meant by *ge*, as a particular term, is to remove the fur from the skin, but when used in general terms there is no difference (with *pi*). What is meant by *zhe* 者 is the person who does this, and the *pi* refers to the *ge* removed from the animal. The word *pi* is *bi* 柀, meaning *xi* 析 (to split). See the "Mubu" 木部 where it refers to "remove" as in the skin. As a derivation, the coats of things are called *pi*, and the act of removing the coat can also be called *pi*.
>
> 剝，裂也，謂使革與肉分裂也。云「革」者，析言則去毛曰革，統言則不別也。云「者」者，謂其人也，取獸革者謂之皮。皮，柀。柀，析也。見木部。因之所取謂之皮矣。引伸凡物之表皆曰皮，凡去物之表亦皆曰皮。[11]

In the *Guangya* 廣雅, "Shi yan" 釋言, "*pi/fu* is to peel" (皮，膚，剝也).[12] In transmitted texts, then, we know that *pi* and *ge* were used similarly, and either can represent the skin that is peeled off. In the *Yili* 儀禮, the *ding*-vessel can be filled with animal skin as a sacrificial offering.[13] Records in the *Zhou li* 周禮 and Western Zhou bronze inscriptions mention the use of animal skins as ritual objects.[14] If we combine this data with the examples in the Huadong oracle-bone inscriptions, then we can understand *ge* and *pi* as verbs of sacrifice representing the hides (剝取獸皮). In example 5, the phrase *lai zi pi ding you xing* (來自皮鼎卣興) means coming from the site where Zi will perform the sacrifices of *pi* (peel off skin), *ding* (boil head in a *ding*-vessel), and *you* (wine-libation ritual) to Zixing" (從對子興舉行皮, 鼎, 肜祭祀的地點前來).

A Note on the Omen Branches' Direction for the Diviner Huang Group

The "omen branches" (*yaozhi* 兆枝) on the front of an oracle bone and the drilled and chiseled notches on the backs are arranged in patterns of opposition. If the notches on the back went to the right, then the cracks on the front went to the left. Generally, in the case of turtle plastrons, the omen cracks are distributed on either side of the central vertical line. Dong Zuobin 董作賓(1896-1963) understood this symmetry as a Shang aesthetic that persisted over time no matter how the rituals changed (see fig. 10.1).[15] The

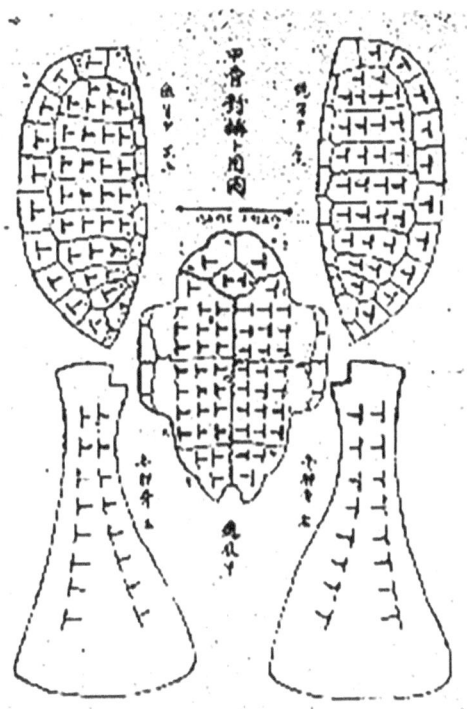

Figure 10.1. Illustration of Symmetry in Oracle Bone Cracks. *Source:* Author's graphic adapted from Dong Zubin, Zhongyang yanjiu lishi yuyan yanjiusuo jikan 中央研究院歷史語言研究所集刊 29 (November 1957), 105.

cracks are aligned along the central vertical lines on both the carapaces and plastrons.[16] We see that plastron omen cracks when on the left side of the center face right and those on the right side face left. Carapace omen cracks likewise face the central line. There are exceptions however. For example, after examining turtle bones from different burial grounds and excavation sites in Yinxu, Liu Yiman 劉一曼 points out that this tradition is applied to turtle bones found at Xiaotun 小屯, Houjiazhuang South 侯家莊南地, and Huayuanzhuang East, but not to those from other locations in Yinxu. Moreover, in the cases of Miaopu North 苗圃北地 and Huayuanzhuang South turtle bones, most were chiseled and burned on the outer rim of the notch along opposite sides of the central vertical line.[17] It is important to note that, besides two examples of turtle shell pieces with incised practice graphs (*xikezi* 習刻字) found in Miaopu North, the rest of the shells found were not inscribed. Liu Yiman 劉一曼 explains that this was due to the fact that these bones were produced by commoners or others who were not members of the royal house.[18]

One particularly curious aspect of this issue is that those bones under the supervision of the Diviner Huang 黃 group seem most likely to adhere to this crack-making protocol. If we look at thirteen examples (*Heji* 35376, 35659, 37469, 37763, 38167, 38776, 38847, 38878, 38849, 38850, and *Hebu* 11175, 11946, 12463), we find that seven pieces have notches with omen cracks along the central vertical axis: *Heji* 35376 (see fig. 10.2),

35376

Figure 10.2. *Heji* 35376. *Source:* Author's graphic adapted from Guo Moruo and Hu Houxuan, ed., *Jiaguwen heji* 甲骨文合集, 13 vols. (Beijing: Zhonghua, 1978–1982).

35659, 37763, 38878, 38849, 38850, and *Hebu* 12463.[19] At least four of them used the central ridge as the pivot for directing the omen cracks to the left or right (*Heji* 35376, 37763, 38849, *Hebu* 12463) and three, being incomplete, only reveal partial views.

Of these, I was able to personally inspect *Heji* 35376, which now belongs to the Palace Museum Collection (number *xin* 160250). In the rubbing of the front view available in *Heji*, only one crack is visible; but a closer look reveals that there are two cracks on either side of the central line with clear notches on the back. See also the case of *Heji* 37763 (fig. 10.3).

In oracle bones supervised by Diviner Huang, the fact that cracks face away from, rather than toward, the central line contradicts the supposition of a general Shang royal style. The Diviner Huang inscriptions probably date to around Yinxu fourth period during the time of Di Yi 帝乙 and Di Xin 帝辛. By this time oracle bone divination was standardized and extremely regular, yet, as we see, an individual diviner group could maintain a singular practice.

In this essay, I looked at two relatively small points concerning late Shang oracle bone practice. The cache of turtle plastrons from the Huayuanzhuang South site and the Diviner Huang bones both date after the heyday of King Wu Ding 武丁. In the first point, I noted the practice of using animal skin in sacrificial rites to ancestral spirits. While these rites were being performed by Shang heirs outside the Shang court, diviner

Figure 10.3a. *Heji* 37763. *Source:* Author's graphic adapted from Guo Moruo and Hu Houxuan, ed., *Jiaguwen heji* 甲骨文合集, 13 vols. (Beijing: Zhonghua, 1978–1982).

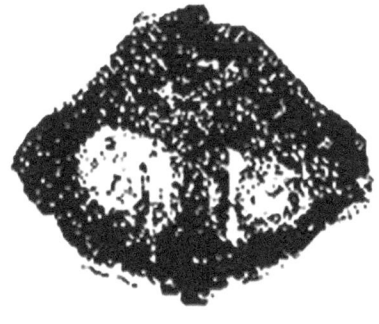

Figure 10.3b. Rubbing of *Heji* 37763.

groups in the central court supervised the cracking of bones in ways that suggested styles particularized by group rather than the need to follow a centralized style. New oracle bone finds allow us over time to have a more refined view of Shang practice.

Notes

1. *Editor's note: Huadong* inscriptions are referred to by the number assigned in Zhongguo shehui kexueyuan *kaogu* yanjiusuo 中國社會科學院考古研究所, ed., *Yinxu Huayuanzhuang dongdi jiagu* 殷墟花園莊東地甲骨, 6 vols. (Kunming: Yunnan renmin, 2003).

2. *Yinxu Huayuanzhuang dongdi jiagu*, vol. 6, 1742.

3. Liu Yuan 劉源, *Shang Zhou jizuli yanjiu* 商周祭祖禮研究 (Beijing: Shangwu, 2004), 110–11; Zhu Fenghan 朱鳳瀚, "Lun youji" 論肜祭, *Guwenzi yanjiu* 古文字研究, vol. 24 (Beijing: Zhonghua, 2002), 87–94.

4. Qiu Xigui, "Shuo 'XX Bai Dai shi wu'" 說'叀𦄋白大師武,'" in *Qiu Xigui xueshu wenji* 裘錫圭學術文集, vol. 3 (Shanghai: Fudan daxue, 2012), 19.

5. See Yu Xingwu 于省吾 and Yao Xiaosui 姚孝遂, *Jiagu wenzi gulin* 甲骨文字詁林 (Beijing: Zhonghua, 1996), 2707.

6. Ji Xusheng 季旭昇, *Shuowen xinzheng* 說文新證 (Taipei: Yiwen, 2014), 187.

7. *Yinxu Huayuanzhuang dongdi jiagu*, vol. 6, 1618.

8. See Huang Tianshu 黃天樹, "Yinxu Huayuanzhuan dongdi jiagu zhong suojian xuci de dapei he duiju" 殷墟花園莊東地甲骨中所見序辭的搭配和對舉, in *Huang Tianshu guwenzi lunji* 黃天樹古文字論集 (Beijing: Xueyuan, 2006), 405, 407–08.

9. Editor's note: *Heji* inscriptions are numbered based on Guo Moruo and Hu Houxuan, ed., *Jiaguwen heji* 甲骨文合集, 13 vols. (Beijing: Zhonghua, 1978–1982).

10. Qiu Xigui 裘錫圭, "Shi 'wu' 'fa'" 釋'勿' '發,' in *Qiu Xigui xueshu wenji* 裘錫圭學術文集, vol. 1 (Shanghai: Fudan daxue, 2012), 151, 153. For the *Yi Zhoushu* passage, see Huang Huaixin 黃懷信, Zhang Maorong 張懋鎔, and Tian Xudong 田旭東, *Yi Zhoushu huijiao jizhu* 逸周書彙校集注, rev. ed. (Shanghai: Shanghai guji, 2007), 438.

11. Xu Shen 許慎 (ca. 120?), *Shuowen jiezi zhu* 說文解字注, annot. Duan Yucai (Shanghai: Shanghai guji, 1988), 122.

12. Wang Niansun 王念孫 (1744–1832), *Guangya shuzheng* 廣雅疏證 (Nanjing: Jiangsu guji, 2000), 135.

13. See Ling Tingkan 凌廷堪 (1757–1809), "*Yili shi sheng*" 儀禮釋牲, in *Jiaoli tang wenji* 校禮堂文集 (Beijing: Zhonghua, 1998), vol. 15, 137–38; Zhang Wenjie 張聞捷, "Zhoudai yong ding zhidu shuzheng" 周代用鼎制度疏證, *Kaogu xuebao* 2012.2: 131–62.

14. See Li Xueqin 李學勤, "Yicheng Dahekou Shang yu mingwen shishi" 翼城大河口尚盂銘文試釋, *Wenwu* 2011.9: 67–68; He Jingcheng 何景成, "Ba Bo yu yu Zhoudai pibi zhidu" 霸伯盂與周代皮幣制度, *Chutu wenxian yu guwenzi yanjiu* 出土文獻與古文字研究 2 (2017): 6–18.

15. Dong Zuobin 董作賓, "Jiagu shiwu zhi zhengli" 甲骨實物之整理, *Jiagu wenxian jicheng* 甲骨文獻集成, vol. 34 (Sichuan: Sichuan daxue, 2001), 103. Originally published in *Zhongyang yanjiu lishi yuyan yanjiusuo jikan* 中央研究院歷史語言研究所集刊 29 (November 1957): 909–21.

16. Chen Mengjia 陳夢家, *Yinxu buci zongshu* 殷墟卜辭綜述 (Beijing: Zhonghua, 1988), 11; Huang Tianshu, "Guanyu bugu de zuoyou wenti" 關於卜骨的左右問題, in *Huang Tianshu jiagu jinwen lunji* 黃天樹甲骨金文論集 (Beijing: Xueyuan, 2014), 250.

17. Liu Yiman 劉一曼, "Anyang Yinxu jiagu chutudi ji qi xiangguan wenti" 安陽殷墟甲骨出土地及其相關問題, *Kaogu* 1997.5: 55–58.

18. Liu Yiman, "Anyang Yinxu jiagu chutudi," 59.

19. Editor's note: *Hebu* inscriptions are found based on numbers assigned in Zhongguo shekeyuan lishi yanjiusuo 中國社科院歷史研究所, ed., *Jiaguwen heji bubian* 甲骨文合集補編 (Beijing: Yuwen, 1999).

11

Notes on a Cornerstone of Early Chinese Argumentative Rhetoric

The Function Word *gù* 故

RUDOLF G. WAGNER

Introduction

During the Warring States period, and perhaps already during the Chunqiu period, a toolbox of new function words as well as structural devices for argumentation emerged that went a long way to increase the precision and explicitness of the connections within and between sentences.[1]

This came with an exponential increase of argumentative texts, such as the *Laozi*, *Sunzi*, *Mozi*, or *Xunzi* compared to predominantly narrative texts, such as the *Zuo zhuan*. In order to accurately understand the connections between and within clauses and sentences, or, to put it more bluntly, to actually understand the argument made, it seems self-evident that the precise function of these function words needs to be ascertained.

There is a general consensus that the word *gù*, written in standardized script 故 and placed at the point of contact between a preceding clause that offers an explanation and a succeeding clause with the statement that has been explained, is a function word of linkage. We will refer to this word as "linkage *gù*." The function-word pair *shigu* 是故 is frequently used in highly argumentative texts that also often use the simple *gù*. This pair appears in the same position as *gù*. The difference is that it nearly always is followed by a full sentence with a subject and a verb, while phrases following the simple *gù* tend to imply the subject of the phrase before the *gù*. The *shi* 是 in this case stresses the innovative character of the argument provided in the previous phrase and might best be read as an exclamation mark following the "that is why . . ."[2] In some early manuscript copies as well as in transmitted texts, a *gù* might be replaced by a *shiyi* 是以, which indicates that the meaning of the two was considered very similar or identical.[3]

The following definitions reflect the consensus in most available scholarship: A conjunction. Used in most cases at the beginning of the last clause of a complex sentence, it indicates a "cause-and-effect" (*yinguo* 因果) relationship between the preceding and the succeeding text. May be translated as "therefore" (*suoyi* 所以) or "for this reason" (*yin ci* 因此).[4] A more recent study specializing on the "empty characters" (*xuzi* 虛字) in excavated texts from the Zhanguo (Warring States) period argues in a similar manner: *gù* and *shigu* both appear in excavated Zhanguo texts in multi-clause cause-and-effect sentences, or in the effect clause of multi-clause sentences, or at the beginning of such a clause, indicating the effect.[5]

Yang Shuda was among the first Chinese scholars using linguistic terminology to suggest for *gù* the definition of a function word for linkage between two clauses, the *yinguo* formula, and the *suoyi* translation in 1928.[6] There is little bandwidth of interpretation in Chinese handbooks of "empty words" (*xuci* 虛詞) in the classical language. They all draw on the same commentarial glosses and on the same earlier standard works on the subject.

There are three problems with this definition: (1) the "cause and effect" definition is too generic to provide an accurate understanding; (2) the "at the beginning of the concluding clause" definition misidentifies the place "in between" the two clauses; and (3) the definitions implausibly assume that this and similar terms do not change over time. The otherwise fine recent study by Zhang Yaru 張亞茹 (discussed later in this chapter) made this into a general linguistic proposition for argumentative texts that has been mistakenly followed: "As one can see, the presence or absence of the *gù* has no influence on the content expressed, its function is simply to establish a link between the *explicans* and the *explicandum*."[7]

Some Initial Suggestions for Addressing These Problems

The definition that *gù* links "cause and effect" seems valid insofar as it points to a connection between the phrases preceding and succeeding the *gù*, but the "cause and effect" is an umbrella explanation that fails to address the actual logic of the argument offered. Cause and effect relationships have the form of factual propositions. The "effect" might be a known phenomenon for which now a "cause" is given or consist of a number of familiar phenomena connected as "cause" to suggest an "effect" that had been hitherto unknown. The presence of *gù*, however, indicates a dialogic argumentation with an interlocutor or reader in which the speaker/writer expresses his or her rational explanation for a historical phenomenon or abstract notion that is assumed to be familiar to the reader. There is, thus, a relatively static asymmetry in terms of time and form between the phrases preceding and succeeding the *gù*. Given the dialogic framework of *gù*, its presence changes the statement preceding it from one of fact into one of reasoned opinion that critically rejects other explanations as unconvincing. In this rejection, the existence of other options is implied and to a degree preserved. At the same time, the explanation offered before the *gù* does not leave the element after the *gù* unaffected but changes it from an empty or misunderstood statement into a meaningful utterance. Instead of the "cause and effect" formula, the pair of terms—*explicandum* for the statement after the *gù* and *explicans* for the statement preceding it—would seem to be more appropriate.[8] The notion of the *explicandum* suggests that it is familiar and known but in need of an *explicans* for its validity. The notion of the *explicans* ties this segment directly to the *explicandum* in a manner stressing its dialogic character of explaining something not understood or misunderstood to an interlocutor or reader.

The notion that linkage *gù* is "at the beginning" of the concluding clause suffers from an understanding that Chinese sentences only have a one-dimensional linear sequence of words that can be sufficiently structured with the help of the Western-style punctuation as is now common in the modern editions of premodern Chinese texts. There is no established punctuation for two-dimensional structures as they occur in interlocking parallel style, for hierarchical structures of phrases of different status, for content linkages through rhyme, or for linear but discontinuous and asymmetrical structures as in the case of *gù*.[9] This absence results in the graphic streamlining of complex structures to unidimensional linearity and the loss of an understanding of the crucial role the dynamics of such two-dimensional structures play in the configuration of the argument.

None of the grammatical handbooks and studies, furthermore, interrogate the historical trajectory of this argumentative toolbox as a whole or in terms of its individual parts. Handbooks imply that these function words and rhetorical structures emerged fully armed like Athena from Zeus's head and, again like Athena, did not change over time. Occurrences of linkage *gù* that did not fit the definition were assigned other functions or meanings based on the assumed meaning that might "reasonably" be expected in the given place in a manner following the methodology of earlier glossators or commentators. This led to long lists of presumable meanings. As far as the historical record is known to us, however, we clearly see an exponential growth in argumentative or, as some scholars have called it, "expository," texts during the Warring States period. It is reasonable to assume that their authors would develop strategies to finetune the connections within and between their arguments, as well as to disambiguate their particular use of the new and widely shared key terms. This already suggests the historicity of the results.[10] Arguments, it should be added, were not just made in visibly argumentative texts but also in narrative texts such as the *Zuo zhuan*. Zhang Yaru's recent paper began this discussion by arguing for a difference in the use of linkage *gù* in these two types of texts, but we will have to see whether this division, useful as it may be otherwise, accurately captures key differences. Since the intellectual climate of imperial China greatly differed from that of the Warring States period, it is legitimate to question whether, with the standardization of script and the consolidation of canons, we also find a standardization of the argumentative toolbox that implies a discontinuation of what might be seen as an experimental diversity characteristic of the earlier stage.

In terms of the study of pre-Buddhist Chinese argumentation, the most important questions that have not been addressed at all in the definitions of *gù* would be where the new contribution of the author is to be found—before or after the linkage *gù* or in both—and on what type of authority the *explicandum* and the *explicans* each were based. The present study is primarily concerned with paving the way for answering these questions.

Testing Relevancy

A quantitative assessment of the timeline in the use of linkage *gù* will provide background for the emergence of a new argumentative toolbox in early China and the place of linkage *gù* within it. Linkage *gù* does not appear in oracle bones, and there are only two items in the Western Zhou bronze inscriptions (discussed later), the Da Yu *ding* 大盂鼎, cast around 1003 BCE, and the middle Western Zhou Bronze Ban *gui* 班簋.[11]

Dates for the writing of many of the transmitted texts from pre-Qin China are notoriously controversial, and the unearthed manuscripts only provide data *ante quem*. However, the dates are stable enough to allow for the delineation of an order of magnitude of the spread of linkage *gù* during the Chunqiu and Zhanguo periods. Both the quantitative and temporal frames are short on historical precision, but they are stable enough to show some broad contours. As poetry can be assumed to use linkage *gù* little, if at all, we select two prose texts, the *Zuo zhuan* and *Laozi*, the former mainly narrative and the latter altogether argumentative.[12] This selection is random to avoid prejudging the result, and it has the simple purpose of highlighting the order of magnitude in the appearance of linkage *gù* in texts from the Western Zhou and Zhanguo periods.

From the *Zuo zhuan* we randomly select the records for Dukes Yin (r. 722–712 BCE) and Ding (r. 509–495 BCE), while, for the *Laozi*, the entire text will be analyzed. Both show a near uniform meaning for *gù* that has to do with the reasons or causes of something, and both also show a great majority of uses in the firmly established position between the last and the penultimate clauses. For Duke Yin, the proportion of linkage *gù* to other functions and positions is 27:3, for Duke Ding it is 16:14. There is no *shigu* 是故 in either of these two records. For the *Laozi*, the dominating position of linkage *gù* is even more pronounced with a proportion of 67:3, among them two *shigu*.[13] The argumentative intensity of these two types of text, as expressed in arguments in which a linkage *gù* appears, also greatly differs. As for the *Zuo zhuan*, there are twenty-seven cases of linkage *gù* among a total of 5,906 characters of the Duke Yin record and sixteen out of 10,836 characters in the Duke Ding record, which makes for an average of about 0.4 percent. In contrast, there are sixty-seven cases of linkage *gù* among the roughly 5,000 characters of the *Laozi*, which corresponds to about 1.3 percent, or more than three times as much as the corresponding proportion in the *Zuo zhuan*.

In the two *Zuo zhuan* records, linkage *gù* appears in three contexts: in the presentation of historical background that will explain a historical event (14/43); in direct speeches by historical figures that present an argument, often based on abstract concepts (18/43); and in commentarial explanations for the wording or the absence of pieces of information in the *Chunqiu* entry at hand (9/43, all of them in Duke Yin). In the *Laozi*, all occurrences are in abstract conceptual discussions, with the post-*gù* outcome determined by the timeless and spaceless logic of the argument, and by a factual historical occurrence. The strong presence of linkage *gù* in direct speeches by dukes and other elite members in the two previously mentioned Western Zhou bronzes and in the *Zuo zhuan* might be seen as evidence that the argumentative structure in which *gù* appears developed in oral court discussions that tried to determine a way to deal with a present-day situation by drawing on earlier precedents or invoking a principle, or by analyzing the motives driving one's opponents.[14] Already in the *Zuo zhuan* speeches, the argumentation involving *gù* often involves abstract concepts. While the difference between the argumentative stress in narrative and argumentative texts remains, the narrative texts also record or offer arguments; the difference is less pronounced between argumentative texts and the direct speeches in narrative texts.

To highlight the dominant status of linkage *gù* among function words that act as connectors, we might compare its occurrences with that of another function word that occurs in a similar position with a connecting function: *ze* 則. In the records of the two dukes selected from the *Zuo zhuan*, *ze* occurs twenty-nine times in this function compared to the forty-three occurrences of linkage *gù*; in the *Laozi*, the number for *ze* is thirty-six, just above half the numbers for *gù*. While the full content of the argumentative toolbox has not been mapped and no statistics are available for the relative frequency in the use of the function words contained therein, the comparison with *ze* allows for a statement that linkage *gù* is among the more frequently used function words in this set.

At this moment, we are primarily interested in the substantial presence and general stability in the uses of linkage *gù* during the Chunqiu and Zhanguo periods as compared to its uses in the Shang and Western Zhou periods. I propose to take this substantially increased presence as an indicator of the emergence of a toolbox for rational argumentation developed by the Zhanguo period.[15] It is possible that the degree to which the ingredients in this toolbox are used might be a rough indicator of the original date of a given text.[16] Needless to say, these are hypotheses with good initial plausibility, but which will have to be tested and developed through a specialized study that cannot be offered at this stage. The presence of this toolbox provides the context for the emergence of linkage *gù*, and this function word in turn significantly contributes to define this new set of instruments as primarily devoted to rational argumentation.

In the selected cases, the stability in the use of linkage *gù*, as seen from its position in sentences, was very high. It would be a miracle if this were the case throughout, as it might be assumed that the routines needed to result in such a stability might take time to develop. We will return to this issue later.

Disambiguating the Character

In the previous section, the focus was on the way in which writers were using *gù*. We focused on the position of the word within the sentence and its parts, basing ourselves on transmitted versions in which the writing for *gù* had been disambiguated after the Qin reforms. We now turn to the labor of the reader during the pre-Qin period.

The character 故 in the linkage position previously described is not attested in oracle-bone inscriptions. Only the bronze inscription on the Ban tureen (Ban *guǐ*) from the middle of the Western Zhou is known to have used this form in the place and function analyzed here.[17]

The word is occasionally used in the 故 form in Zhanguo period manuscripts, but there is no record during this period of linkage *gù* being written in this way. The character appearing in the position of linkage *gù* is always written *gu* 古. This character has been used during this period as a loan character to write a number of words. A comparison of transmitted texts in standardized script with Zhanguo manuscripts and a check in the transliterations of Zhanguo texts into standardized script by modern scholars shows that 古 has been assumed to have been used to write the following words, which I list here in their pinyin transcription, Old Chinese reconstruction, following Baxter/Sagart with their standard script form added in parentheses: *gǔ* OC *kˤaʔ (古), *gù* OC *kˤa(ʔ)-s (故), *gù* *[k]ˤa-s (固), *gū* (辜), and *gǔ* (詁).[18] The last three loans are extremely rare. The pronunciations of the different words were close but not identical, a fact that survives in the different tones of their modern pronunciation. To identify the word actually pointed at by a given character 古, the reader of the Zhanguo manuscript would have to disambiguate this character, a process involving four aspects: location within sentence, phonetics, context, and, finally, graphics. I will shortly go through them in sequence.

Disambiguation Based on Indication of Grammatical Function by Location within the Sentence

The character 古 occurs in the beginning of sentences as a noun. Read *gǔ* OC *kˤaʔ, it opens statements about the way things were "in antiquity." If placed between an *explicans* and an *explicandum* at the end of a sentence, it cannot be a noun but must be a function word linking these two elements. As *gǔ* OC *kˤaʔ does not occur as a function word, this position makes a reading *gù* OC *kˤa(ʔ)-s for these occurrences plausible. As the vast majority of occurrences of 古 are in this position, the reader can rely on a reading routine to identify this character as representing the word *gù* OC *kˤa(ʔ)-s. The character 古 also appears in other positions within sentences. Examples are 為其君之古 (故), 殺其身者 (someone killing himself for the cause of his lord),[19] or at the beginning of phrases such as 何古 (故) (what is the reason for / cause for something).[20] Here *gù* is a noun. While, in these places, the readings *gǔ* OC *kˤaʔ or *gù* OC *[k]ˤa-s, both of which mean "antiquity" (or the even rarer other loans) are not impossible, the standard references to "antiquity" are at the beginning of sentences. The reader's decision in these cases ultimately depends on context (plausibility). We conclude that the location of 古 in a sentence in pre-Qin times provided the most important clue for its disambiguation with the linkage *gù*, being an easy case because of its frequency.

Phonetic Disambiguation

Reading was not done silently during this period but aloud.[21] The content was identified from what one heard oneself reading. As the pronunciations for the words written during the Zhanguo period with the character 古 varied, readers had to define which word they were reading when faced with the character 古. If they identified it as meaning "antiquity" or "ancient," they would read it *gǔ* OC *kˤaʔ; if they identified it as the word later written 故, they would read it as *gù* OC *kˤa(ʔ)-s with the final "s." Such an identification was not done randomly. Its most important anchor was the position of the word within a sentence.

Context Disambiguation

The context of a sentence is not random. It comes with the criterion of a meaningfulness of the sentence within the immediate environment and a heavy reliance on the broader standard ways to talk about the issue under consideration. Let us take the example from the previous section: 為其君之古 (故), 殺其身者 (someone killing himself for the cause of his lord).

The discussion here is about the criteria for a loyal minister, one example of which is given in this sentence. Reading "someone killing himself for the antiquity of his lord" would not make sense. Given the substantial number of phonetic and graphic loans in pre-Qin writing, the burden for a Zhanguo reader to identify the intended words was substantial. The path eventually taken to relieve it was to enlarge the pool of available characters in order to establish, at least for the majority of cases, a one-to-one relationship between the character and the word it was supposed to represent.

Graphic Disambiguation

A comparison of Zhanguo manuscripts and Western Han manuscripts containing the same or very similar textual elements (such as the Western Han *Laozi* manuscript at Peking University and the two *Laozi* manuscripts from Mawangdui on the one hand with the three *Laozi* manuscripts from Guodian on the other)[22] shows a systematic identification of the character 古 in the linkage position previously defined as signaling the word *gù* OC *kˤa(ʔ)-s and followed by a transcription into the character 故.

From the newly excavated manuscripts it seems that, already during the Qin, the writing of 故 had become the norm.[23] This transcription was the work of a reader who identified the intended word and then wrote it down in the disambiguated character. The character 故 retained this writing to the present day, even though it was in turn occasionally used as a loan character for the words *gǔ* OC *kˤaʔ (古) and *gù* OC *kˤaʔ-s (故).

Defining the Meaning

The noun *gù* OC *kˤa(ʔ)-s points to the reason/cause for an action or statement. Given that the word is attested since the Western Zhou in this function, Zhang Yujin's assumption that the function word (meaning "it is because of this/that" or "therefore") is derived from the noun is plausible.[24]

Given the options of location-based, phonetic, and context disambiguation, it is possible to identify early uses of *gù* OC *kˤa(ʔ)-s as a function word. Its earliest use known today is on the inscription of the bronze Da Yu tripod (Da Yu *ding*). In the relevant passage, the Zhou king (Kang) is speaking to his subordinate Yu about how, in the past, King Wu succeeded King Wen and managed to set up the Zhou state:

> As to those engaged in ceremonial matters, woe! There was no permission for excess with regard to alcoholic beverages and

[even] at the *chai* and *zheng* rites [of the king] there was no permission for excess. That is why heaven guarded and kept watch over [its] son (?) and in a great way secured the former kings' possession of the four quarters!

I have heard that, as to the loss of the mandate by the Yin, it was due to the greater and lesser lords of the Yin as well as the officials assisting Yin frequently abandoning themselves to alcoholic beverages. That is why they lost the people!

In the transcription into modern characters, the quotation reads:

在於御事 虡! 酒無敢酖 有紫蒸祀無敢擾 故天翼臨子 法保先王 敷有四方
我聞殷墜命 唯殷邊侯 甸與殷正百辟率肆於酒 故 喪師.²⁵

There are different transcriptions, word identifications, and translations of this inscription including the passage quoted.²⁶ Most of these differences are irrelevant for my analysis of the linkage *gù* here. For my own rendering, I have selectively followed the transliterations and translations that seemed to me most convincing.

We have two linkage *gù* in this inscription, both in the same position and with the same function. In the first *gù*, King Kang explains the success of his predecessor, the *explicandum*, in what purports to be a record of a speech he made to Yu. In his *explicans*, he attributes this success to the prevention of alcohol abuse by officials during ritual ceremonies. He then takes the inverse example, the demise of the Yin. Drawing on the oral record, he (in the *explicandum*), attributes this demise to the rampant alcohol abuse during the last stage of the Yin dynasty, the *explicans*, to this day associated with an entire artificial "lake" of the brew laid out by the king. Presumably, the Yin's demise is familiar to the implied reader, as are the stories about the extensive alcohol consumption. But the demise could be, and presumably was, attributed to many factors: superior armaments, overwhelming coalition, economic causes, divine intervention, and so forth. The king now principally attributes it to rampant alcohol abuse and uses the outcome of the two different treatments of alcohol consumption as a positive model and negative warning for later rulers.²⁷

The location, function, and meaning of the linkage *gù* in the Da Yu *ding* inscription are all in place. This indicates that at least, in the "spoken" language of members of the political elite, the argumentative pattern involving linkage *gù* was already in place. In this case, the statements before and after the *gù* both derive their authority not from the timeless and spaceless logic of abstract concepts, but from historical facts of an earlier time whose relevance is that they pertain to the same place.

Less than a century later, an argumentation involving abstract concepts is recorded. The King Mu–period Ban tureen, mentioned earlier, uses 故 instead of 古 and records that, after the king had ordered the subjugation to the Zhou of peoples in the East within three years, the official in charge inscribed the result onto this tureen: "Lord [Mao herewith] reports this historical process [of the war against the Rong] hereon [saying]: 'These people have failed with the ritual vessels and have been blind to Heaven's commands. That is why they were annihilated!'" (公告乎事于上 唯民亡茁 才彝 昧天令 故 亡).[28] The *explicandum* is a historical fact, the annihilation of these people. The *explicans* draws both on historical realities, presumably the lack of respect shown for ritual vessels of the Zhou, and on the very abstract notion that they were "blind to heaven's commands," although even this might be a concrete historical reference to their refusal to submit to the Zhou. The Shi Xun *gui* 師詢簋 inscription, from the late tenth or early ninth century BCE offers the last of only four Western Zhou examples known. Here the king contrasts the present day with the glorious times of Kings Wen and Wu, who were assisted by excellent advisors. Heaven is now sending down disaster and, as the king's / Shi Xun's virtue is deficient, "that is why there is no succor from the former kings (?)!" (古 (故) 亡承 (抍) 于先王).[29] The inscription poses many challenges, but it seems that the *explicandum* is a present-day disaster, explained by heaven's response to a lack of virtue in the king or Shi Xun.

At this stage, without being able to provide further evidence, we may hypothesize that linkage *gù* started its career in an assumption of a rationally explainable dynamics of the world with the higher powers, such as heaven sharing the values of the best among human beings. We might further assume that the first field where these rationally explainable dynamics were explored were discussions about the logic of historical developments that were adduced to provide lessons for the present, rather than logic linking general and abstract concepts.

While, theoretically, function words might be used in any context, in cultural and historical reality, they tend to be tied to certain rhetorical tropes. In the case of early Chinese writing, three such tropes may be discerned. These are: (1) explanations for the occurrence of an historical event, a trope mostly found in argumentative statements in narrative texts and, as we have seen, within such texts, often in records of oral statement; (2) explanations for the presence or absence of statements or formulations in texts, accepted by the author as authoritative, such as the *Spring and Autumn Annals*. These will be found both in predominantly narrative texts, such as the *Zuo zhuan*, and in predominantly argumentative texts, such as commentaries to or essays on classical texts. In general terms, this form is commentarial in nature; (3) explanations supporting the validity of an abstract conceptual statement. In the following sections, I will offer examples of all three.

Explanations for the Occurrence of a Historical Fact

The *Zuo zhuan*, referring to the *Chunqiu* passage about Duke Yin and recording the event "in the third month, the Duke and Zhu, the *yifu*, made a covenant at Mie" (公及邾儀父盟于蔑), writes: "After his ascending the throne, the Duke [of Lu] wished for friendly relations with Zhu [a territory appended to Lu]. That is why the covenant was made in Mie [a place in Lu close to Zhu]!" 公攝位而欲求好於邾, 故為蔑之盟.[30] Here we have an historical fact recorded in the authoritative entry from the chronicle of Lu. The *Zuo zhuan* provides meaning for the seemingly dry fact that this covenant was concluded in Mie. The implication is that the *Chunqiu* does not record dry facts even though the meaning in this case might only become clear to readers who check where Mie is in relation to Zhu.[31] *Gù* here does not link a cause and an effect but an explanation and a fact. The *explicandum*, which is the point of departure of the argument, comes after the *gù*. What comes before is the *explicans*. This *explicans* relies on other historical facts, not on abstract notions. The explanation takes up the dialogic frame of arguing with a *gù*. Although not presented as direct speech, it is in dialogue with a reader who presumably cannot make sense out of the fact that the covenant was made in Mie or who has heard other explanations.

Explanations for the Presence or Absence of Statements or Formulations in Texts Accepted by the Author as Authoritative

Following the preceding explanation, the *Zuo zhuan* continues: "The ruler of Zhu is Ke; [He] had not yet been officially appointed by the [Zhou] king.

That is the reason why no noble title is recorded for him! If [the *Chunqiu*] says [= calls him] Yifu [ceremonious elder], this is to honor him" 邾子克也。未王命,故不書爵。曰「儀父」,貴之也。³²

The *Zuo zhuan* posits that it is the habit in the *Spring and Autumn Annals* to provide the title of such high-ranking partners in diplomacy. It notes the absence of this information and offers the reader a rational explanation. The starting point, *explicandum*, is the historical fact of the formulation in a canonical work after the *gù* (the unusual form of which might have eluded the reader altogether). The *explicans* again comes before the *gù*. It creates a difference between the formulation used for the ruler of Zhu and the routine presumably guiding *Chunqiu* entries involving high-ranking personalities in such diplomatic relations. As the entry under question is right at the beginning of the *Chunqiu*, the routine has been extracted from later records but was thought to have been in place at least since the beginning of the *Chunqiu*. The *explicans*, which might actually have alerted the reader to the presence of an *explicandum*, treats these recording routines as historical facts. The statement operates in a dialogue with a reader who might have heard other explanations and whom it tries to convince with a rational argument. However, while not using abstract conceptual language or reasoning, it explains the textual practice of an authoritative text extracted from the majority of entries, not an historical event. The *gù* here does not link a cause and an effect but a recording routine of an authoritative text as the *explicandum* and an historical fact as the *explicans*. In the *Zuo zhuan* rhetoric, the *explicans* is not presented as an inference from the *explicandum* ("perhaps the reason for the absence of the nobility rank might be that . . .") but as unquestionable historical fact. In the process of the development of the argument, a seemingly meaningless name turns into a rationally explained fact.

Moving from a text of historical narrative to one of abstract argumentation, I may be excused for matching the *Zuo zhuan*'s dealing with *Chunqiu* entries with Wang Bi's dealing with *Laozi* statements, because it was, during my work on Wang's commentary that I first became aware of the need for some further study on *gù*.

Laozi 14.2 writes in Wang Bi's version:

一者——其上不皦 其下不昧 繩繩兮不可名 復歸於無物 是謂無狀之狀無物之象.

Wang Bi comments:

欲言無耶 而物以成　　　　欲言有耶 而不見其形
　　　故曰
無狀之狀　　　　　　　　　無物之象.

This comment translates as: "One wishes to say that it [the One] does not exist? [The fact still remains] that the entities are based on it for their completion. One wants to say it [the One] exists? [The fact still remains] that it does not show its form. That is why [the text] says: 'Shape of the shapeless, appearance of a no-thing!'" (If one extrapolated from this commentary and modernized Wang Bi's reading of the *Laozi* passage, it would be: "As to this One—its upper side is not bright;—its lower side is not dark. Dim it is, and impossible to name. It returns and relates [the entities] back to the no-thing. This [I] call the shape of something shapeless, the appearance of a no-thing.")[33]

For Wang Bi, the *Laozi* is an authoritative text. This gives a high standing to the *Laozi*'s utterances and determines the stance of the commentator as explaining what is darkly indicated in the *Laozi*, rather than being the critic who takes the text to task.[34] Wang Bi's interaction with his readers is even more complex than the *Zuo zhuan*'s. While the *Zuo zhuan* was not the only text and, definitely, not the most authoritative in offering meaning to the *Chunqiu* entries during the Warring States period, Wang Bi competed with at least a dozen other commentaries for the *Laozi* when he wrote his own. Readers at the time would normally read a text together with and through a commentary. Wang's work thus implicitly engages not simply with a reader in need of an explanation for a dense and abstract text, but with a diversity of readers whose reading of the *Laozi* has already been informed by a wide range of other commentaries. This plethora of counter-texts leaves its invisible traces in the elements stressed in Wang Bi's commentary.

The reader of Wang's commentary has just read the *Laozi* passage quoted at the end. It is not new to him. The assumption is, however, that he has read it through a different commentary, which would have given another explanation. It has the authority of a *Laozi* statement but remains dead or misunderstood without a proper *explicans*. It still is an *explicandum*, and Wang Bi's *explicans*, coming before the *gù* 故, is the new element. Only in the light of this *explicans* does the *Laozi* passage, quoted after the *gù yuē* 故曰, get what Wang Bi would consider its true meaning. The reader is therefore encouraged to reread the familiar quotation in light of this explanation, but, while the understanding of it is new, the statement itself is not. To emphasize the agonistic nature of this *gù* 故, the last phrase of Wang's comment should end with a (perhaps double) exclamation mark. "THAT is why [the *Laozi* text] says: '[The One has] the shape of something shapeless, the appearance of a no-thing'!"

The authority of the *Laozi* statement is anchored in the stature of the *Laozi*, but its true authority and claim to philosophical truth hinges on its being properly understood. As we saw, the *Zuo zhuan* anchors its own *explicans* of the entry in an analysis and understanding of the *Chunqiu*'s overall recording practice (referred to as "routine" earlier). In a similar manner, the Wang Bi commentary gets its authority as an *explicans* from cross-linking the different *Laozi* statements—with their great bandwidth of abstract concepts, metaphors, comparisons, and onomatopoeia—into a philosophically homogeneous whole for which he creates a new and abstract philosophical terminology. In the present case, he does so by drawing on statements in other chapters about the basis for the ten thousand kinds of entities (which, in order to be this *basis*, cannot have any of their features). This is an authority coming from explaining the *Laozi* through a philosophical system extracted from the *Laozi*.[35] Through his comment, a *Laozi* statement that just states—without arguing—its case becomes a meaningful philosophical proposition. The transition to meaningfulness is indicated by the *gù*, and the new and crucial part of Wang Bi's comment comes before the *gù*. Again, we do not have a statement of a cause-and-effect relationship linked by *gù* but an argument offering an *explicans* for an *explicandum*. In the process, the *explicandum* is transformed from a dead authoritative letter into a philosophical proposition that deserves this authority.

We can thus observe that both the *explicandum* and the *explicans* operate with abstract concepts, not historical facts. The relationship between the two is not situated in a time sequence but in a purely abstract logical connection that has a validity unbound by space and time.

Explanations Supporting the Validity of an Abstract Conceptual Statement

The Later Han author Wang Fu 王符 (82–167 CE) writes the following in his *Qianfu lun* 潛夫論, rendered here in a two-dimensional format that highlights the internal parallels and linkages:

凡為治之大體

莫善於抑末而務本　　莫不善於離本而餙末

夫為國者

以富民為本　　　　　以正學為基

民富乃可教　　　　　學正乃得義

民貧則背善　　　　　學淫則詐偽

　　　　　　入學則不亂　　得義則忠孝

故

明君之法　務此二者　以為

成太平之基　　　　　致休徵之祥

(It is a widely held opinion)[36] with regard to the grand substance of managing political order that nothing is superior to putting down what is secondary ["the branches"] and focusing on what is fundamental ["the root"], and nothing is worse than letting go of the fundamental and bringing to full embellishment what is secondary. As a matter of principle, someone properly managing a state will take making the people prosperous as fundamental and rectifying learning as basic. Once the people are prosperous, it will become possible to educate them and once learning has been rectified, [the learned elite] will attain to justice; [but] once the people are impoverished, they will turn their backs on what is good; and once learning has become decadent, fakery and deception [will afflict the learned] while if [they] enter into [correct] learning, they will not create chaos and, if they attain to justice, they will be loyal and abide by filial piety. That is why it has been the rule for enlightened rulers to abide by these two [e.g., principles] to put down what is secondary and focus on [what is fundamental], considering this to be the basis for bringing about Great Peace and the blissful sign of bringing proof that one is doing the right thing![37]

The statement after the *gù* (the *explicandum*) is introduced from the outset as a familiar rule for which the author now provides a new *explicans*. It defines "enriching the people" and "rectifying learning" as the concrete forms of "putting down what is secondary and focusing on what is fundamental." This in turn transforms the statement after the *gù* from a flat commonplace one or a metaphysical proposition—that the ruler "hold on to the one" rather than becoming one of the many as in the *Laozi*—into a meaningful and concrete political strategy that can be translated, as was done by Wang Fu, into a critique of the present government's favoring luxury production and trade (the "branches") rather than agriculture (the "root"). In his own argumentation, Wang Fu in the first sentence draws on a general proposition that has often (as in the *Laozi*) been stated. It is introduced by *fan* 凡, which provides a framework of validity for most cases (rather than in principle). He then elaborates on this proposition by linking it to a general principle that comes from different sources (such as the *Mengzi*). But this combination of enriching the people and rectifying learning is his own.

In the next step of the elaboration, he draws on Confucius's statement that people can be instructed only after having been made prosperous, as well as on a plethora of earlier claims for the need to rectify learning, both accompanied by a grim picture of the fallout from policies not following this line. This in turn will form the argumentative basis for his attacks on the prevailing urban consumerism and the dominance of "learning about the empty and negative" of his time, which had obviously not been rectified and had opened the door for fakery and deception. In light of this layered *explicans*, the *explicandum* at the end is translated not only into a concrete and meaningful general political strategy, but also into the fundament of an acerbic attack on the powers-that-be of Wang Fu's own time.

If my reading accurately catches the overall drift of Wang Fu's argument, then I propose he follows the pattern already seen in the two previous forms of the use of *gù*. The innovative and potentially provocative element is in the *explicans* before the *gù*, but the *explicans* also transforms the *explicandum*, already developed in the beginning of the argument, into a meaningful and presumably correctly understood maxim for good governance, which could be a critical litmus test for the actual performance of government. In both the *explicans* and the *explicandum*, the language used is highly abstract and conceptual; no reference is made to recorded historical fact; but indirect reference to previously articulated abstract principles abound. The *explicans* and the *explicandum* do not get their logic from the "before and after" of time or the "here and not there" of space, but from a purely conceptual rationality.

Tracking the Timeline

Looking back at earlier texts, the pattern observed here was not (or not yet) used pervasively. A case in point is the *Sunzi*. The *textus receptus* of the *Sunzi* has 104 occurrences of linkage *gù*. This very high number for such a short text (1.55%) marks it as exceedingly argumentative. In terms of their place in the phrase, these *gù* are situated, in most cases, between a familiar *explicandum* and a new *explicans*, but, in quite a few cases, both the argument and the element after *gù* are new. For example, "As a matter of principle, it has never happened that a protracted war is of benefit to the state. That is why someone who does not fully understand the damage of making use of war will not be able to fully understand the benefits of making use of war" (夫兵久而國利者 未之有也. 故不盡知用兵之害者 則不能盡知用兵之利也).[38] The text is articulating a general principle that itself is new, even though it claims support from available historical evidence. The statement after the *gù*, however, is also new, but it is a simple proposition without claiming historical support. Its logic and meaning hinge on the segment before the *gù* in the same manner as what we observed in the Wang Fu quotation.

Victor Mair has offered a detailed critique of the use of *gù* in the *Sunzi*. He attributes the high frequency of the use of *gù*, in comparison to other military treatises, to the *Sunzi*'s close relationship to an oral tradition. However, Mair also notes that "well over half of the succeeding clauses in the *Sunzi* manifestly do not follow from the preceding clauses."[39] In this respect the *Sunzi* is an extreme outlier, and we lack a clear explanation of why this text should so sharply deviate from what was already a well-established and widely used practice.

A second, but different, case in point is the much-discussed beginning of the first chapter of the *Xunzi*, "Encouragement to Study" ("Quan xue" 勸學). To quantify the size of the problem, it might be noted that this chapter has altogether twenty-one cases of linkage *gù* (of which three are *shìgù*). Of these twenty-one, three or about 15 percent do not at first sight correspond to the pattern outlined earlier. We are thus dealing with uses that even within this text are exceptional and small in number. Two of them occur right at the beginning. The chapter starts, according to Hutton's recent translation:

> The gentleman says: Learning must never stop. Blue dye derives from the indigo plant, and yet it is bluer than the plant. Ice comes

from water, and yet it is colder than water. Through steaming and bending, you can make wood as straight as an ink-line into a wheel. And after its curve conforms to the compass, even when parched under the sun, it will not become straight again, because the steaming and bending have made it a certain way. **Likewise**, when wood comes under the ink-line, it becomes straight, and when metal is brought to the whetstone, it becomes sharp. The gentleman learns broadly and examines himself thrice daily, and then his knowledge is clear and his conduct is without fault.

And so, if you never climb a high mountain, you will not know the height of Heaven. If you never visit a deep ravine, you will not know the depth of the Earth. If you never hear the words passed down from the former kings, you will not know the magnificence of learning. The children of the Han, Yue, Yi, and Mo peoples all cry with the same sound at birth, but when grown they have different customs, because teaching makes them thus.[40]

The words marked bold are *gù* in the original. In the Knoblock translation, the first is rendered as "so, too," and the second as "truly."[41] Both translators felt that anything akin to "therefore" would not make sense and decided to render the word as an empty fill-in. The modern Chinese translations render the *gù* in both cases as *suoyi* 所以, but their division of the text is such that the reader in neither case finds out why and how what follows should be connected to what precedes.[42] The problem already appears in the graphic organization of the text in some modern editions. The segmentation offered here by the CHANT database is followed by Knoblock and Hutton, as well as, for this section, in the recent study by Martin Kern. It runs:

君子曰: 學不可以已. 青, 取之於藍而青於藍; 冰, 水為之而寒於水. 木直中繩, 輮以為輪, 其曲中規, 雖有槁暴, 不復挺者, 輮使之然也. 故木受繩則直, 金就礪則利, 君子博學而日參省乎己, 則智明而行無過矣.

　　故不登高山, 不知天之高也; 不臨深谿, 不知地之厚也; 不聞先王之遺言, 不知學問之大也. 干, 越, 夷, 貉之子, 生而同聲, 長而異俗, 教使之然也.

While the first linkage *gù* is graphically placed at the beginning of an extensive final clause, the second *gù* is placed at the beginning of a new second paragraph without any pretense of a logical link to the preceding. The segmentation, the meaning, and the function of the two *gù* in this text have all been discussed in scholarship, most extensively by Kern. Concerning the first *gù*, Kern follows the assumption that the phrase about wood being bent to form a wheel is another instance of transformation by education. He writes:

> The first analogies of blue/indigo and ice/water, for example, are ready-for-use, disposable items from the general store of rhetorical analogies; the second analogy—the wood bent by steam and then remaining bent even when dried again—is a more original comparison to a person's permanent transformation by learning. It is followed by *gu* 故, an introductory sentence adverbial that often does not have a strong logical force (as in "therefore"), as it does not function as the hinge between the immediately preceding sentence or section and the subsequent one. Instead, it frequently serves as the introduction of another piece of traditional wisdom: what follows *gu* (which I translate as "thus [it is said]" to indicate that the following is again a quotation or otherwise marked speech) is a general maxim, usually bound by rhyme or rhythm, that is supported by the preceding illustration.⁴³

While this comment does not evade the problem and offers with the "thus [it is said]" a way to a solution, its own solution remains unsatisfactory because it deprives linkage *gù* of its core function. For the second *gù*, Kern offers an altogether new general definition of the function of linkage *gù*, "the sentence adverbial to introduce a concluding commonplace," but does not offer an explanation about what is being concluded.

Under the assumption that the linkage *gù* is not an empty word, I suggest that the *Xunzi* segment quoted here consists of a series of independent short statements that are focused on the theme of the *junzi*'s need for study. I therefore propose to graphically organize the pieces belonging together, highlight their internal structure through two-dimensional writing, and translate the relevant segments as given in the brackets:

君子曰學不可以已
青 取之於藍而青於藍　　　　　　冰 水為之而寒於水
木直中繩 輮以為輪 其曲中規 雖有槁暴 不復挺者 輮使之然也
　　　　　　　　　故
受繩則直　　　　　　　　　　　金就礪則利.

If a piece of wood that is straight to fit the [ink] line is bent to form a wheel, its crookedness will fit [the circle described by] compasses.⁴⁴ That even though there is extreme dryness it will not stretch straight again is due to this bending. That is why [only] a piece of wood that is made to abide by the [ink] line will be straight and [only] a piece of metal that is handled with the whetstone will be sharp.

The notion of *qu* 曲 (crooked) is used negatively in the *Xunzi*.⁴⁵ I therefore assume that the first sentence gives a negative example. A piece of wood that, in its original condition, was straight as the ink line could be permanently made round or crooked by violent bending; this is like someone with an excellent original disposition who might become permanently crooked if he did not consolidate his straightness through correct study. The linkage suggested by the *gù* implies the insertion of the "only" to mark the fundamental difference between improvement by correct study and being bent by imposition.

君子
博學而日參省乎己
則
智明而行無過矣
　　　　　　　　　故
不登高山 不知天之高也　　不臨深谿 不知地之厚也
不聞先王之遺言 不知學問之大也

As a gentleman will [constantly] broaden his learning and thrice daily examine himself, his knowledge will be clear and his conduct will be without fault. That is why [by contrast] someone who does not climb a high mountain will not know the height of heaven, someone who does not get close to a deep ravine, will not know the thickness of the earth, and someone who does not listen to the words handed down from the former kings will not know the magnificence of learning.

Again, *gù* here starts a statement that is dealing with the exact opposite of the segment preceding the *gù*, namely with a practice that is dealing not with a true *junzi* but with that of someone who utterly disregards the essential steps of becoming such a *junzi*. This kind of inversion requires a simple and quite logical step from the reader, because it follows from the broadening of learning of the *junzi* that someone who does not broaden his learning will not become a *junzi*. The sententious phrasing of this inversion points to the possibility suggested by Martin Kern that this passage had already become a fixed commonplace. The simple insertion of a *yue* 曰 after the *gù* (this is why it is said) would have made this reading even more plausible, especially since the *gù yue* is a very frequent formula.

The first question is how these uses of *gù* should be characterized: as flaws in textual transmission or experiments in using an established argumentative tool for different purposes?[46] And, second, did these new uses become incorporated into a regular argumentative practice over time, or did they fall by the wayside?

I would suggest that the practice of occasionally demanding that the reader fill in the intermediary steps that would make the *gù* meaningful did not, however, become part of the routine of the use of linkage *gù*. This suggestion is based on a cursory reading through later argumentative texts, namely of the Eastern Han, Sanguo, and Jin. To become falsifiable, this suggestion clearly would have to be backed up by systematic qualitative and quantitative study. Given the small volume of such exceptions as early as during the Warring States, a check with the help of a random number (such as every eighteenth occurrence of linkage *gù* in a random selection of texts) is not likely to produce reliable results, whereas it would involve a disproportionate investment of time and energy. At this stage, I simply want to stress the possibility and plausibility that some writers of argumentative prose during the Warring States period might have experimented with the argumentative toolbox that was then available to offer argumentative shortcuts; that these experiments were, from the outset, outliers in an already highly homogeneous practice; and that, as the uses of these argumentative tools became ever more standardized, these experimentations were discontinued during the early Western Han. A systematic study would have to test the following hypothesis: the use of linkage *gù* underwent a standardization similar to that observed for initial *fú* during this time.

Conclusions

These notes set out to develop a number of hypotheses with indications of their initial plausibility concerning the uses of *gù* within an evolving argumentative toolbox in early and early medieval China together. These hypotheses are as follows:

Drawing on earlier routines, a vastly expanded argumentative toolbox developed during the Warring States period that became standardized and routinized since the Western Han. This toolbox included a broad array of function words; structural elements such as parallelisms; topical features such as implied references to generally accepted principles or direct references to authoritative classics; and hierarchy markers for different kinds of statements. (This toolbox operates on the assumption of a rationally explainable world in which the higher powers such as Heaven share the same values as the sages among men rather than being unpredictable.) *Gù*, like other parts of this toolbox, has a history. It is characterized by the gradual standardization of the use of the components in this toolbox.

The use of linkage *gù* implies a dialogic situation, as it emphatically rejects other available explanations for the *explicandum*. The sizeable proportion of the use of linkage *gù* in what purports to be dialogue in pre-Qin texts, including Western Zhou bronze inscriptions, is an indicator that this use became routinized in elite discussions about the dynamics of history, which came with the assumption that these dynamics followed regular patterns that, if properly understood, could serve to explain present-day *explicanda*. As the *explicanda* were anchored in texts coming with the authority of sages or in propositions associated with sagely teaching, the counter-texts with which the *explicans* were engaging often had the form of commentaries through the new *explicans*, these counter-texts are preserved in their shadow form in the emphatic rejection.

Within this toolbox, *gù* (OC *kˤa(ʔ)-s), normally written 古 in pre-Qin times and then uniformly transcribed into 故, played the role of a function word that provided the linkage between an *explicandum* and an *explicans*, rather than between a cause and an effect as scholarly convention has it. In the standardized form, the *explicandum* is a known historical fact or statement of abstract principle. The argumentative purpose of the *explicans* is (1) to overcome a non- or misunderstanding of the *explicandum* in the reader's mind that is based on other explanations and (2) to establish a rationally convincing explanation. The new contribution of the author is the *explicans*. If accepted, it will also give the known *explicandum* a new meaning. In a small number of cases in pre-Qin texts, both the *explicandum* and the *explicans* seem to be new, but such exceptions will not be found later.

The word *gù* (OC *kˤa(ʔ)-s), written 古, is disambiguated principally based on the position of this character between an *explicans* and an *explicandum* at the end of a sentence with context providing supplementary evidence. This is confirmed by the nearly uniform transcription of 古 in this place as 故 since the Qin.

Broadly speaking, linkage *gù* was used in two types of arguments. One explained a historical event or practice, the *explicandum*, by suggesting in the *explicans* other historical events or practices that brought it about. The connection between the two was provided by sequence in terms of time and proximity in terms of space. The *explicandum* derived its authority from being recorded in a canonical source or being an uncontested fact; the suggested meaning, the *explicans*, derived its authority by suggesting, in a rationally convincing manner, other historical facts that might account for the occurrence of the *explicandum*. This type of use of linkage *gù* dominates in the argumentative parts of narrative, typically historical, texts. The other type of argument explained a general maxim or principle, with high canonical authority or general acceptance, with conceptual propositions as the *explicans*. The connection between the two was exclusively based on the rational persuasiveness of the *explicans* for the uncontested *explicandum* after the *gù*. The latter came with a level of authority that allowed or even called for explanation but was never to be questioned. This type of use of linkage *gù* dominates in predominantly argumentative texts, such as those assigned to the "masters" (*zhuzi* 諸子) of the pre-Qin period. Quantitatively, linkage *gù* is used much more frequently in such argumentative texts.

The status asymmetry between the *explicandum* and the *explicans* ultimately reflects that between the canonical authority of the "sages" of earlier times with their insuperable levels of insight, and the much lower rank of the later born, who forever try to make sense of the sages' bequests because this is the only access to truth they have.

The earliest known and datable occurrences of linkage *gù* in the Western Zhou already show the core features of location within the sentence, the asymmetry between *explicans* and *explicandum*, and the dialogical context. During the Zhanguo and possibly Chunqiu periods, the use of linkage *gù* greatly expanded. The overwhelming majority of these uses corresponded to the basic pattern outlined in this chapter. There was, however, a small number of cases with experimental uses of linkage *gù* that required the reader to either disambiguate the linkage by inserting some implied logical steps or that actually offered both, a new *explicandum* and a new *explicans*; there was also a further number of cases in texts, such as the *Sunzi*, that represented outliers for which we lack explanations. By the Western Han, however, the use of linkage *gù* as well as that of other parts of the new argumentative toolbox had become standardized to the point that such exceptions were few and far between if they still occurred at all.

The arguments presented in these notes have the form of propositions for reasons of the economy of space. Given the lack of detailed statistical evidence, especially for the historical process of standardization, that follows from the methodological difficulty of producing falsifiable data for the presence or disappearance of already rare exceptions in the use of linkage *gù*, these propositions must be read as hypotheses with some initial plausibility that might be used to frame a larger research program, but which need more evidence to become fully falsifiable.

Notes

1. The reference to the Chunqiu period here rather than, as is usual, only to the Warring States period, is a reaction to the growing uncertainty about the date of the composition of pre-Qin texts following the recent discoveries of manuscripts that have seriously undermined the assumptions about the late date of composition routinely ascribed to texts *associated* with authors of the Chunqiu period (such as the *Sunzi*). My reference is intended to signal that it is a possibility that this toolbox had already developed during this earlier period. I am not aware of any systematic study of the development and content of this toolbox in any language. A listing of some Chinese case studies will be found in Zhang Yujin 張玉金, *Chutu Zhanguo wenxian xuci yanjiu* 出土戰國文獻虛詞研究 (Beijing: Renmin, 2011), 56–57. *Literary Forms of Argument in Early China*, ed. Joachim Gentz and Dirk Meyer (Leiden: Brill, 2015), is the first book-length effort known to me that assembles a wide array of studies focusing on this toolbox. A fine bibliography of earlier case studies on formal rather than verbal devices of structuring arguments is found in Martin Kern, "Style and Poetic Diction in the *Xunzi*," in *Dao Companion to the Philosophy of Xunzi*, ed. Eric L. Hutton (Dordrecht: Springer, 2016), 4n16.

2. Christoph Harbsmeier, *Clavis Syntactica: A Key to Some Basic Syntactic Categories in Classical Chinese* (unpublished manuscript, rev. version, December 2018, kindly sent to me by the author), 47, suggests that initial *gù* "always implies a *shì*."

3. An example is Guodian *Laozi* A's 是以聖人 (slip 31), compared to the Western Han *Laozi* manuscript at Peking University, which reads here 故聖人 (*Shangjing* 上經, slip 56). See the synopsis in Beijing daxue chutu wenxian yanjiusuo 北京大須阿出土文獻研究所, ed., *Beijing daxue cang Xi-Han zhushu* 北京大學藏西漢竹書, vol. 2 (Shanghai: Shanghai guji, 2012), 181.

4. He Leshi 何樂士 et al., *Gudai Hanyu xuci tongshi* 古代漢語虛詞通釋 (Beijing: Beijing daxue, 1985), 186.

5. Zhang Yujin, *Chutu Zhanguo wenxian xuci yanjiu*, 368.

6. Yang Shuda 楊樹達, *Ci quan* 詞詮 (Shanghai: Shangwu, 1928), 133–34. Georg von der Gabelentz had already in 1881 treated the *gù* as a linkage term in composite sentences together with *suoyi*; see his *Chinesische Grammatik* (Leipzig: T. O. Weigel, 1881), par. 1405–06. This definition as *suoyi* was taken up by Pei Xuehai 裴學海 in his *Gushu xuci jishi* 古書虛詞集釋 (1932; rpt. Beijing: Zhonghua, 1954), 308.

7. Zhang Yaru 張亞茹, "Yuti chayi yu yinguo guanxici 'gu'" 語體差異與因果關係詞"故," *Gu Hanyu yanjiu* 2016.4: 63. A similar argument was made by Yu Yue 俞樾 many years ago in his *Gushu yiyi juli* 古書疑義舉例, with examples from the *Liji* and *Xunzi*; see Zhang Cheng 張赬, "Shanggu Hanyu lianci 'gu' de pianzhang gongneng yanjiu" 上古漢語連詞"故"的篇章功能研究, *Gu Hanyu yanjiu* 2014.2: 26–34. It may be that the infelicitous designation of words such as *gù* as "empty words" (*xuci*) perpetuates the problem of not taking seriously the meaning in rhetorical context.

8. Zhang Yaru recently used a Chinese form of this terminology by talking about a *beishizhe* 被釋者, which would correspond to the *explicandum*, and a *jiangshizhe* 將釋者, which would match the *explicans*. The title of the article, however, maintains the old formula ("Yuti chayi yu yinguo guanxici 'gu,'" 63–64).

9. Authors have tried to overcome this flaw through a form of textual arrangement that reflects the structure of the text through a two-dimensional arrangement. See Joachim Gentz, "Defining Boundaries and Relations of Textual Units: Examples from the Literary Tool-Kit of Early Chinese Argumentation," in *Literary Forms of Argument*, 120; David Schaberg, "On the Range and Performance of *Laozi*-Style Tetrasyllables," in *Literary Forms of Argument*, 87–111. See especially my "Technique and the Philosophy of Structure: Interlocking Parallel Style in *Laozi* and Wang Bi," in *The Craft of a Chinese Commentator: Wang Bi on the Laozi* (Albany: State University of New York Press, 2000), 53–114; "A Building Block of Chinese Argumentation: Initial *Fu* 夫 as a Phrase Status Marker," in *Literary Forms of Argument*, 37–66; "The Importance of Context Structures on Paleography, Translation and Analysis: Notes on a Unit of the *Ziyi* 緇衣 in Honor of Professor Pang Pu," in *Pang Pu jiaoshou bashi shouchen jinian wenji* 龐朴教授八十壽辰紀念文集, ed. Wang Shouchang 王守常 and Yu Jin 余瑾 (Beijing: Zhonghua, 2008), 278–300, esp. 291 and 299–300.

10. It might also suggest a regional diversity, but this is beyond the purview of the present study.

11. For this, see Zhang Yujin 張玉金, *Xi-Zhou Hanyu yufa yanjiu* 西周漢語語法研究 (Beijing: Shangwu, 2004), 173, and Zhou Baohong 周寶宏, "Xi-Zhou Shi Xun gui mingwen huishi" 西周師訇簋銘文匯釋, *Zhongguo wenzi yanjiu* 2005.1: 26–31.

12. As the issue here is the order of magnitude rather than the exact numbers, I have left the differences between the different *Laozi* manuscripts, transmitted and reconstructed versions, aside and used the text offered in the CHANT database (http://www.chant.org/).

13. For the study of the order of magnitude, it is not really relevant that, in the Han dynasty manuscripts of the *Laozi*, quite a few of these initial *gù* do not appear. The proportion still remains very high.

14. These quotations from direct speeches use a highly formulaic rhetoric and their relationship to actual direct speech is unclear.

15. There are, to be sure, many ways to make a case other than with reason-based argumentation; to name just a few: religious, political, or other authority, or trust, violent imposition, bribes, seduction, or a claim that the outcome would be irrelevant either way.

16. In the *Tang zai Chimen* 湯在啻門, from the Tsinghua University trove, for example, no linkage *gù* appears at all, although it is a dialogic text offering formulaic answers to questions (although no real arguments). See Joachim Gentz, "Literary Forms of Argument in the Tsinghua University Manuscript *Tang zai Chimen* 湯在啻門," in *Qinghua daxue cang Zhanguo zhujian (wu)* guoji xueshu yantaohui lunwenji》《清華大學藏戰國竹簡 (伍)》國際學術研討會論文集, ed. Li Xueqin 李學勤, Sarah Allan 艾蘭, and Michael Lüdke 呂德凱, *Qinghua jian yanjiu* 清華簡研究 3 (2019): 194–221.

17. Zhongguo shehui kexueyuan kaogu yanjiusuo 中國社會科學院考古研究所, comp., *Yin-Zhou jinwen jicheng* 殷周金文集成, vol. 8 (Beijing: Zhonghua, 1987), 303–05 (no. 4341).

18. I follow William Baxter and Laurent Sagart, *Old Chinese: A New Reconstruction* (Oxford: Oxford University Press, 2014). For my argument it is only relevant that these different words written 古 were pronounced differently and had to be disambiguated.

19. *Lu Mu Gong wen Zisi* 魯穆公問子思, in *Guodian Chu mu zhujian* 郭店楚墓竹簡, ed. Jingmen shi bowuguan 荊門市博物館 (Beijing: Wenwu, 1998), 23 (slip 5).

20. 子羔曰：何故以得為帝？孔子曰：昔者而歿世也，善於善相受也，故能治天下; *Zi Gao* 子羔, in *Shanghai bowuguan cang Zhanguo Chu zhushu* 上海博物館藏戰國楚竹書, ed. Ma Chengyuan 馬承源, vol. 2 (Shanghai: Shanghai guji, 2002), 184 (slip 1). I follow the transcription of Ma Chengyuan with the exception of the 故 in 故能, which he wrongly left as 古能.

21. As far as I can tell, no one felt the need to state this explicitly, because it was the common practice in China as well as in the Middle East and Europe until relatively recent times. As late as the Song dynasty, however, reading was routinely done aloud in China, and it was noted as exceptional if someone was reading silently. For references, see Li Yu, "A History of Reading in Late Imperial China," PhD diss., Ohio State University, 2003, esp. 59–61.

22. Cf. *Laozi jiayibing* 老子甲乙丙, in *Guodian Chu mu zhujian*, 1–10; *Laozi* in *Beijing daxue cang Xi-Han zhushu*, vol. 2; Mawangdui Han mu boshu zhengli xiaozu 馬王堆漢墓帛書整理小組, ed., *Mawangdui Han mu boshu: Laozi* 馬王堆漢墓帛書: 老子 (Beijing: Wenwu, 1976).

23. Yi Qiang 伊強, *Qin jian xuci ji jushi kaocha* 秦簡虛詞及句式考察 (Wuhan: Wuhan daxue, 2017), 191–93.

24. Zhang Yujin, *Chutu Zhanguo wenxian xuci yanjiu*, 369. There have been many different proposals for the etymology of *gù* OC *kˤa(ʔ)-s, some directly deriving them from the words now written 古 or 固. See Axel Schuessler, *ABC Etymological Dictionary of Old Chinese* (Honolulu: University of Hawai'i Press, 2007), 263, quoting Pulleyblank for the first option.

25. The reproduction of the rubbing of the text, together with a transcription and a free translation (which I have in part followed), is in W. A. C. H. Dobson, *Early Archaic Chinese* (Toronto: University of Toronto Press, 1962), 220–26.

26. For English translations, see Dobson, *Early Archaic Chinese*, 220–26; Robert Eno, "Inscriptional Records of the Western Zhou," unpublished manuscript, 2017, 23–24, https://hdl.handle.net/2022/23466. Constance A. Cook, "Da Yu ding," in *A Source Book of Ancient Chinese Bronze Inscriptions*, ed. Constance A. Cook and Paul R. Goldin, rev. ed. (Berkeley: Society for the Study of Early China, 2020), 32–34.

27. Dobson's reading of the last phrase, "this is why [Yin] failed in the discipline of [its] officials," cannot stand. This phrase contains the *explicandum*, which is the demise of the Yin, not a summary of the *explicans*. Furthermore, even though it is possible that both the *explicans* and the *explicandum* here are subordinate to "I have heard" as assumed by Eno and Cook, this would be a nearly unique case. The *explicandum* is the demise of the Yin and the king draws for his *explicans* on data from the oral tradition, to end with the *explicandum* to which he has now given a new meaning. Dobson only deals with the *gù* in the second statement, which he defined as a causal conjunction occurring "before the clause of consequence." He adds examples from the "Jiu Gao" 酒誥 chapter of the *Shangshu*, the *Mengzi*, and the *Mozi*.

28. Ban *gui* 班簋, in *Yin-Zhou jinwen jicheng*, vol. 8, 303–05 (no. 4341).

29. See Zhou Baohong, "Xi-Zhou Shi Xun gui mingwen huishi," 26–31.

30. *Chunqiu Zuo zhuan zhengyi* 春秋左傳正義, in *Shisanjing zhushu* 十三經註疏, ed. Ruan Yuan 阮元 (Beijing: Zhonghua, 1987), 1715 (Yin 1.2).

31. This implication is spelled out by Dong Zhongshu 董仲舒 (179–104 BCE): "The *Chunqiu* records the successes and failures in all-under-Heaven and shows the causes which brought them about. What is hidden in darkness, it makes clear, for that which there is no transmission, and it makes known, one cannot but carefully probe it" 《春秋》記天下之得失, 而見所以然之故. 其幽而明, 無傳而著, 不可不察也. See *Chunqiu fanlu yizheng* 春秋繁露義證, ed. Su Yu 蘇輿 (Beijing: Zhonghua, 1992), 56 (3 "Zhulin" 竹林).

32. *Chunqiu Zuo zhuan zhengyi*, 1715.

33. For the text and the translation, which has been made slightly more explicit here, see Rudolf G. Wagner, *A Chinese Reading of the Daodejing* (Albany: State University of New York Press, 2003), 162.

34. I am aware of only one commentary that explicitly refused such a subordination and claimed the right to develop what it considered the initial dim insights of a text, otherwise considered authoritative, to full philosophical propositions. This is Guo Xiang's *Commentary on the Zhuangzi*.

35. Cf. Rudolf G. Wagner, *The Craft of a Chinese Commentator: Wang Bi on the* Laozi (Albany: State University of New York Press, 2000), 298.

36. *Fan* 凡 is a phrase status marker indicating a higher level of general validity for a statement. It is anchored in a quantitative assessment. *Fu* 夫, which Wang Fu uses in the next sentence, is a phrase status marker indicating the general validity of a principle. It is anchored in a qualitative assessment. See Wagner, "A Building Block of Chinese Argumentation," 37–66.

37. Wang Fu 王符, *Qianfu lun* 潛夫論 (Shanghai: Shanghai guji, 1978), 15.

38. *Sunzi shijia zhu* 孫子十家注, comm. Sun Wu 孫武 et al., in *Zhuzi jicheng* 諸子集成, vol. 6 (Shanghai: Shanghai shudian, 1988), 2.25–26.

39. *The Art of War: Sun Zi's Military Methods*, trans. Victor Mair (New York: Columbia University Press, 2007), 32–33.

40. *Xunzi: The Complete Text*, trans. Eric L. Hutton (Princeton, NJ: Princeton University Press, 2014), 1, emphasis added.

41. John Knoblock, *Xunzi: A Translation and Study of the Complete Works*, vol. 1 (Stanford: Stanford University Press, 1988), 136.

42. An example is Zhang Jue 張覺, *Xunzi yizhu* 荀子譯注 (Shanghai: Shanghai guji, 1995), 2.

43. Kern, "Style and Poetic Diction in the *Xunzi*," 8.

44. *Gui* 規 here refers to a device to make circles, not to the later (Han) invention of a magnetic compass.

45. In chapter 13, the *Xunzi* deals with human nature's evilness, which he compares to a crooked piece of wood, *gou mu* 枸木, that needs straightening and to a dull piece of metal that needs sharpening just as humans need education. Commentators have glossed *gou* 枸 as meaning *qu* 曲 (crooked).

46. Given that the character 古 also occurs in the initial position of a sentence, where it refers to the word *gǔ* OC *kˤaʔ with the meaning "antiquity," there are cases where the transcription is questionable. A comparison between Zhanguo and Western Han manuscripts of the *Laozi* also shows a substantial increase in initial *gù* for the later manuscripts.

Contributors

Roger T. AMES is Humanities Chair Professor at Peking University and Academic Director of the Berggruen China Center.

Erica BRINDLEY is Professor of Asian Studies at Pennsylvania State University.

Shirley CHAN is Associate Professor in the Department of Media, Communications, Creative Arts, Language, and Literature Department at Macquarie University.

CHEN Wei 陳偉 is Professor in the School of History and Chair of the Center of Bamboo and Silk Manuscripts at Wuhan University.

CHEUNG Kwong-yue 張光裕 is Head and Chair Professor in the Department of Chinese at the Hang Seng University of Hong Kong.

Constance A. COOK is Professor and Chair in the Department of Modern Languages and Literatures, Lehigh University.

GU Man 顧漫 is Researcher in the Institute for the History of Medicine and Medical Literature at the China Academy of Chinese Medical Sciences.

HAN Yujiao 韓宇嬌 is managing editor of the *Journal of Chinese Linguistics*, Institute of Linguistics at Beijing Language and Culture University.

Vivienne LO is Professor in the Department of History at University College London.

Gil RAZ is Associate Professor in the Department of Religion at Dartmouth College.

Edmund RYDEN was, before his retirement, Associate Professor in the Faculty of Law at Fu Jen Catholic University.

Rudolf G. WAGNER was Senior Professor at the Department of Chinese Studies at Heidelberg University. Wagner passed away in 2019 before the completion of this volume.

Index

acupuncture: and homology of water, 37–38, 44–45, 46; and Laoguanshan figurine, 31–33, 39; and *qi*, xiii, 27, 28–29, 30–32; and turtle divination, 118, 119, 144n52

Allan, Sarah, xi, 57, 137, 164; on conceptual metaphor theory, xii–xiii, xv, 53, 187n46; and *li* metaphor, 75–80, 84, 87, 88; on sages, 93–94, 95; and *tianren* relationship, 112; and turtle divination, 117, 119, 121; on water and cosmos, 1–2, 15; on water and plants, 19, 75, 76, 77–78, 80, 84, 87–88, 187n47; and water as homology, 19, 20, 21, 29–30

Analects (*Lunyu*), 82, 104, 151, 172, 184n21, 186n36; and archery, 195–96; on Confucius, 110–11; on *de*, 112, 178

ancestral spirits: vs. Daoism, 60, 61; as deities, 1, 13, 16n9, 120, 166, 167, 168; and illness and healing, 120, 121, 123–31, 133, 142n27; sacrifices to, 201–3, 207; and *tian*, 94, 103, 105. *See also* deities; *shenming*

archery, xiv, 189–200

Aristotle, 100

art: archery as, 194–97; as metaphor, 166–67, 169, 181

Bodde, Derk, 5–6, 7

body, human: acupuncture points on, 28, 31–32, 144n52; and cosmos, 23, 185n32; and heart, 147–48, 150; and homology of water, xiii, 19–50; and *li* (propriety), 104, 197; parts of, 126, 141n22, 164; as political state, xiv, xv, 170–77, 179–81; *qi* in, 21, 24–25, 27–30, 34, 63–65

body, royal: as political state, 119, 120, 121, 122; and turtle divination, xiv, 118–23, 131, 133, 139

bronze inscriptions: on archery, 191–93, 195; Ban *gui*, 214, 217, 221; Da Yu *ding*, 214, 219–20; *gù* in, 214–17, 219, 233, 234; Ling *ding*, 191, 193; on sacrifice, 204; Shi Xun *gui*, 221; Yi *hegai*, 191, 193; Yu *fangding*, 191, 193; Zuoce Ban *yuan* (bronze turtle), 191

Buddhism, 88

Butler, Joseph, 113n3

Cai Shen, 156

calendar: day signs in, 121, 123–33, 136; in turtle divination, 117, 118–21, 122, 123, 129, 131, 139

Cao Jiao, 109

Chang Kwang-chih, 5

Chen Chi-yun, 63
Chen Gang, 104
Chen Jing, 69
Chen Wenzi, 68
Chen Ziqin, 111
Cheng Hao, 79, 86, 87
Cheng Xuanying, 80, 149, 157
Cheng Yi, 79, 83, 86, 87
Christianity/Abrahamic religions, 94, 95–103, 105–6, 112, 113n3
Chu, state of, 5, 21, 47, 138; script of, 17n12, 170; texts excavated from, 24, 137, 190, 195. *See also* Guodian manuscripts; Mawangdui manuscripts
Chu ci, 172
Chu Silk Manuscript, 16n9
Chunqiu (Spring and Autumn Annals), 156, 215, 222–23, 224, 238n31
Chunqiu period, 211, 215, 216, 234, 235n1
Chunyu Kun, 153
Confucianism, 3, 107, 186n42; vs. Abrahamic religions, 98, 106, 113n3; and archery, 195; dichotomies in, 86–87; vs. Greek philosophy, 99–102; vs. religion, 102–5; *tianren heyi* in, 94, 95, 110–12; and water, 19, 21, 57, 185n27. *See also* Ruists
Confucius, 110–11, 112, 227
Conrad, Cecilia A., 15
conversion narratives, 51–74
cooking, xiv, 53, 163, 165–66, 171–77, 181, 182, 186n40
correlative cosmology, 4, 5, 13–14, 15, 168, 169. *See also* Five Phases
cosmologies of flow, 1–18; and Constancy (*heng*), 6–9, 11; vs. correlative cosmology, 13–14, 15; and creativity, 3, 5–9, 10–11, 15, 16n4; *Taiyi sheng shui* on, 5, 9–13, 14
cyclical processes, 9–11, 12, 23, 31–32, 78; calendrical, 119, 121–26, 128, 131; hydrological, 38–39, 46

Da Dai liji, 151, 153
Dao (the Way): and archery, 194; and Celestial Master *zhengyi*, 62–64, 70, 71; and cosmologies of flow, 1, 2, 11; and *de*, 177; and harmony, 12, 90n14; and human-cosmos relationship, 95, 101, 102, 112; and *li* (pattern), 81, 82, 84, 85, 87; name (*ming*) of, 11, 17nn26–27; and plant metaphor, 77–78; and *qi*, 53, 55, 63; translations of, 113n3, 154–55; and water, xii, 21, 22, 76–77, 78, 89n3, 164
Daodejing. See *Laozi*
Dao-embodiment, 2–5, 8, 9, 11–14, 15
Daoism: and cosmologies of flow, xiii, 3, 5, 14–15; and metaphor, 164, 185n27; and Ruism/Confucianism, 21, 185n27, 186n42; Shangqing, 70
Daoism, Celestial Master, xiii, 51–74; conversion to, 67–70; and demonic illness, xiii, 55–61, 65, 66–67, 71; development of, 53–55; and healing, 67–70; metaphors in, 52–53, 61–64; ritual protocol of, 64–67; vs. traditional ritual, 60–61
Daoxuezhuan (Traditions of Students of the Dao), 58, 67
Daxue (Great/Expansive Learning), 79, 83, 107, 197
de (moral virtuosity, integrity): and archery, 195, 197; bad (*ede*), 180; as *eudemonia*, 187n55; and harmony (*he*), 107–8; and *qi*, 178–81; in statecraft, 112, 169, 176, 177–81; and *tian*, 106–7, 108–9

Declarations of the Perfected (*Zhen'gao*), 69
deities: ancestral spirits as, 1, 13, 16n9, 120, 166, 167, 168; animistic, 1, 18n34; Christian/Abrahamic vs. Chinese, 95–103, 105–6, 112, 113n3; and correlative cosmologies, 4, 13; creator, 5, 9, 10, 16nn9–10, 22–23, 38, 46; local, 54–55, 61, 66–67, 69; Shang, 1, 3, 103, 112, 120, 166, 167; and turtle divination, 117, 120. See also Shangdi; *shenming* (spirit illumination)
Demon Statutes of Lady Blue (*Nüqing guilü*), 55–57, 58, 59, 62, 71
demons: and illness, xiii, 51–52, 54–61, 62, 65, 66–68, 70, 71, 120–21, 125; and *qi*, 26–27, 55–61
Dewey, John, 97, 98–99
ding (vessel, to sacrifice), 203–5
Disputers of the Tao (Graham), 85–86
Dobson, W.A.C.H., 238n27
Documents. See *Shangshu*
Dong Zhongshu, 238n31
Dong Zuobin, 205
Du Jiong, 67–69
Du Yu, 154
Duan Yucai, 204
Dushu zazhi (Wang Niansun), 156

Emerson, Ralph Waldo, 95–99
Erya, 35
exorcism, 141n17, 142n24; and healing, 117, 119–31, 133, 134, 138, 139, 203

Fan Boci, 69, 70
Fang Yizhi, 79
Fazang, 82–83, 88

Five Modes of Virtuosic Conduct (*Wuxingpian*), 106–7, 109, 110, 112, 115n32
Five Phases (*wuxing*), xiii, 5, 31–32, 119, 169, 185n32. See also correlative cosmology
Fu Hao, 124

Gabelentz, Georg von der, 236n6
Gao You, 156
ge (skin, leather), xiv, 201–3, 207; and *pi*, 203–5
Graham, A. C., 12, 18n36, 80–81, 82, 85–86, 101
Granet, Marcel, 99, 101, 105–6
Greek philosophy, 99–102
gù (function word; that is why), xv, 211–39; and abstract statements, 225–27; and authoritative texts, 222–25, 234; change over time of, 214–16, 228–32; definition of, 219–22; disambiguation of, 217–19; and historical facts, 222, 233, 234; standardization of, 232, 235; in two-dimensional sentence structures, 213, 225, 230, 236n9
Gu Huan, 58, 59, 72n10
Gu Jihong, 37
Guan Zhong, 155, 156
Guangya, 158, 161n67, 204
Guangyun, 157, 158
Guanzi, 19, 34, 151, 153, 177, 178, 190
Guo Xiang, 239n34
Guodian manuscripts, 17n12, 21, 110, 115n32, 149; on archery, 195, 197; *Laozi* in, 22, 219, 235n3. See also *Five Modes of Virtuosic Conduct*; *Taiyi sheng shui*
Guoyu (Discourses of the States), 149, 153, 155, 158, 168, 173–74, 183n11, 184n21

Gushu xuzi jishi (Pei Xuehai), 150

Hall, David, 99
Han dynasty, 15, 118, 120, 123
Han Fei, 77
Han Feizi, 81, 172, 187n53
Han Odes (*Han shi*), 190
Han shi waizhuan, 151
Han shu, 150, 156, 161n67
Hanson, Marta, 121
Harper, Donald, 22–23, 46, 119, 120–21, 142n24
he (harmony, harmonization), xiv, 102, 171–79, 181, 182; and cosmologies of flow, 12, 14, 15; and *de*, 107–8; and *li* (pattern), 79, 80, 90n14; and sages, 110, 111, 112
Hebu (*Jiaguwen heji bubian*), 206, 207, 209n19
Heji collection (*Jiaguwen heji*, eds. Guo Moruo and Hu Houxuan), 133, 134, 137, 138, 144n53, 203–4, 206
Hengxian (The Primordial State of Constancy), 6–11, 14, 15
historicity, 163–71, 184nn20–21; vs. divination, 168, 169; and mythology, 168, 169, 183n10, 184n25; and statecraft, 168–70, 181–82
Hopkins, Gerard Manly, 86, 92n41
Houjiazhuang South site, 206
Hu Houxuan, 119
Hua Qiao, 69–70
Huainanzi, 3, 12, 14, 75, 153, 156, 185n32
Huang, Diviner, xiv–xv, 206–8
Huang Chang, 62
Huang Di (Yellow Emperor), 34, 38, 40, 41, 42
Huang Di neijing (Yellow Emperor's Inner Classic), 32, 41, 46, 119, 140n11; *Lingshu* recension of, 34–35, 40, 43
Huang Tianshu, 203
Huangfu Mi, 44
Huayuanzhuang East oracle-bone inscriptions (Huayuanzhuang dongdi jiagu): *ge* in, xiv, 201–10; and turtle divination, 117, 123–38
human-cosmos relationship, xiv, xv, 16n5; and correlative cosmologies, 13–14; and cosmologies of flow, 1–13, 14–15; individuality in, 95–99; in medical theory, 19–50, 121; and sages, 93–95, 107, 108–13; and *shen xin* (body and heart), 147–48; *Tang chuyu Tangqiu* on, 163–64, 165–66, 169, 177; *tian* in, xiii, 93–95, 105–8, 109, 112–13, 147, 166–69, 179, 186n33; and transcendence, xii, 95, 96, 99–102
humanism, European, 98
Hutton, Eric L., 228–29

illness, corruption, affliction (*ji*), 174–75, 177–80, 187n53; in conversion narratives, 52, 65, 68, 69; in turtle divination, 121, 122–23, 124–38
illness and healing, xiv; and conversion, 67–70, 71; and demons, xiii, 51–52, 54–61, 62, 64–68, 70, 71, 120–21; and exorcism, 117, 119–31, 133, 134, 138, 139, 203; and king's body, 121–23; and military metaphors, 65–67, 137
Instructions for Entering the Oratory (*Rujingfa*), 64

James, William, 98, 115n20
Jao Tsung-I, 119
Ji Xusheng, 202
Jia Yi, 150

Jie, King (Xia), 170, 171, 174–75, 182
Jingci yanshi (Wu Changying), 151
Jingdian shiwen (Lu Deming), 157, 161n67
Jinshizi (Golden Lion; Fazang), 82–83
Jiyun (comp. Ding Du), 157
Johnson, Mark, xii, 52–53

Keightley, David, 120, 137
Kern, Martin, 183n11, 229, 230, 232
Kleeman, Terry, 62
Knoblock, John, 229
Kong Yingda, 191
Kongzi jiayu, 151
Kongzi shilun, 189

Lakoff, George, xii, 52–53
Laoguanshan (Tianhui) lacquered figurine, 31–33, 39
Laoguanshan manuscripts (Tianhui), 21, 31–33
Laozi (*Daodejing*): as argumentative text, 211, 215; on cooking, 186n40; and Dao-embodiment, 3, 11, 14; on *de*, 177; and demonic illness, 58; *gù* in, 215–16, 227; Guodian manuscript of, 22, 219, 235n3; and *li* (pattern), 77, 82, 87; Mawangdui manuscript of, 47n3, 154, 219; Wang Bi on, 223–25; on water, 20, 21–22, 76–77, 89n5; in Zhanguo vs. Western Han, 239n46
Legge, James, 94, 113n3
li (principle, pattern, grain of jadeite), xiii, 75–92; history of, 80–83; as metaphor, 84–85; and Song concepts, 78–80; translation of, 85–87, 91n37; and water and plant metaphors, 76–80, 84, 85, 87–88
li (ritual propriety), 94, 102, 103–5, 106; and archery, 195–96, 197; as metaphor, 166–67; and music, 195, 196; in statecraft, 178–79, 181
Li Maoxi, 150
Li Shan, 151, 156
Li Zhouhan, 149
Liji (Book of Rites), 35, 104, 151, 152, 155, 236n7; on archery, 191, 195, 196; on *de*, 177–78
Lingshu (*Huangdi Neijing*), 34–35, 40, 43
Liu de, 195
Liu Lang, 150
Liu Shao, 81, 86
Liu Yiman, 206
Lu Xiujing, 59–60, 61
Lüshi chunqiu (Master Lü's Spring and Autumn Annals), 14, 27–28, 30, 81, 164

Ma Jianzhong, 150
Ma Shi wentong (Ma Jianzhong), 150
Mair, Victor, 228
Master Lu's Abridged Codes for the Daoist Community (*Lu xiansheng daomen kelüe*), 59–60, 64–67, 70
Master Red Pine's Almanac of Petitions (*Chisongzi zhangli*), 53, 54, 57, 59, 61
Mawangdui manuscripts, 21, 24, 32, 107, 115n32, 154; *Laozi* in, 47n3, 219. See also *Five Modes of Virtuosic Conduct*
medical practice: and homology of water, 19–50; and human-cosmos relationship, 121; and *qi*, xiii, 21, 27, 30–31, 119; regional variations in, 32; vs. ritual war, 55, 58, 67; texts on, xiii, 20, 34–37, 119, 120, 122, 140n4. See also acupuncture; illness and healing

Mencius (*Mengzi*), 71, 79, 80, 149, 153, 227; on archery, 190, 196–97; vs. Christianity, 113n3; history in, 184n21; on moral virtuosity, 106–7, 109; on *qi*, 29–30, 61; on water, 57–58, 76
Meng Kang, 156, 161n67
Meng Sheng, 62
metaphor theory, conceptual, xii–xiii, xv, 52–53
metaphors, root, 2, 19, 76, 78–80
Metaphors We Live By (Lakoff and Johnson), xii, 52
Miaopu North site, 206
military metaphors, xiii, 52, 53, 61, 70, 71, 75, 77; and illness, 54–55, 58, 59, 66–67, 137
Mote, Frederick, 5, 16n10
moxibustion, 37, 119
Mozi, 80–81, 164, 172, 184n21, 186n36, 211
music, 152, 167, 178, 181, 186n42; and archery, 191, 194–96, 197; and ritual (*li*), 104, 110, 196
mythology: animals in, 57, 184n15; and art and writing, 166–67, 181; of creation, 5–6, 9, 16n4, 16n9; and historicity, 168, 169, 183n10, 184n25; and metaphor, xii, 2, 166–67

Nanjing (Classic of Difficulties), 38, 43–44, 49n39
Needham, Joseph, 5, 46, 91n36, 99
Neo-Confucianism, 83–84

Odes. See *Shijing*
oracle bones, xiii–xv; and acupuncture, 119; graphs on, 63, 103, 104, 121, 141n17, 214, 217; styles of, xiv–xv, 207–8; vs. turtle divination, 117.

See also Huayuanzhuang East oracle-bone inscriptions; turtle divination
oral transmission: and argumentative texts, 216, 220, 222, 228, 238n27; and reading aloud, 218, 237n21; of rhetoric, 164, 167, 185n27

Pace of Yu (exorcism), 120, 142n24
Peng Zu, 178
plant metaphors, xii, 187n47; dichotomies in, 87; and *li* (pattern), 76–80, 84, 85, 87–88
Plato, 100, 114n19
politics. See statecraft
Primordial State of Constancy, The (*Hengxian*), 6–11, 14, 15
Puett, Michael, 4, 15, 142n27

qi: and acupuncture, xiii, 27, 28–29, 30–32; in Celestial Master Daoism, 62–64; and cosmologies of flow, 6–7, 10, 11; and Dao, 53, 55, 63; and *de*, 178–81; and demons, 26–27, 55–61; deviant, 43, 61, 63, 66, 67, 119–20, 121; and homology of water, 19–47; in human body, 21, 24–25, 27–30, 34, 63–65; and illness, 119–20; and *li* (pattern), 75, 78, 84, 85, 87; in medical practice, xiii, 21, 27, 30–31, 119; reverse flow of, 55–61, 66; as root metaphor, 78, 79; and sexual practices, 24–25, 27, 28; as water, 52–53, 61, 63, 64, 71, 79
Qi, state of, 32
Qi Bo, 39, 40, 41
Qianfu lun (Wang Fu), 225–26
Qin dynasty, 26–27, 138, 140n4, 190; *gù* in, 217, 219, 234
Qin Shi Huangdi, 165

Qiongda yi shi (Guodian bamboo-slip manuscript), 197
Qiu Xigui, 123, 202, 204

ren (humaneness, consummatory conduct), xii, 83; and archery, 195, 196, 197; and *de*, 102, 106, 109, 110, 113n3
Renwu zhi (Gazette of Human Nature; Li Shao), 81
resonance, cosmologies of, xiii, 5, 13–14, 15, 46, 93, 95. *See also* correlative cosmology
rhetoric: argumentative, xv, 211, 214–16, 220–21, 228, 232, 233; Greek, 164; of metaphor, 163–68, 177, 181, 182, 183n11, 185n27; and *qi*, 64, 67; in *Tang chuyu Tangqiu*, 170–73
Ricci, Matteo, 94
ritual. *See li* (ritual propriety)
Royal Record of Yü (Shun), 93–94
Ruists, 169, 185n27, 195, 197. *See also* Confucianism

sacrifice: and conversion, 52, 58, 61; and exorcism, 117, 118, 120–35, 139, 143n40; and homology of water, 35; and *li* (propriety), 103; and term *ge*, xiv, 201–5
sages, 15, 46; in argumentative texts, 233–34; and healing, 30–31; and human-cosmos relationship, 93–95, 107, 108–13; kings as, 169, 173, 175, 181, 182; and water, 22, 44
Schleiermacher, Friedrich, 98, 112
Schwartz, Adam, 126
seasons, 9, 10, 23, 119, 172; and plant metaphor, 77–78, 84, 85
Secret Instructions for Ascending to Perfection (*Dengzhen yinjue*; Tao Hongjing), 53, 54, 57, 59, 64, 69, 70
self-cultivation, 24, 27–29, 46, 104, 106; and archery, 190, 195, 197; sexual, 24–25, 27, 28
self-divinization, 4, 15
self-generation, 3, 5–9, 12, 14, 15, 16n10, 22, 101
shamanism, 4, 137, 167
Shan Yuchen, 149
Shang dynasty, 184n20, 184n25, 191; deities of, 1, 3, 103, 112, 117, 118, 120, 166, 167; turtle divination in, 117–39, 201, 205–8. *See also* oracle bones; Tang, King; Wu Ding, King
Shangdi (God on high, Supreme Thearch), 1, 3, 103, 112, 166
Shanghai museum manuscripts, 16n12, 149, 155, 156, 189
Shangshu (Book of Documents), 151, 152, 156, 158; and historicity, 167, 168, 170, 183n11, 184nn20–21
Shanhaijing, 157
Shen Yue, 150
shenming (spirit illumination), 23–26, 46
shenqidu (to internalize conduct), 107
Shenxianzhuan (Traditions of Divine Transcendents), 58–59
Shi Bo, 173
Shiji, 151, 154
Shijing (Book of Odes), 110, 155, 167, 168, 184n21, 189, 190
Shiming, 153
Shu, state of, 21, 32
Shuangbaoshan tomb (Mianyang), 31
Shui Zhigan, 155
Shun (sage-king), 107, 109, 111
Shuowen jiezi, 117, 152, 154, 155, 156, 157, 202, 204
Shuoyuan, 156, 172

Shusun Wushu, 110
Sima Qian, 14, 26
Sima Tan, 14
Sima Xiangru, 149
Sivin, Nathan, 121
Slingerland, Edward, 52–53
Song dynasty, 32, 197, 237n21; *li* (pattern) in, xiii, 75, 78, 82, 83–84, 87, 88
Spirit Turtle (Shen Gui, Ling Gui), 118
spontaneity, 1, 3, 5–9, 12, 14, 15, 18n36; of water, 19, 24, 29
statecraft: and cooking, xiv, 163, 165–66, 171–72, 173, 176, 181, 182, 186n40; and cosmologies of flow, 13; *de* in, 112, 169, 176, 177–81; and *gu*, 226–27; and historicity, 168–70, 181–82; and human body, xiv, xv, 170–77, 179–81; and *li* (pattern), 81–82; *li* (ritual propriety) in, 103, 178–79, 181; and royal body, xiv, 119, 120, 121, 122; and water management, 26–27, 57, 71; and writing, 166–67, 169, 181
Su Dongpo (Su Shi), 88
Sunzi, 211, 228, 235
Supreme Ultimate (*taiji*), 83, 87, 90n14
Suwen, 40–41, 42

Taiyi (creator deity), 9, 10, 17n26, 22–23, 24, 26, 38, 46
Taiyi sheng shui (Taiyi Gives Birth to Water), 5, 9–13, 14, 22–23, 46, 76
Takashima Kenichi, 134, 135
Tang, King (Shang), 163, 170–77, 181, 182, 186n33
Tang chuyu Tangqiu (Tang Resides Near the Mound of Tang), xiv, 163, 170–77, 180, 181, 182
Tang Junyi, 99, 102

Tang Yijie, 105, 108, 111
Tang zai Chimen, 140n11, 164, 171, 179, 181, 185n33, 237n16
Tao Hongjing, 51–52, 54, 64, 74n25
Thinking Through Confucius (Hall and Ames), 99
tian (the cosmic, Heaven), 113n3; in argumentative texts, 221; in Confucianism, 105–8; and cosmologies of flow, 1–3, 8, 9–13; in human-cosmos relationship, xiii, 93–95, 105–8, 109, 112–13, 147, 166–69, 179, 186n33; and *li* (pattern), 84–85; and *qi*, 39, 55, 61, 81; and sages, 93–95, 110–13, 233; and spirit illumination, 22–23; and *taiji* (Supreme Ultimate), 83, 90n14; and transcendence, xii, 95, 96, 99, 103
tiandi (heaven and earth), 3, 22, 24, 83, 87, 94, 110, 111, 113
Tianhui Laoguanshan figurine, 31–33, 39
tianming (Heaven's Mandate), 167, 168, 171, 182, 184n20, 186n39
tianren heyi (mutuality of *tian* and humanity), xiii, 94, 105–6, 109, 112–13
Transcendentalism, 95–99
Tsinghua University manuscripts, xiv, 147–62, 163–64. See also *Tang chuyu Tangqiu*; *Tang zai Chimen*
turtle divination, 117–46; on afflictions (*ji*), 121, 122–23, 124–38; and exorcism, 117, 119–31, 133, 134, 138, 139, 203; royal body in, xiv, 118–23, 131, 133, 139; and spirit of plastron, 135, 144n52; symmetry in, 201, 205–8

Wang Bi, 82, 83, 223–25
Wang Bing, 42

Wang Fu, 225–27, 228
Wang Fuzhi, 79, 90n14
Wang Guanjun, 150
Wang Li, 150
Wang Niansun, 156, 161n67
Wang Ning, 149
Wang Sheng, 62
Wang Su, 151
Wang Tingxiang, 79
Wang Xianqian, 155
Wang Yangming, 79, 87
Wang Yao, 58–59
Warring States period, 235n1; argumentative texts in, 214, 233; calendar in, 123, 144n56; cosmologies of flow in, 3, 13–15; demonic illness in, 120, 137, 138; *gù* in, 211, 212, 215–19, 224, 232, 233, 234, 239n46; statecraft in, 165, 169, 171, 172, 181, 182; texts from, 16n9, 21, 178, 181, 212, 235n1; turtle divination in, 135, 141n21; water metaphor in, xiii, 19, 22, 26, 27. *See also* Tsinghua University manuscripts
water, xii–xiii, xiv; Allan on, xii, 1–2, 15, 19–21, 29–30, 75–78, 80, 84, 87–88, 187n47; in Confucianism, 19, 21, 57, 185n27; and cosmologies of flow, 1–2, 8–11, 13, 15; cycles of, 38–39, 46; and Dao, xii, 21, 22, 76–77, 78, 89n3, 164; homology with body of, xiii, 19–50; and *li* (pattern), 76–80, 84, 85, 87–88; management of, 26–27, 44, 46, 57–58, 71; *Mencius* on, 57–58, 76; and plants, xii, xiii, 19, 75, 76–80, 84, 85, 87–88, 187n47; and *qi*, 19–47, 52–53, 55–61, 63, 64, 71, 79; in rivers and watercourses, 27, 30, 34–39, 44, 76–77, 79, 80, 84–85, 87, 89n5; *Taiyi sheng shui* on, 5, 9–13, 14, 21–26, 46, 76; and women, 20, 21
Watson, Burton, 12
Way of Water and Sprouts of Virtue, The (Allan), xii, 19, 29–30, 53, 75, 164, 187nn46–47
weaving metaphor, 89n5
Wei Huacun, 73n23
Wei Zhao, 149, 153, 155, 158
Wen (sage-king), 110, 111
Wenxuan, 149–50, 151, 156
Western Han period: argumentative texts in, 232–33, 235; figurine from, 30–33; texts from, 20, 21, 32, 140n4, 219, 239n46
When Red Pigeons Gathered on Tang's House (*Chijiu zhi ji Tang zhi wu*), 183n9
"Withered Tree and Strange Rock" (painting: Su Shi), 88
writing: standardization of, 214; and statecraft, 166–67, 169, 181
Wu (sage-king), 111
Wu Changying, 151
Wu Ding, King (Shang), 118, 122, 123, 124
wuwei (non-action), xii, 3, 15, 19, 22
Wuwei manuscripts (Gansu), 32, 140n4
Wuxing (Guodian manuscript), 149

Xia dynasty, 167, 170, 172–77
Xiang Zonglu, 156
Xiaotun site, 206
xin (heart, mind), xii, 87, 122, 125, 197; and body (*shen*), 147–50, 152, 153, 155, 157; as heartminding, 105, 107, 109; and water, 78–79
Xin, Lady, 171–72
Xin shi wei zhong (The Heart is Called the Center), xiv, 147–62
Xingqing lun (Shanghai Museum manuscript), 155

Xinxu, 151
Xu Shen, 63
Xunzi, 150–55, 184n21, 197, 236n7; as argumentative text, 211; *gù* in, 228, 230–32; on *li* (pattern), 81, 91n40; on *li* (propriety), 178–79

Yan Shigu, 156
Yang Feng, 62
Yang Liang, 155
Yang Shuda, 212
Yang Xuancao, 38
Yao (sage-king), 109, 111, 178
Yao Xiaosui, 135, 202
Yi Yin, xiv, 138, 170–77, 179–81, 186n33, 186n36
Yi Zhou shu, 204
Yijing (*Zhouyi*; Book of Changes), 81, 82, 83, 87, 111, 152, 154
Yili, 190, 191–93, 194, 204
yin and *yang*, 9, 23, 113, 169; and turtle divination, 118, 119, 123; and water, 20, 26, 35
Yin Zhizhang, 153
Yu the Great, 26, 46, 57–58, 178
Yu Yue, 236n7
yu-exorcism, 120, 123–25, 128, 129, 131, 134, 138, 203
Yupian, 140n12, 157, 161n67, 162n69

Zhang Dainian, 80, 82
Zhang Daoling, 55–57, 73n23
Zhang Jiebin, 42–43
Zhang Pu, 62
Zhang Yaru, 212, 214, 236n8
Zhang Yujin, 219

Zhang Zai, 79
Zhang Zhicong, 42
Zhangjiashan (Jiangling) manuscripts, 21, 28–29, 30, 31, 32
Zhanguo zonghengjia shu (Mawangdui manuscript), 154
Zhao Guang, 62
Zhejiu jiayijing (A-B Classic of Acupuncture and Moxibustion), 44
Zheng Xuan, 151, 152, 191
Zhongyong (Focusing the Familiar), 106, 110, 111
Zhou dynasty: deities of, 1, 103, 167; historicity in, 168, 171, 181, 184n20; *li* (ritual) in, 103; schools of thought in, 3, 20; and Shang (Yin), 123, 138. *See also* bronze inscriptions
Zhou li, 194, 204
Zhouyi (Book of Changes). See *Yijing*
Zhouyi lüeli (Simple Exemplifications of the Principles of the Book of Changes; Wang Bi), 82
Zhu Peng, 37
Zhu Xi, 80, 83–85, 86, 87–88, 112
Zhuangzi, 3, 12, 14, 77, 157, 161n67, 177; on *li* (pattern), 80, 86
Zhuge Liang, 61
Zigong, 110, 111
Ziyi, 149, 156
Zong Mi, 77
Zun de yi, 195
Zuo zhuan, 151, 154, 211, 214, 224, 225; on archery, 190–91; *gù* in, 215–16, 222–23; historicity of, 168, 183n11, 184n21

www.ingramcontent.com/pod-product-compliance
Lightning Source LLC
Chambersburg PA
CBHW030533230426
43665CB00010B/877